D1669794

THE MILITARY BALANCE 1977-1978

The International Institute for Strategic Studies
18 Adam Street London WC2N 6AL

All rights reserved. No part of this publication may be reproduced, stored in a retrieval system, or transmitted in any form or by any means, electronic, mechanical, photocopying, recording or otherwise, without the prior permission of the International Institute for Strategic Studies.

ISBN 0 86079 011 8

ISSN 0459-7222

Printed in Great Britain by
Adlard & Son Ltd, Bartholomew Press, Dorking

© The International Institute for Strategic Studies 1977

CONTENTS

PREFACE

The Military Balance is an annual, quantitative assessment of the military power and defence expenditure of countries throughout the world.

It examines the facts of military power as they existed in July 1977, and no projections of force levels or weapons beyond this date have been included, except where specifically stated. The study should not be regarded as a comprehensive guide to the balance of military power; in particular, it does not reflect the facts of geography, vulnerability or efficiency, except where these are explicitly touched upon.

In general, national entries are grouped geographically, but with special reference to the principal regional defence pacts and alignments. Information about some smaller countries, whose military forces are of a size which has not seemed to warrant fuller description at this stage, has been set out in tabular form. Other tables give comparative information on nuclear delivery vehicles and static measurements of the strategic nuclear balance, defence expenditure (with historical trends), military manpower (active and reserve), major naval ship construction, army divisional establishments and arms-transfer agreements. There is a list of peace-keeping forces now deployed, a table giving the characteristics of offensive support aircraft and an index of the NATO code-names for Soviet aircraft. A separate essay assesses the European theatre balance between NATO and the Warsaw Pact and summarizes the statistics of forces and weapons in Europe which are the subject of negotiations for mutual force reductions.

Notes, which follow this Preface, will help the reader to use the current edition of *The Military Balance*. It is important to read them, since they amplify and give precision to the data in the national sections and tables. In addition, because some items have not appeared annually, an index is given on p. 111 which provides a guide to such occasional features in this and previous editions.

The Institute assumes full responsibility for the facts and judgments which this study contains. The co-operation of governments has been sought and, in many cases, received. Not all countries have been equally co-operative, and some figures have necessarily been estimated. The Institute owes a considerable debt to a number of its own members and consultants, who have helped in compiling and checking material.

The Military Balance is complemented by the Institute's other annual handbook, *Strategic Survey*, published each spring, which reviews the most significant issues of international security and strategic policy in every major country and area of the world during the previous calendar year and is designed to enable subsequent events to be followed.

September 1977

READERS' NOTES

Regions and Countries

The main geographical regions are indicated in the Table of Contents on p. iii. An alphabetical list, showing where each country entry is to be found, is on p. 2, following these notes. To the extent that national variations permit, each country entry (with the exception of those for some smaller countries) is arranged in a standard form: general information about population, military service, total military manpower strength, Gross National Product (GNP) and defence expenditure is followed by separate sections on the main armed services (army, navy, air force), each of which contains, where the information is available, sub-sections on reserves and, where relevant, on deployment of forces of a significant size.

Defence Pacts and Agreements

A short description of multilateral and bilateral pacts and military aid agreements introduces each of the main regional sections of the study. Defence assistance given under less formal arrangements is also noted. Agreements which cover only economic aid are not included.

Defence Expenditure

For defence expenditure the latest available budget figures are quoted. Table 2 on pp. 82–3 shows current and past expenditures, expressed in United States dollars so as to afford international comparisons; however, as many countries update these each year, the figures will not necessarily correspond with those shown in previous editions of *The Military Balance*. In Table 4 there are comparisons of NATO defence expenditures 1960–1976 in current and constant prices. In this table, and for the NATO countries in Table 2, a NATO definition of defence expenditure is used, but in all other cases national definitions are used. The defence expenditures of the Soviet Union and the People's Republic of China are estimates. The problem of arriving at Soviet defence expenditure and at a suitable exchange rate to afford comparability is discussed on p. 10 whilst a note on p. 54 gives an indication of the difficulty of arriving at a figure for China.

Gross National Product (GNP)

GNP figures are usually quoted at current market prices (factor cost for East European countries). Where figures are not currently available from published sources, estimates have been made, and Table 2 uses both published and estimated GNP figures. Wherever possible, the United Nations System of National Accounts has been used, rather than national figures, as a step towards greater comparability. For the Soviet Union GNP estimates are made in roubles, following R. W. Campbell, 'A Shortcut Method for Estimating Soviet GNP' (*Association for Comparative Economic Studies*, vol. XIV, no. 2, Fall 1972). East European GNPs at factor cost are derived from Net Material Product, using an adjustment parameter from T. P. Alton, 'Economic Growth and Resource Allocation in Eastern Europe', *Reorientation and Commercial Relations of the Economics of Eastern Europe*, Joint Economic Committee, 93rd Congress, 2nd Session (Washington: USGPO, 1974). For the People's Republic of China two estimates of GNP have been given in a note on p. 54.

Currency Conversion Rates

To make comparisons easier, national currency figures have been converted into United States dollars, using the rate prevailing at the end of the second quarter of the relevant year. In all cases the conversion rates used are shown in the country entry but may not always be applicable to commercial transactions. An exception has been made in the case of the Soviet Union, since the official exchange rate is unsuitable for converting rouble estimates of GNP. Various estimates of more appropriate conversion rates have been made, but they have shortcomings too great to warrant their being used here; the official rate is, however, given in the country section. Further exceptions are certain East European countries which are not members of the IMF and Romania (which is), for which the conversion rates used are those described in Alton's study mentioned above.

Manpower

Unless otherwise stated, the manpower figures given are those of active forces, regular and conscript. An indication of the size of militia, reserve and para-military forces is also included in the country entry where appropriate. Para-military forces are here taken to be forces whose equipment and training goes beyond that required for civil police duties and whose constitution and control suggest that they may be usable in support, or in lieu, of regular forces. Further manpower information is also included in Table 3.

Equipment

The equipment figures in the country entries cover total holdings, with the exception of combat aircraft, where front-line squadron strengths are normally shown. Except where the contrary is made clear, naval vessels of less than 100 tons structural displacement have been excluded. The term 'combat aircraft' comprises only bomber, fighter-bomber, strike, interceptor, reconnaissance, counter-insurgency and armed trainer aircraft (i.e. aircraft normally equipped and configured to deliver ordnance); it does not include helicopters. Basic technical details of the nuclear delivery vehicles (missiles, artillery and aircraft) available to NATO and Warsaw Pact countries are given in Table 1 on pp. 77–81. Where the term 'mile' is used to indicate the range or radius of weapons systems, it means a statute mile.

Strength of Military Formations

The table below gives the average establishment strength of the major military formations used in the text (further information about certain of the divisions is given in Table 8 on pp. 92–3). The figures should be treated as approximate, since military organization is flexible, and formations may be reinforced or reduced. The manning of formations may, of course, be well below these levels.

| | Division | | | | | Brigade | | | | Squadron |
| | Armoured | | Mechanized | | Airborne | Armoured | | Mechanized | | Fighter aircraft |
	Men	Tanks	Men	Tanks	Men	Men	Tanks	Men	Tanks	
United States	16,500	324	16,000	216	15,000	4,200	108	4,500	54	12–14
Soviet Union	11,000	325[a]	12,700	266[a]	7,000	1,300[b]	95[b]	2,300[b]	40[b]	10–14
China	10,000	270	12,000[c]	30[c]	9,000	1,200[b]	90[b]	2,000[b]	—	9–10
Britain[d]	11,700	212	—	—	—	4–5,000	106	—	—	8–15
Germany	17,000	300	17,500	250	8–9,000	4,500[e]	108[e]	5,000[e]	54[e]	15–21
India	15,000	200	17,500[c]	—	—	6,000	150	4,500	—	12–20
Israel	—	—	—	—	—	3,500	80–100	3,500	36–40	15–20
Egypt	11,000	300	12,000	190	—	3,500	96	3,500	36	10–12

[a] These tank strengths are for Soviet divisions in Eastern Europe; other Soviet divisions have fewer.
[b] Strength of a regiment, which is the equivalent formation in the Soviet and Chinese command structures. (The term 'regiment' is, however, often employed, particularly in West European countries, to describe a battalion-size unit, and it is so used in *The Military Balance*.)
[c] Infantry division.
[d] Britain is proposing to eliminate the brigade as a formation and have armoured divisions smaller than above and a new infantry formation of about brigade size, known as a Field Force.
[e] Proposed new armoured brigades will have 3,026 men and 99 tanks, mechanized brigades 3,730 men and 66 tanks.

Divisional strengths cover organic units only and exclude support units or services outside the divisional structure. Warsaw Pact formations and squadrons have establishments similar to those of the Soviet Union. NATO formations and squadrons not included in the table above have similar totals to those of Germany unless otherwise mentioned in the text. Iran, Pakistan, the Philippines, Thailand, Japan, South Korea and Taiwan have tended to adopt American military organization, while Australia, New Zealand, Malaysia and Singapore have generally followed British practice.

Arms Transfers

Major arms supply agreements identified as being made during the year which ended on 1 July 1977 are listed, under geographical regions, in Table 11 on pp. 96–101. Because the actual transfer of arms may take place outside that year, an indication is also given there of expected delivery dates, where these are known. Licensing arrangements, which are very widespread among the larger countries, are not normally included.

Abbreviations and Terms

A list of the abbreviations used in the text is on p. viii, immediately following these notes. For the convenience of the reader, certain important abbreviations are explained again when first used. Where a $ sign appears it refers to United States dollars, unless otherwise stated. The term billion equals 1,000 million.

ABBREVIATIONS

AA	Anti-aircraft	Log	Logistic
AAM	Air-to-air missile(s)	LPH	Landing platform, helicopter
AB	Airborne	LRCM	Long-range cruise missile(s)
ABM	Anti-ballistic missile	LST	Landing ship, tank
Ac	Aircraft	Lt	Light
AD	Air defence		
AEW	Airborne early warning	M	Million
AFV	Armoured fighting vehicle(s)	MARV	Manoeuvrable re-entry vehicle(s)
ALBM	Air-launched ballistic missile(s)	MCM	Mine counter-measures
ALCM	Air-launched cruise missile(s)	Mech	Mechanized
Amph	Amphibious	Med	Medium
APC	Armoured personnel carrier(s)	MGB	Motor gunboat
Armd	Armoured	MICV	Mechanized infantry combat vehicle(s)
Arty	Artillery	MIRV	Multiple independently-targetable re-entry vehicle(s)
ASM	Air-to-surface missile(s)		
ASW	Anti-submarine warfare	Mk	Mark
ATGW	Anti-tank guided weapon(s)	Mor	Mortar(s)
ATK	Anti-tank	Mot	Motorized
AWACS	Airborne warning and control system	MR	Maritime reconnaissance
AWX	All-weather fighter	MRBM	Medium-range ballistic missile(s)
		MRV	Multiple re-entry vehicle(s)
Bbr	Bomber	Msl	Missile
Bde	Brigade	MT	Megaton (1 million tons TNT equivalent)
Bn	Battalion *or* billion		
Bty	Battery	MTB	Motor torpedo boat(s)
Cav	Cavalry	n.a.	Not available
Cdo	Commando	NATO	North Atlantic Treaty Organization
CENTO	Central Treaty Organization		
CEP	Circular error probable	OCU	Operational Conversion Unit
COIN	Counter-insurgency		
Comd	Command	Para	Parachute
Comms	Communications	Pdr	Pounder
Coy	Company		
		RCL	Recoilless rifle(s)
Det	Detachment	Recce	Reconnaissance
Div	Division	Regt	Regiment
		RL	Rocket launcher(s)
ECM	Electronic counter-measures	RV	Re-entry vehicle(s)
Engr	Engineer		
Eqpt	Equipment	SAM	Surface-to-air missile(s)
EW	Early warning	SAR	Search and rescue
		Sig	Signal
FB	Fighter-bomber	SLBM	Submarine-launched ballistic missile(s)
Fd	Field	SLCM	Sea-launched cruise missile(s)
FGA	Fighter, ground-attack	SP	Self-propelled
Flt	Flight	Spt	Support
FPB	Fast patrol boat(s)	Sqn	Squadron
FPBG	Fast patrol boat(s), guided-missile	SRAM	Short-range attack missile(s)
		SRBM	Short-range ballistic missile(s)
GDP	Gross Domestic Product	SSBN	Ballistic-missile submarine(s), nuclear
GNP	Gross National Product	SSM	Surface-to-surface missile(s)
GP	General purpose	SSN	Submarine(s), nuclear
Gp	Group	Sub	Submarine
GW	Guided weapon(s)		
		Tac	Tactical
Hel	Helicopter(s)	Tk	Tank
How	Howitzer(s)	Tp	Troop
HQ	Headquarters	Tpt	Transport
Hy	Heavy	Trg	Training
ICBM	Inter-continental ballistic missile(s)	UN	United Nations
Incl	Including	UNDOF	United Nations Disengagement Observation Force
Indep	Independent		
Inf	Infantry	UNEF	United Nations Emergency Force
IRBM	Intermediate-range ballistic missile(s)	UNFICYP	United Nations Force in Cyprus
		UNTSO	United Nations Truce Supervisory Organization
KT	Kiloton (1,000 tons TNT equivalent)		
		Veh	Vehicle(s)
LCT	Landing craft, tank	V(/S)TOL	Vertical (/short) take-off and landing
LHA	Amphibious general assault ship(s)		

1

COUNTRIES AND
PRINCIPAL PACTS

COUNTRY INDEX

The United States and the Soviet Union

Strategic Forces

As negotiations to limit offensive forces continued at the Strategic Arms Limitations Talks (SALT), the two super-powers modernized, and in some areas expanded, their capabilities within the limits imposed by the 1972 five-year Interim Agreement and the guidelines for a second accord reached at Vladivostok in 1974. The Interim Agreement, which set ceilings on numbers of sea and land-based missile launchers, is scheduled to lapse on 3 October 1977.

The United States concentrated on improvements to the existing triad of ICBM, SLBM and bombers and continued to fund development programmes for new systems for deployment in the 1980s. The size of the ICBM force – 550 *Minuteman* III (each with 3 MIRV), 450 single-warhead *Minuteman* II and 54 single-warhead *Titan* II – did not change. Plans to improve *Minuteman* III yield and accuracy with procurement of the 370KT Mk 12A MIRV warhead and NS-20 guidance system went ahead. These programmes, together with improvements to *Minuteman* software, would increase accuracy (measured in CEP) from about 0.25 nautical miles (nm) to 700 feet by the end of the decade and significantly enhance the ability to destroy hardened targets. Development of MARV proceeded, and component development began on an 8–10-MIRV mobile ICBM, the MX, to replace parts of the *Minuteman* force in the 1980s and further enhance hard-target capability.

At sea, the SLBM force of 496 *Poseidon*, each with 10–14 MIRV, in 31 submarines and 160 *Polaris*, each with 3 MRV, in 10 submarines remained in operation. Construction of the first ten 24-tube *Trident* boats continued (initial funding has been approved for others), and testing began on the 4,000nm-range C4 *Trident* I missile. When operational in 1978, the C4, armed with 8×100KT MIRV, will almost double the effective range of American SLBM and increase their accuracy to a CEP of less than 1,500ft. A second-generation SLBM for the *Trident* class, the 6,000nm D5, reportedly with a 14×150KT MIRV warhead and possibly able to manoeuvre, was under early development.

In the air, structural and avionics improvements were made to the B-52G/H bomber force. Flight testing continued on three B-1 bomber prototypes, and a fourth began construction, but plans to procure further aircraft were cancelled.

Flight testing proceeded of versions of the air-launched cruise missile (ALCM) for deployment aboard the B-52 and possibly other aircraft. The terminally-guided version for possible deployment in the early 1980s would have a maximum range of 1,500nm. Cruise missiles were also tested from other platforms. The *Tomahawk* sea-launched cruise missile (SLCM) was fired successfully from surface vessels and submarines, and feasibility studies were begun for adapting this 2,000nm-range missile for ground launch.

American ICBM, SLBM and long-range bombers totalled 2,083, over 200 fewer than in 1967. However, this force had the capability to deliver over 11,000 warheads, almost twice as many as a decade earlier. With the introduction of the *Trident* submarine force, warhead totals will approach 14,000 (10,000 on ICBM and SLBM) in the early 1980s.

The improvement of strategic defensive forces continued at a slower pace. Interceptor aircraft continued to be phased out, but a new interceptor was planned. Development of an advanced bomber and missile attack radar went on, but the *Seafarer* submarine communications system met political obstacles. Several programmes to enhance satellite survivability began, including satellite 'hardening', manoeuvrability and, possibly, development of an anti-satellite capability.

The Soviet Union proceeded with broad modernization of ICBM, SLBM and bomber capabilities. Although total ICBM numbers fell to 1,477 (as older ICBM were replaced by new SLBM), at least 80 new ICBM – SS-17, SS-18 and SS-19 – were deployed in MIRV and single-warhead modes. These were said to be notably more accurate than the SS-9 and SS-11, SS-19 accuracy reportedly approaching that of existing US systems. The mobile SS-X-16 remained under development, but an intermediate-range MIRV version, the SS-20, began deployment (with reloads) in the Western USSR. A new ICBM family for possible late 1980s deployment was reported in the early development stage.

Soviet SLBM increased to 909 in 82 submarines. Four *Delta*-II-class submarines were launched, each with 16 4,800nm-range SS-N-8. Two new SLBM were tested during the year; the SS-NX-17, a solid-propellent replacement for the SS-N-6, and the SS-NX-18, a 3-MIRV replacement for the SS-N-8. Development of a longer-range replacement for the SS-N-3 SLCM continued.

Deployment of the *Backfire* B bomber continued at a rate of approximately 25 per year, and development proceeded on new ASM.

Compared with 837 in 1967, Soviet ICBM, SLBM and long-range bombers numbered 2,521. This force can deliver roughly 3,800 warheads against the United States. With the replacement of the remainder of the ICBM force with the new MIRV-equipped missiles, this total would rise to over 7,500 in the early 1980s, individual warheads having significantly higher yields than US ones.

Both air defence interceptors and SAM were modernized. The 64 ABM launchers around Moscow remained in operation, and tests were reported of new transportable radars and endo-atmospheric missiles. Civil defence activities and satellite interceptor tests continued, and there were reports of work on a charged-particle beam for use in ballistic missile defence.

General-purpose Forces

Numbers in the American and Soviet armed forces remained at last year's levels of 2.09 million and 3.67 million respectively, compared with roughly 3 million for each in the mid 1960s. Both steadily improved conventional capabilities. By reducing support personnel, the United States added one to her 13 army divisions and proceeded with plans to raise two more by 1978; two infantry divisions were also being mechanized. Programmes concentrated on new direct- and indirect-fire anti-armour weapons. The procurement of 30,000 *TOW* missiles was completed, and *Dragon* procurement continued. Cannon-launched guided projectiles and scatterable mines were under development, as were new precision-guided munitions for helicopters, and procurement of new surveillance and target-acquisition aids began. Tank production was increased, but the number of medium tanks (around 10,000) was roughly the same as in 1967. The XM-1 tank and the Mechanized Infantry Combat Vehicle (MICV) were under development. Modernization of the theatre nuclear weapon stockpile began, with development under way on enhanced-radiation weapons for use on the battlefield.

The Soviet Union continued to increase holdings of BMP MICV and T-62 and T-72 tanks, and tank numbers rose to some 43,000 compared with some 34,000 in 1967. The deployment of helicopters, SAM, ATGW and self-propelled artillery also continued.

In the US Navy plans were made to reverse the decline in major surface combatants from over 300 to less than 200 in a decade. The building of a new nuclear-powered carrier was cancelled, however, and planning concentrated on a new class of smaller, conventionally-engined carrier. Two 688-class attack submarines were delivered, and funding for a further three was approved. Development continued of the *Aegis* ship defence system (to be deployed aboard a new strike cruiser), the *Harpoon* anti-shipping missile and a tactical version of the *Tomahawk* SLCM. Research also accelerated on the development of a new generation of naval VTOL aircraft.

The Soviet Navy continued its gradual growth in size and quality. The first of three *Kiev*-class aircraft carriers became operational, construction continued of *Kara*- and *Kresta*-II-class missile cruisers, and development of a class of missile cruiser for the 1980s was also reported. Procurement of V- and T-class nuclear and F-class diesel attack and C-II-class cruise-missile submarines proceeded. New anti-shipping and anti-submarine missiles were under development and being deployed, and the naval air force received *Forger* VTOL and *Backfire* aircraft.

The United States continued deployment of the Air Force F-15 and the Navy F-14 fighters, and development of the less costly F-16 and F-18 continued in order to enable combat aircraft force levels to be kept above 2,500 as older aircraft are retired. Production of the A-10 close air support aircraft began and is to be completed by the early 1980s. Procurement of at least 16 E-3A AWACS aircraft was approved (but no decision to buy it was taken by NATO). Modification of the F-4C for electronic warfare roles proceeded, as did development work on converting the F-111A for this.

The deployment of new Soviet fighters with improved range, payload and avionics continued, including the Su-17 *Fitter* C, MiG-23 *Flogger* B and Su-19 *Fencer*. With the introduction of more multi-role aircraft, the Soviet Union has over twice as many fighters suitable for ground-attack missions as in the 1960s, many nuclear-capable. There were reports of new air-to-air and air-to-surface missiles under development, and of work on ECM equipment to enhance aircraft penetration.

THE UNITED STATES

Population: 217,030,000.
Military service: voluntary.
Total armed forces: 2,088,000 (119,600 women).
Estimated GNP 1976: $1,692.4 bn.
Defence expenditure 1977–78: $109.7 bn.*

Strategic Nuclear Forces:†

OFFENSIVE:
(a) *Navy:* 656 SLBM in 41 subs.
31 SSBN (*Lafayette*-class), each with 16 *Poseidon* C3.
10 SSBN (5 *Washington*-, 5 *Allen*-class), each with 16 *Polaris* A3.
(2 *Trident*-class SSBN, each with 24 *Trident* C4, building.)
(b) *Strategic Air Command* (SAC): some 644 combat aircraft.
ICBM: 1,054.
450 *Minuteman* II, 550 *Minuteman* III, 54 *Titan* II.
Aircraft:
Bombers: 441, in 24 sqns.
68 FB-111A in 4 sqns ⎱with
226 B-52G/H in 15 sqns ⎰1,500 SRAM
75 B-52D in 5 sqns.
Training: 72 B-52D/F.
Storage or reserve: 153, incl B-52D/F/G.
Tankers: 519 KC-135 in 32 sqns.
Strategic Reconnaissance and Command: 18 SR-71A in 2 sqns; U-2C/K; 4 E-4A/B; 28 RC/EC-135.

DEFENSIVE:
North American Air Defense Command (NORAD), HQ at Colorado Springs, is a joint American–Canadian organization. US forces under NORAD are in Aerospace Defense Command (ADCOM).

ABM: Safeguard system (msls deactivated).

Aircraft (excluding Canadian and tac units):
Interceptors: 331
(i) Regular: 6 sqns with 141 F-106A.
(ii) Air National Guard (ANG): 3 sqns with 80 F-101B, 1 with 20 F-4D, 6 with 90 F-106A.
AEW aircraft: 1 reserve sqn with 8 EC-121.

Warning Systems:
(i) *Satellite-based early-warning system:* 3 DSP satellites, 1 over Eastern Hemisphere, 2 over Western; surveillance and warning system to detect launchings from SLBM, ICBM and Fractional Orbital Bombardment Systems (FOBS).

(ii) *Space Detection and Tracking System* (SPADATS): USAF *Spacetrack* (7 sites), USN *SPASUR* and civilian agencies. Space Defense Center at NORAD HQ: satellite tracking, identification and cataloguing control.
(iii) *Ballistic Missile Early Warning System* (BMEWS): 3 stations (Alaska, Greenland, England); detection and tracking radars with ICBM and IRBM capability.
(iv) *Distant Early Warning* (DEW) *Line:* 31 stations roughly along the 70°N parallel.
(v) *Pinetree Line:* 24 Stations in Central Canada.
(vi) *474N:* 3 stations on US East, 1 on Gulf, 3 on West coast (to be replaced by *Pave Paw* phased-array radars: 1 on East, 1 on West coast); SLBM detection and warning net.
(vii) *Perimeter Acquisition Radar* (PAR): 1 north-facing phased-array 2,000-mile system at inactive ABM site in North Dakota).
(viii) *Back-up Interceptor Control* (BUIC): system for AD command and control (all stations but 1 semi-active).
(ix) *Semi-Automatic Ground Environment* (SAGE): 6 locations (2 in Canada); combined with BUIC and Manual Control Centre (MCC) in Alaska (to be replaced by Joint Surveillance System (JSS) with 7 Region Operations Control Centres, 4 in US, 1 in Alaska, 2 in Canada); system for co-ordinating surveillance and tracking of objects in North American airspace.
(x) *Ground radar stations:* some 51 stations manned by ANG, augmented by the Federal Aviation Administration (FAA) stations (to be replaced as surveillance element of JSS).

Army: 789,000 (51,900 women).
4 armd divs.
5 mech divs.‡
5 inf divs.‡
1 airmobile div.
1 AB div.
1 armd bde.
1 inf bde.
3 armd cav regts.
1 bde in Berlin.
2 special mission bdes in Alaska and Panama.
Army Aviation: 1 air cav combat bde, indep bns assigned to HQ for tac tpt and medical duties.
1 *Honest John*, 3 *Pershing*, 8 *Lance* SSM bns.
Tanks: some 10,000 med, incl 3,300 M-48, 6,700 M-60 (M-60A2 with *Shillelagh* ATGW); 1,600 M-551 *Sheridan* lt tks with *Shillelagh*.
AFV: some 22,000 M-577, M-114, M-113 APC.

---

* Expected Outlay in Fiscal 1978. Budget Outlay $117.7 bn; Total Obligational Authority $120.4 bn.
† Manpower included in Army, Navy and Air Force totals. Msl and ac characteristics given in Table 1, pp. 77–81.

‡ One National Guard bde is incorporated in 1 mech and 3 inf divs. Two of the divs will not achieve deployment until 1978.

Arty and Msls: some 5,000 175mm SP guns and 105mm, 155mm and 203mm SP how; 105mm, 155mm towed guns/how; 3,000 81mm, 3,000 107mm mor; 6,000 90mm and 106mm RCL; *TOW, Dragon* ATGW; *Honest John, Pershing, Lance* SSM.

AA arty and SAM: some 600 20mm, 40mm towed and SP AA guns; some 20,000 *Redeye* and *Chaparral/Vulcan* 20mm AA msl/gun systems; *Nike Hercules* and *HAWK* SAM. (*Roland* SAM on order.)

Aircraft/Hel: about 500 ac, incl 300 OV-1/-10, 200 U-8/-21; 8,000 hel, incl 1,000 AH-1G/S, 4,000 UH-1/-19, 500 CH-47/-54, 2,500 OH-6A/-58, H-13. Trainers incl 100 T-41/-42 ac; 700 TH-55A hel.

DEPLOYMENT:

Continental United States
   Strategic Reserve: (i) 1 armd, 1 mech, 3 inf, 1 air-mobile, 1 AB divs. (ii) To reinforce 7th Army in Europe: 1 armd, 2 mech divs, 1 armd cav regt.*

Europe: 198,400.
(i) Germany: 189,000. 7th Army: 2 corps, incl 2 armd, 2 mech divs, 3 mech bdes plus 2 armd cav regts; 3,000 med tks.†
(ii) West Berlin: 4,400. HQ elements and 1 inf bde.
(iii) Greece: 800.
(iv) Italy: 3,000.
(v) Turkey: 1,200.

Pacific
(i) South Korea: 30,000. 1 inf div, 1 AD arty bde.
(ii) Hawaii: 1 inf div less 1 bde.

RESERVES: 591,000.
(i) Army National Guard: 379,000; capable after mobilization of manning 2 armd, 1 mech, 5 inf divs, 20 indep bdes‡ (3 armd, 6 mech, 11 inf) and 3 armd cav regts, plus reinforcements and support units to fill regular formations.
(ii) Army Reserves: 212,000 in 12 trg divs, 3 indep combat bdes; 49,000 a year do short active duty.

Marine Corps: 192,000 (3,900 women).
3 divs.
2 SAM bns with *HAWK*.
575 M-60 med tks; 950 LVTP-7 APC; 175mm SP guns; 105mm, 155mm how; 155mm, 203mm SP how; 230 81mm and 107mm mor; 106mm RCL; *TOW, Dragon* ATGW.
3 Air Wings: 365 combat aircraft.
   12 FGA sqns with 144 F-4N/S with *Sparrow* and *Sidewinder* AAM.

---

* One armd div, 1 mech div, 1 armd cav regt have hy eqpt stockpiled in W. Germany.
† Includes those stockpiled for the strategic reserve formations.
† There are, in addition, 4 indep bdes incorporated in active army divs.

13 FGA sqns: 3 with 80 AV-8A *Harrier*, 5 with 60 A-4E/F/M, 5 with 60 A-6A/E.
2 recce sqns with 21 RF-4B, 2 AEW sqns with 17 EA-6A (to be replaced by EA-6B).
3 observation sqns with 54 OV-10A.
3 assault tpt/tanker sqns with 36 KC-130F.
3 attack hel sqns with 54 AH-1J.
4 lt hel sqns with 84 UH-1E/N.
9 med hel sqns with 162 CH-46F.
6 hy hel sqns with 126 CH-53D.

DEPLOYMENT:
(i) *Continental United States:* 2 divs, 2 air wings.
(ii) *Pacific:* 1 div, 1 air wing.

RESERVES: 33,500.
   1 div and 1 air wing: 2 fighter sqns with F-4B, 5 attack sqns with A-4E, 1 observation sqn with OV-10A, 1 tpt/tanker sqn with KC-130, 7 hel sqns (1 attack with AH-1G, 2 hy with CH-53, 3 med with CH-46, 1 lt with UH-1E), 2 tk bns, 1 assault amph bn, 1 SAM bn with *HAWK*, 1 fd arty gp.

Navy: 536,000 (23,800 women); 175 major combat surface ships, 78 attack submarines.

Submarines, attack: 68 nuclear, 10 diesel.

Aircraft carriers: 13; 2 nuclear-powered (*Nimitz*, 96,000 tons, *Enterprise*, 91,000 tons).
   8 *Forrestal/Kitty Hawk*-class 78/87,000 tons).
   3 *Midway*-class (64,000 tons).
   These normally carry 1 air wing (85–95 ac, 75 in *Midway* class) of 2 fighter sqns with F-14A or F-4B/J, 3–4 attack sqns (1 AWX) with A-7 or A-6; RA-5C recce; 2 asw sqns (1 with S-3A, 1 with SH-3A/D/G/H hel); 1 ECM sqn with EA-6B; 1 AEW sqn with E-2B/C; EA-3B/KA-6 tankers and other specialist ac.

Other surface ships:
5 nuclear-powered GW cruisers with SAM, *ASROC*.
19 GW cruisers with SAM, *ASROC*.
2 GW lt cruisers with SAM.
38 GW destroyers with SAM, *ASROC*.
34 gun/asw destroyers, most with SAM or *ASROC*.
6 GW frigates with SAM, *ASROC*.
58 gun frigates.
7 patrol gunboats with SAM.
62 amph warfare ships, incl 7 LPH, 1 LHA.
3 MCM ships.
110 log and operations support ships.
(13 SSN, 2 nuclear-powered carriers, 3 nuclear-powered GW cruisers, 17 destroyers, 1 GW frigate, 4 LHA, 1 patrol msl hydrofoil building.)

Missiles:
   Standard SSM/SAM, *Tartar, Talos, Terrier, Sea Sparrow* SAM, *ASROC, SUBROC* ASW.

Ships in reserve:
   4 subs, 6 aircraft carriers, 4 battleships, 10 cruisers, 10 amph warfare, 9 MCM ships, 46 log

support and 41 troop, cargo and tanker ships. (239 cargo ships, 162 tankers could be used for auxiliary sea-lift.)

Aircraft: 13 attack carrier air wings; some 1,200 combat aircraft.
26 fighter sqns: 12 with F-14A, 14 with F-4.
39 attack sqns: 12 with A-6, 27 with A-7.
10 recce sqns with RA-5C, RF-8.
24 land-based MR sqns with 216 P-3A/B/C.
11 ASW sqns each with 10 S-3A.
12 AEW sqns each with E-2B/C.
11 ASW hel sqns with 8 SH-3A/D/G/H.
17 misc support sqns with 20 C-1, 15 C-2, 8 C-9B, 12 C-130F/LC-130, 12 CT-39, 7 C-118, 26 C-131, 6 C-117, 36 EA-6B ac; 21 RH-53D, CH-46, SH-3, SH-2B/C hel.
20 trg sqns with T-1A, T-2B/C, T-28/-29B/-34/-38/-44, TA-4J/F, TA-7C, TS-2A, TE-2 ac; TH-1, UH-1D, TH-57A hel.

DEPLOYMENT (average strengths of major combat ships; some in Mediterranean and Western Pacific based overseas, rest rotated from US):
Second Fleet (Atlantic): 5 carriers, 62 surface combatants.
Third Fleet (Eastern Pacific): 4 carriers, 65 surface combatants.
Sixth Fleet (Mediterranean): 2 carriers, 15 surface combatants, 1 Marine Amphibious Unit (MAU).*
Seventh Fleet (Western Pacific): 2 carriers, 20 surface combatants, 1 MAU, 1 Marine Bn Landing Team.

RESERVES: 98,000. Ships in commission with the Reserve include 30 destroyers, 7 patrol gunboats, 3 amph warfare, 22 MCM ships.
2 carrier wings: 6 A-7, 1 A-4E/L attack, 4 F-4N fighter, 2 RF-8G recce, 2 KA-3B tanker, 2 E-1B/-2B AEW, 3 EA-6A/EKA-3 ECM sqns.
13 MR sqns: 11 with P-3A, 2 with SP-2H.
3 tpt sqns with C-9/C-118.
7 hel sqns: 4 with SH-3A/G, 2 with HH-1K, 1 SAR with HH-3.

Air Force: 571,000 (40,000 women); about 3,400 combat aircraft.†
80 fighter/attack sqns: 49 with F-4, 2 with F-105G (to be replaced by F-4G), 13 with F-111E/F, 6 with F-15, 6 with A-7D, 1 with A-10A, 3 with F-5E.
9 tac recce sqns with RF-4C.
1 AWACS sqn with 1 E-3A (15 on order).

---

* Marine Amphibious Units are 5–7 amph ships with a Marine bn embarked. Only 1 in Mediterranean and 1 in Pacific are regularly constituted. 1 Battalion Landing Team (MAU less hel) also deployed in the Pacific; 1 occasionally formed for the Atlantic.
† Excluding ac in SAC and NORAD; incl ac in ANG and Air Force Reserve.

1 ECM sqn with EB-57 (2 with 42 EF-111A due).
11 tac air control sqns: 6 with OV-2/-10, 1 with C-130E, 1 with EC-135 ac, 3 with CH-3/-53 hel.
5 special operations sqns: 4 with C/AC-130 ac, 1 with CH-3, UH-1 hel.
1 tac drone sqn with DC-130.
15 tac airlift sqns with 272 C-130.
17 hy tpt sqns: 4 with 77 C-5A, 13 with 271 C-141.
5 SAR sqns with 32 HC-130 ac, 79 HH-3/-53, 11 HH-1 hel.
1 medical tpt sqn with 23 C-9.
2 weather recce sqns with 14 WC-130.
Hel incl some 300 UH-1N, HH-3E, HH-43, HH-53B/C.
Trg sqns with some 1,600 T-37/-38/-39/-41/-43.

DEPLOYMENT:
Continental United States (incl Alaska):
(i) Tactical Air Command: 82,000; 9th and 12th Air Forces. 42 fighter sqns, 5 tac recce sqns.
(ii) Military Airlift Command (MAC): 64,500. 21st and 22nd Air Forces.
Europe: US Air Force, Europe (USAFE): 76,000. 3rd Air Force (Britain), 16th Air Force (Spain; units in Italy, Greece and Turkey), 17th Air Force (Germany and Netherlands). 1 AD sqn in Iceland. 24 fighter sqns (plus 4 in US on call) with 400 F-4C/D/E, 72 F-15, 156 F-111E/F; 3 tac recce sqns (plus 3 in US on call) with 60 RF-4C; 2 tac airlift sqns (plus 6 in US on call) with 32 C-130.
Pacific: Pacific Air Forces (PACAF): 31,100; 5th Air Force (Japan, Okinawa, 1 wing in Korea), 13th Air Force (Philippines, Taiwan). 9 fighter sqns, 1 tac recce sqn.

RESERVES: 148,000.
(i) Air National Guard: 94,000; about 900 combat aircraft.
  10 interceptor sqns (under ADCOM, see p. 5); 29 fighter sqns (13 with F-100C/D, 3 with F-105B/D, 2 with F-4C, 9 with A-7, 2 with A-37B); 8 recce sqns (1 with RF-101, 7 with RF-4C); 18 tac tpt sqns (17 with C-130A/B/E, 1 with C-7); 6 tac air spt gps with 0-2A; 13 tanker sqns (10 with KC-135, 3 with KC-97); 3 ECM sqns with 8 C/EC-121 (ADC), 18 EB-57B; 2 SAR sqns with HC-130/HH-3.
(ii) Air Force Reserve: 54,000; about 200 combat aircraft.
  3 fighter sqns with F-105D; 4 attack sqns with A-37B; 18 tac tpt sqns (12 with C-130/A/B, 4 with C-123K, 2 with C-7); 1 AEW sqn with EC-121 (ADC), 2 tanker sqns with KC-135; 2 special operations sqns with AC-130, CH-3; 4 SAR sqns (2 with HC-130, 2 with HH-1H/-3); 1 weather recce sqn with WC-130. 18 Reserve Associate Military Airlift sqns (personnel only): 4 for C-5A, 13 for C-141A, 1 aero medical for C-9A.
(iii) Civil Reserve Air Fleet: 225 long-range commercial ac (131 cargo/convertible, 94 passenger).

THE SOVIET UNION

Population: 257,890,000.
Military service: Army and Air Force 2 years.
Navy and Border Guards 2–3 years.
Total armed forces: 3,675,000.*
Estimated GNP 1976: 490 bn roubles.†
Estimated defence expenditure 1977: see pp. 10–11.

Strategic Nuclear Forces:‡
OFFENSIVE:
(a) *Navy:* 909 SLBM in 82 subs.
8 D-II-class SSBN, each with 16 SS-N-8.§
13 D-I-class SSBN, each with 12 SS-N-8.
34 Y-class SSBN, each with 16 SS-N-6 *Sawfly.*
7 H-class SSBN, each with 3 SS-N-5 *Serb.*
11 G-II-class diesel, each with 3 SS-N-5.‖
9 G-I-class diesel, each with 3 SS-N-4 *Sark.*‖
(b) *Strategic Rocket Forces* (SRF): 375,000.¶
ICBM: 1,477.
109 SS-7 *Saddler* and SS-8 *Sasin* (being phased out).
238 SS-9 *Scarp* (being replaced).
840 SS-11 *Sego* (being replaced).
60 SS-13 *Savage.*
40 SS-17.
50 SS-18.
140 SS-19.
IRBM and MRBM: some 620 deployed (most in Western USSR, rest east of Urals).
100 SS-5 *Skean* IRBM.
20 SS-20 IRBM (mobile).
500 SS-4 *Sandal* MRBM.
(c) *Long-Range Air Force* (LRAF): 741 combat aircraft.**
Long-range bombers: 135.
100 Tu-95 *Bear.*
35 Mya-4 *Bison.*
Medium-range bombers: 476.
305 Tu-16 *Badger.*
136 Tu-22 *Blinder.*
35 *Backfire* B.
Tankers: 53.
9 Tu-16 *Badger.*
44 Mya-4 *Bison.*

---

* Excludes some 750,000 uniformed civilians.
† See Readers' Notes: official exchange rate 1976, $1=0.75.
‡ Characteristics of nuclear delivery vehicles and notes on numbers and types under construction and test are given in Table 1 on pp. 77–81.
§ One may be a new D-III class.
‖ These 60 launchers are not considered strategic missiles under the terms of the Strategic Arms Limitation (Interim) Agreement.
¶ The SRF and *PVO-Strany,* separate services, have their own manpower.
** About 75 per cent based in the European USSR, most of the remainder in the Far East; there are also staging and dispersal points in the Arctic.

ECM: 94.
94 Tu-16 *Badger.*
Recce: 36.
4 Tu-95 *Bear.*
22 Tu-16 *Badger.*
10 Tu-22 *Blinder.*

DEFENSIVE:
Air Defence Force (PVO-Strany): 550,000:¶ early warning and control systems, with 6,000 early warning and ground control intercept (EW/GCI) radars; interceptor sqns and SAM units.

Aircraft: about 2,650.
Interceptors: incl some 80 MiG-17 (*Fresco* D), 170 MiG-19 (*Farmer* B/E), 650 Su-9 *Fishpot* B, Su-11 *Fishpot* C, 320 Yak-28P *Firebar,* 150 Tu-28P *Fiddler,* 850 Su-15 *Flagon* A/D/E, 110 MiG-23 *Flogger,* 300 MiG-25 *Foxbat* A.
Airborne Warning and Control Aircraft: 9 modified Tu-126 *Moss.*

ABM: 64 *Galosh,* 4 sites around Moscow, with *Try Add* engagement radars. Target acquisition and tracking by phased-array *Dog House* and *Chekov,* early warning by phased-array *Hen House* radar on Soviet borders. Range of *Galosh* believed over 200 miles; warheads nuclear, presumably in megaton range.

SAM:
Fixed-site Systems: 12,000 launchers, at over 1,000 sites.
SA-1 *Guild:* HE warhead, med/high altitude, obsolescent.
SA-2 *Guideline:* 3,500, HE warhead, slant range about 25 miles, effective 1,000–85,000 ft.
SA-3 *Goa:* 1,500, HE warhead, slant range 15 miles, low-altitude, effective 500–60,000 ft.
SA-5 *Gammon:* slant range 50–150 miles, high-altitude (100,000 ft).

Mobile Systems:
SA-4 *Ganef:* Twin mounted, tracked carrier, med-/long-range.
SA-6 *Gainful:* Triple mounted, tracked carrier, short-/med-range.
SA-7 *Grail:* man-portable, short-range, low-altitude.
SA-8 *Gecko:* 4 msls, mounted on 6-wheeled vehicle with fire-control radar.
SA-9 *Gaskin:* 4 msls, mounted on BRDM, short-range, low-altitude.

Army: 1,825,000.
45 tk divs.
115 motor rifle divs.
8 AB divs.
Tanks: 43,000: IS-2/-3, T-10, T-10M hy, T-54/-55/

-62/-72 med, PT-76 lt (most tks fitted for deep wading).

AFV: 47,000: BRDM scout cars; BMP MICV; BTR-40/-50/-60/-152, GT-T/M-1970, BMD APC.

Artillery: 19,000 100mm, 122mm, 130mm, 152mm, 180mm, and 203mm fd and SP guns/how; 7,200 82mm, 120mm, 160mm and 240mm mor; 2,700 122mm, 140mm, 200mm, 240mm, 250mm and 280mm multiple RL; 10,800 ASU-57 and ASU-85 SP, 76mm, 85mm and 100mm ATK guns; *Swatter, Sagger* ATGW.

AA Artillery: 9,000 23mm and 57mm, 100mm towed, ZSU-57-2, ZSU-23-4 SP guns.

SSM (nuclear capable): about 1,200 launchers (units organic to formations), incl *FROG* (range 10–45 miles), *Scud B* (range 185 miles), *Scaleboard* (range 500 miles).

DEPLOYMENT AND STRENGTH:

Central and Eastern Europe: 31 divs: 20 (10 tk) in East Germany, 2 tk in Poland, 4 (2 tk) in Hungary, 5 (2 tk) in Czechoslovakia; 10,500 med and hy tks.*

European USSR (Baltic, Byelorussian, Carpathian, Kiev, Leningrad, Moscow and Odessa Military Districts (MD): 64 divs (about 20 tk).

Central USSR (Volga, Ural MD): 6 divs (1 tk).

Southern USSR (North Caucasus, Trans-Caucasus, Turkestan MD): 24 divs (3 tk).

Sino-Soviet border (Central Asian, Siberian, Transbaikal and Far East MD): 43 divs (about 5 tk), inc 3 in Mongolia.

Soviet divs have three degrees of combat readiness: Category 1, between three-quarters and full strength, with complete eqpt; Category 2, between half and three-quarters strength, complete with fighting vehicles; Category 3, about one-third strength, possibly complete with fighting vehicles (some obsolescent).

The 31 divs in Eastern Europe are Category 1. About half those in European USSR and the Far East are in Category 1 or 2. Most of the divs in Central and Southern USSR are likely to be Category 3. Tk divs in Eastern Europe have 325 med tks, motor rifle divs up to 266, but elsewhere holdings are lower.

Navy: 450,000, incl 50,000 Naval Air Force, 12,000 Naval Infantry and 10,000 Coast Arty and Rocket Troops; 230 major surface combat ships, 234 attack and cruise-missile subs (82 nuclear, 152 diesel).

Submarines:

Attack: 39 nuclear (13 N-, 17 V-I, 3 V-II, 5 E-I, 1 A-class), 128 diesel (56 F-, 10 R-, 10 Z-, 40 W-, 4 B-, 3 T-class, 5 coastal Q-class).

---

* Excluding tks in reserve (replaced by new ones but not withdrawn from the area).

2

Cruise Missile: 43 nuclear:
  1 P-class.
  13 C-class, each with 8 SS-N-7.
  29 E-II-class, each with 8 SS-N-3 *Shaddock*.
24 diesel:
  16 J-class, each with 4 SS-N-3.
  6 W-*Long Bin* class, each with 4 SS-N-3.
  2 W-*Twin Cylinder* class, each with 2 SS-N-3.

Surface Ships:
  1 *Kiev*-class carrier (40,000 tons) with SSM, SAM, 12 VTOL ac, 20 hel (2 building).
  2 *Moskva*-class ASW hel cruisers, each with 2 twin SAM, about 20 Ka-25 hel.
  5 *Kara*-class ASW cruisers with SAM, 1 hel.
  4 *Kresta*-I-class ASW cruisers with SSM, SAM, 1 hel.
  9 *Kresta*-II-class ASW cruisers with SAM, 1 hel (2 building).
  4 *Kynda*-class cruisers with SSM, SAM.
  10 *Sverdlov*-class cruisers (3 with SAM, 2 with hel).
  1 trg cruiser (*Chapaev*-class).
  14 *Krivak*-class ASW destroyers with SSM, SAM.
  8 *Kanin*-class ASW destroyers with SAM.
  4 *Kildin*-class ASW destroyers with SSM.
  19 *Kashin*-class ASW destroyers with SAM (5 with SSM).
  8 modified *Kotlin*-class destroyers with SAM.
  38 destroyers, 18 *Kotlin*-, 20 *Skory*-class.
  103 frigates: 20 *Mirka*, 45 *Petya*, 35 *Riga*, 3 *Kola*.
  17 *Nanuchka*-class msl patrol ships with SSM, SAM.
  244 sub chasers (25 *Turya*, 25 *Pchela* hydrofoils, 25 *Grisha*, 64 *Poti*, 65 *Stenka*, 65 SO-1).
  120 *Osa*- and 5 *Komar*-class FPBG with *Styx* SSM.
  100 MTB (*Shershen* and P-6/-8/-10 classes).
  About 330 minesweepers (150 coastal).
  About 100 amph ships, incl 14 *Alligator*, 7 *Ropucha* LST, 60 *Polnocny* LCT.
  90 landing craft (incl MP-4).
  60 oilers, 80 supply ships.
  20 depot, 30 repair ships.
  54 intelligence collection vessels (AGI).

Ships in reserve: 90 W-, 15 Q-class subs, 2 cruisers, 15 *Skory*-, 10 *Riga*-class destroyers.

NAVAL AIR FORCE: some 662 combat aircraft.
280 Tu-16 *Badger* med bbrs with ASM.
30 *Backfire* B med bbrs with ASM.
48 Tu-22 *Blinder* med bbrs, MR, ECM ac.
10 Il-28 *Beagle* lt bbrs.
Some 10 Yak-36 *Forger* VTOL FGA, 10 *Fitter* FGA.
39 Tu-16 *Badger* E/F recce, 30 Tu-16 ECM ac.
205 MR ac: 45 Tu-95 *Bear* D, 15 *Bear* F, 55 Il-38 *May*, 90 Be-12 *Mail* amphibians.
80 Tu-16 *Badger* tankers.
260 ASW hel: Mi-4 *Hound*, Mi-14 *Haze*, Ka-25A/B *Hormone*.
270 misc tpts and trainers.

NAVAL INFANTRY (Marines):
5 naval inf regts, each of 3 inf, 1 tk bn, one assigned to each of Northern, Baltic and Black Sea fleets,

two to Pacific fleet. T-54/-55 med, PT-76 lt tks, BTR-60P series APC; BM-21 122mm RL; ZSU-23-4 SP AA guns; SA-9 SAM.

COASTAL ARTILLERY AND ROCKET TROOPS:
Hy coastal guns, *Samlet* and SS-C-1B *Sepal* SSM (similar to SS-N-3) to protect approaches to naval bases and major ports.

DEPLOYMENT (average strengths only, excl SSBN):
Northern Fleet: 110 subs, 50 major surface combat ships.
Baltic Fleet: 35 subs, 50 major surface combat ships.
Black Sea Fleet (incl Caspian Flotilla and Mediterranean Squadron): 20 subs, 60 major surface combat ships.
Pacific Fleet: 70 subs, 60 major surface combat ships.

Air Force: 475,000; about 4,600 combat aircraft.*
Tactical Air Force: aircraft incl 175 Il-28 *Beagle*, Yak-28 *Brewer*, 220 MiG-17 *Fresco*, 500 Su-7 *Fitter* A, 1,100 MiG-23/-27 *Flogger*, about 1,450 MiG-21 *Fishbed*, 300 Su-17 *Fitter* C, 120 Su-19 *Fencer* A FGA; about 250 *Beagle, Brewer,* 115 MiG-25 *Foxbat* B, 300 *Fishbed* recce; 45 *Brewer* E, 6 An-12 *Cub* ECM ac; 250 tpts; 3,000 lt, med and hy hel; 1,050 tac trg ac.

---

* Excluding *PVO-Strany* and Long-Range Air Force.

Air Transport Force: 1,500 aircraft: An-14 lt, 50 An-8, 780 An-12, 180 An-24/-26, 235 Il-14, 15 Il-18, Il-62, 35 Il-76, 100 Li-2, 10 Tu-104, 5 Tu-134 med, Tu-114, 50 An-22 hy.
3,660 hel, incl 800 Mi-1/-2, 410 Mi-4, 490 Mi-6, 1,610 Mi-8, 10 Mi-10, 310 Mi-24 *Hind* A.
1,300 Civil Aeroflot med- and long-range ac available to supplement military airlift.

DEPLOYMENT:
16 Tactical Air Armies: 4 (1,700 ac) in Eastern Europe and 1 in each of 12 MD in the USSR.

RESERVES (all services):
Soviet conscripts have a Reserve obligation to age 50. Total reserves could be 25,000,000, of which some 4,200,000 have served in last five years.

Para-Military Forces: 450,000.
200,000 KGB border troops, 250,000 MVD security troops. Border troops equipped with tks, SP guns, AFV, ac and ships; MVD with tks and AFV. Part-time military training organization (DOSAAF) conducts such activities as athletics, shooting, parachuting and pre-military training given to those of 15 and over in schools, colleges and workers' centres. Claimed active membership 80 million, with 5 million instructors and activists; effectives likely to be much fewer.

SOVIET DEFENCE EXPENDITURE

No single figure for Soviet defence expenditure can be given, since precision is not possible on the basis of present knowledge. The declared Soviet defence budget is thought to exclude a number of elements such as military R&D, stockpiling and civil defence – indeed some contend that it covers only the operating and military construction costs of the armed forces. The problem of arriving at a correct budgetary figure was discussed in *The Military Balance 1973–1974*, pp. 8–9, and on pp. 109–110 of the 1976–1977 edition.

Furthermore, Soviet pricing practices are quite different from those in the West. Objectives are set in real terms with no requirement for money prices to coincide with the real costs of goods and services. The rouble cost of the defence effort may thus not reflect the real cost of alternative production foregone and, in turn, a rouble value of defence expressed as a percentage of Soviet GNP measured in roubles may not reflect the true burden.

If rouble estimates are then converted into dollars to facilitate international comparisons, the difficulties are compounded, because the exchange rate chosen should relate the purchasing power of a rouble in the Soviet Union to that of a dollar in the USA. The official exchange rate is considered inadequate for this purpose, and there is no consensus on an alternative.

An alternative approach – estimating how much it would cost to produce and man the equivalent of the Soviet defence effort in the USA – produces the index number problem: faced with the American price structure, the Soviet Union might opt for a pattern of spending different from her present one. This particular method tends to overstate the Soviet defence effort relative to that of the USA.

Accordingly, the estimates produced by a number of methods are given opposite, both in roubles and dollars, together with official figures for the defence budget published by the Soviet Union. Estimates produced by China are also given but their basis is not known.

Source		Price base	Defence expenditure		1970–1976	
			1970	1976	% annual growth rate	Burden (% of GNP)
Billions of Roubles						
CIA	(1)	1970	40–45	52–59	4.5	11–13
Lee	(2)	1970	43–50	75–84	—	—
Lee	(2)	Current	43–50	73–82	—	—
China	(3)	Current	49	79	8.26	15+
USSR	(4)	Current	17.9	17.43	—	—
Billions of Dollars						
CIA	(5)	1975	90	120	4.47	—
CIA	(6)	Current	66–99	127–128	—	—
Lee	(7)	Current	80–105	103–140	5	—

(1) *Estimated Soviet Defense Spending in Roubles*, CIA SR 76-10121U, May 1976. Extrapolation to 1976 using CIA growth rate.

(2) Figures for 1970 from W. T. Lee, *Soviet Defense Expenditure for 1955–1975*, Tempo GE75 TMP-42, Washington, DC, 31 July 1975; 1976 figures from W. T. Lee, 'Soviet Defense Expenditures in the 10th FYP' (to appear in *Osteuropa Wirtschaft*, No. 4, 1977).

(3) *Peking Review*, November 1975, January 1976.

(4) Official declared budget.

(5) *A Dollar Cost Comparison of Soviet and US Defense Activities 1966–1976*, CIA SA 77-1000U, January 1977. 1970 figures taken from diagram.

(6) *Ibid.*; 1975 price series converted to current prices using wholesale price index.

(7) W. T. Lee, 'Soviet Defense Expenditures' in W. Schneider and F. P. Hoeber (eds), *Arms, Man & Military Budgets, Issues for Fiscal Year 1977* (New York: Crane Russak, 1976).

The Alliances and Europe

THE WARSAW PACT

Treaties

The Warsaw Pact is a multilateral military alliance formed by the 'Treaty of Friendship, Mutual Assistance and Co-operation' which was signed in Warsaw on 14 May 1955 by the Governments of the Soviet Union, Albania, Bulgaria, Czechoslovakia, East Germany, Hungary, Poland and Romania; Albania left the Pact in September 1968. The Pact is committed to the defence only of the European territories of the member states.

The Soviet Union is also linked by bilateral treaties of friendship and mutual assistance with Bulgaria, Czechoslovakia, East Germany, Hungary, Poland and Romania. Members of the Warsaw Pact have similar bilateral treaties with each other. The essence of East European defence arrangements is not therefore dependent on the Warsaw Treaty as such. The Soviet Union concluded status-of-forces agreements with Poland, East Germany, Romania and Hungary between December 1956 and May 1957 and with Czechoslovakia in October 1968; all remain in effect except the one with Romania, which lapsed in June 1958 when Soviet troops left Romania.

Organization

The Political Consultative Committee consists, in full session, of the First Secretaries of the Communist Party, Heads of Government and the Foreign and Defence Ministers of the member countries. The Committee has a Joint Secretariat, headed by a Soviet official and consisting of a representative from each country, and a Permanent Commission, whose task is to make recommendations on general questions of foreign policy for Pact members. Both are located in Moscow.

Since the reorganization of the Pact in 1969 the non-Soviet Ministers of Defence are no longer directly subordinate to the Commander-in-Chief of the Pact but, together with the Soviet Minister, form the Council of Defence Ministers, which is the highest military body in the Pact. The second military body, the Joint High Command, is required by the Treaty 'to strengthen the defensive capability of the Warsaw Pact, to prepare military plans in case of war and to decide on the deployment of troops'. The Command consists of a Commander-in-Chief and a Military Council. This Council meets under the chairmanship of the C-in-C and includes the Chief-of-Staff and permanent military representatives from each of the allied armed forces. It seems to be the main channel through which the Pact's orders are transmitted to its forces in peacetime and through which the East European forces are able to put their point of view to the C-in-C. The Pact also has a Military Staff, which includes non-Soviet senior officers. The posts of C-in-C and Chief-of-Staff of the Joint High Command have, however, always been held by Soviet officers, and most of the key positions are still in Soviet hands.

In the event of war, the forces of the other Pact members would be operationally subordinate to the Soviet High Command. The command of the air defence system covering the whole Warsaw Pact area is now centralized in Moscow and directed by the C-in-C of the Soviet Air Defence Forces. Among the Soviet military headquarters in the Warsaw Pact area are the Northern Group of Forces at Legnica in Poland; the Southern Group of Forces at Budapest; the Group of Soviet Forces in Germany at Zossen-Wünsdorf, near Berlin; and the Central Group of Forces at Milovice, north of Prague. Soviet tactical air forces are stationed in Poland, East Germany, Hungary and Czechoslovakia.

The Soviet Union has deployed short-range surface-to-surface missile (SSM) launchers and nuclear-capable aircraft in Eastern Europe. Most East European countries also have short-range SSM launchers, but there is no evidence that nuclear warheads for their missiles have been supplied. Longer-range Soviet SSM and aircraft are based in the Soviet Union.

BULGARIA

Population: 8,833,000.
Military Service: Army and Air Force 2 years, Navy 3 years.
Total regular forces: 148,500 (93,000 conscripts).
Estimated GNP 1976: $21.1 bn.
Defence expenditure 1976: 645 m leva ($537.6 m).
$1 = 1.2 leva.

Army: 115,000 (75,000 conscripts).
8 motor rifle divs.*
5 tk bdes.
1 AB regt.
3 SSM bdes with *Scud.*
4 arty, 3 AA arty regts.
1 mountain bn.
2 recce bns.
100 T-34, 1,800 T-54/-55 med tks; 290 BTR-40/ BRDM AFV; 1,500 BTR-60, 35 OT-62 (*TOPAS*) APC; 200 85mm, 400 122mm, 95 152mm guns/ how; 350 120mm mor; BM-21 122mm RL; 36 *FROG*, 20 *Scud* SSM; 76mm ATK guns; 76mm, 130 82mm RCL; *Sagger, Snapper* ATGW; 37mm, 57mm, 85mm, 100mm towed, 200 ZSU-57-2 SP AA guns; SA-6/-7 SAM.

RESERVES: 200,000.

Navy: 8,500 (5,000 conscripts).
4 submarines (2 R-, 2 W-class, ex-Soviet).
2 *Riga*-class escorts.
2 *Kronstadt*- and 6 SO-1-class coastal escorts.
3 *Osa*-class FPBG with *Styx* SSM.
4 *Shershen*- and 8 P-4-class MTB.
6 MCM ships (2 T-43, 4 *Vanya*-class).
24 PO-2-class small patrol/minesweeping boats.
19 landing craft (10 *Vydra*-, 9 MFP-class).
2 Mi-1, 6 Mi-4 hel.

RESERVES: 15,000.

Air Force: 25,000 (13,000 conscripts); 270 combat aircraft.
6 FGA sqns with 72 MiG-17, some MiG-27.
10 interceptor sqns: 4 with 48 MiG-21, 1 with 19 MiG-19, 5 with 60 MiG-17.
3 recce sqns with 10 MiG-21, 24 MiG-15.
1 tpt regt with 6 Il-14, 4 An-24, 2 Tu-134.
1 hel regt with 30 Mi-4, 30 Mi-2 and Mi-8.
Operational trainers incl 27 MiG-15, 10 MiG-21; other trg ac incl 100 L-29, Yak-11/-18, 109 MiG-15/-17/-21UTI.
26 SA-2, 8 SA-3 SAM bns.
1 para regt.

---

* East European Warsaw Pact divs are of three categories with different manning (and hence readiness) levels. Category 1 formations are at up to three-quarters of establishment strength; Category 2 at up to half; Category 3 little more than cadres (see p. 105).

RESERVES: 20,000.

Para-Military Forces: 16,000 border guards with AFV; 12,000 construction troops; 12,000 security police; 150,000 volunteer People's Militia.

CZECHOSLOVAKIA

Population: 14,949,000.
Military service: 2 years.
Total regular forces: 181,000 (110,000 conscripts).
Estimated GNP 1976: $45.7 bn.
Defence expenditure 1977: 18.24 bn koruny ($1.61 bn).
$1 = 11.3 koruny.

Army: 135,000 (95,000 conscripts).
5 tk divs.*
5 motor rifle divs.*
1 AB regt.
3 SSM bdes with *Scud.*
1 ATK bde.
2 arty bdes.
2 AA arty bdes.
3,400 T-54/-55 med tks; 680 OT-65/-66 scout cars; 300 BMP, 2,000 OT-62/-64/-810 APC; 600 122mm, 50 130mm, 120 152mm guns/how; 122mm SP guns; M-51 130mm RL; 40 *FROG*, 27 *Scud* SSM; 125 82mm ATK guns; 110 82mm RCL; 110 *Sagger, Snapper* ATGW; 200 57mm towed and ZSU-23-4, ZSU-57-2 SP AA guns; SA-3/-4/-6/-7 SAM.

RESERVES: 300,000.

Air Force: 46,000 (15,000 conscripts); 558 combat aircraft.
12 FGA sqns with 80 Su-7, 36 MiG-17, 42 MiG-21.
18 interceptor sqns with 250 MiG-21, MiG-15, L-29.
6 recce sqns with 36 MiG-21R, 36 L-29, 11 Il-14.
About 6 An-24, 42 Il-14, 1 Tu-134 tpts.
Hel incl 90 Mi-1/-2, 130 Mi-4, 20 Mi-8.
Operational trainers incl 6 Su-7B, 10 MiG-15, 19 MiG-21, 32 L-29; other trg ac incl 15 MiG-15, 24 MiG-21, 60 L-29, 24 L-39.
28 SA-2/-3 SAM battalions.

RESERVES: 50,000.

Para-Military Forces: 10,000 border troops, some AFV, ATK guns; about 120,000 part-time People's Militia, 2,500 Civil Defence Troops.

GERMAN DEMOCRATIC REPUBLIC

Population: 17,264,000.
Military service: 18 months.
Total regular forces: 157,000 (92,000 conscripts).

Estimated GNP 1976: $48 bn.
Defence expenditure 1977: 11.02 bn Ostmarks
   ($2.89 bn).
   $1 = 3.8 Ostmarks.

Army: 105,000 (67,000 conscripts).
2 tk divs.*
4 motor rifle divs.*
1 SSM bde with *Scud.*
2 arty bdes.
2 AA arty regts.
1 AB bn.
2 ATK bns.
About 2,400 T-54/-55, 600 T-34 (in storage) med
   tks; about 120 PT-76 lt tks; 880 BRDM, FUG-
   70 scout cars; 1,500 BMP, BTR-50P/-60P/-152
   APC; 335 122mm, 100 130mm, 72 152mm guns/
   how; 225 120mm mor; 108 BM-21 122mm RL;
   24 *FROG*-7, 16 *Scud* B SSM; 100mm ATK guns;
   Sagger, Snapper ATGW; 400 23mm, 57mm,
   100mm towed and ZSU-23-4, ZSU-57-2 SP AA
   guns; SA-4/-7 SAM.

RESERVES: 200,000.

Navy: 16,000 (10,000 conscripts).
2 *Riga*-class escorts.
4 SO-1- and 13 *Hai*-class submarine chasers.
15 *Osa*-class FPBG with *Styx* SSM.
70 MTB (15 *Shershen*-, 40 20-ton *Iltis*-, 15 *Libelle*-
   class).
26 coastal patrol craft (coastguard).
52 *Kondor*-class coastal minesweepers.
6 *Robbe*-class, 12 *Labo*-class landing craft.
1 hel sqn with 8 Mi-4, 5 Mi-8.

RESERVES: 25,000.

Air Force: 36,000 (15,000 conscripts); 416 combat
   aircraft.
3 FGA sqns with 35 MiG-17.
18 fighter sqns with 270 MiG-21.
1 recce sqn with 12 MiG-21, 4 Il-14.
2 fighter/trg wings with 45 L-29, 50 MiG-21.
2 tpt sqns with 20 Il-14, 3 Tu-124, 8 Tu-134, some
   An-24.
46 Mi-1, 18 Mi-4, 40 Mi-8 hel.
20 MiG-15UTI, 41 MiG-21UTI trainers.
5 AD regts with 120 57mm and 100mm AA guns.
2 SAM bns with 22 SA-2, 4 SA-3.
2 para bns.

RESERVES: 30,000.

Para-Military Forces: 73,000. 48,000 border guards,
   some tks, AFV, 22 coastal craft; 25,000 security
   troops, 500,000 Workers' Militia.

* See note on p. 13.

HUNGARY

Population: 10,551,000.
Military service: 2 years (incl Border Guard).
Total regular forces: 103,000 (60,000 conscripts).
Estimated GNP 1976: $23.1 bn.
Defence expenditure 1977: 13.15 bn forints
   ($590 m).
   $1 = 22.3 forints.

Army: 83,000 (52,000 conscripts).
1 tk div.*
5 motor rifle divs.*
1 SSM bde with *Scud.*
3 arty regts.
3 AA arty regts.
1 AB bn.
Danube Flotilla: 2 MCM units, 1 AA gunboat unit.
About 1,000 T-34/-54/-55 med, 100 PT-76 lt tks;
   about 600 scout cars; 1,500 BTR-40/-50/-60/-152
   APC; 100 85mm, 250 122mm, 36 152mm guns/
   how; 300 82mm, 100 120mm mor; 75 122mm RL;
   22 *FROG*, 8 *Scud* SSM; 200 57mm, 76mm ATK
   guns; 75 *Sagger, Swatter* ATGW; 200 57mm and
   100mm towed, 100 ZSU-23-4 and ZSU-57-2 SP
   AA guns; SA-6/-9 SAM; 10 100-ton patrol craft
   (MCM and AA), 6 landing craft.

RESERVES: 130,000.

Air Force: 20,000 (8,000 conscripts); 176 combat
   aircraft.
4 fighter sqns with 30 Su-7, 30 MiG-17/-19.
6 interceptor sqns with 116 MiG-21.
About 50 An-2/-24/-26, Il-14 and Li-2 tpts.
About 30 Mi-1/-2, 35 Mi-8 hel.
53 MiG-15UTI, 11 MiG-21UTI, Yak-11/-18, 20
   L-29 trainers.
14 SAM bns with SA-2.

RESERVES: 13,000.

Para-Military Forces: 20,000 border guards (11,000
   conscripts) with AFV, ATK guns; 60,000 part-time
   Workers' Militia (with regular officers).

POLAND

Population: 34,609,000.
Military service: Army, internal security forces,
   Air Force 2 years; Navy, special services 3 years.
Total regular forces: 307,000 (190,000 conscripts).
Estimated GNP 1976: $68.1 bn.
Defence expenditure 1977: 57.28 bn zloty
   ($2.44 bn).
   $1 = 23.5 zloty.

Army: 220,000 (166,000 conscripts).
5 tk divs.*
8 motor rifle divs.*

1 AB div.*
1 amph assault div.*
4 SSM bdes with *Scud*.
3 arty bdes.
6 AA arty regts.
3 ATK regts.
3,500 T-34, T-54/-55/-62 med, 300 PT-76 lt tks;
2,000 FUG-65/-70, BRDM scout cars; 2,200
OT-64, 104 BTR-40/-50/-60/-152 APC; 400 85mm,
700 122mm, 130mm, 150 152mm guns/how; 550
82mm, 120mm mor; 250 122mm, 140mm RL;
46 *FROG*-3/-7, 36 *Scud* SSM; 76mm, 85mm,
100mm towed, ASU-57/-85 SP ATK guns; 82mm
RCL; *Sagger*, *Snapper* ATGW; 400 23mm, 57mm,
85mm, 100mm towed, ZSU 57-2 SP AA guns;
SA-6/-7/-9 SAM.

DEPLOYMENT: *Egypt* (UNEF): 865; *Syria* (UNDOF): 88.

RESERVES: 500,000.

Navy: 25,000, incl Marines and 6,000 conscripts.
4 W-class submarines.
1 *Kotlin*-class destroyer with 2 *Goa* SAM.
12 *Osa*-class FPBG with *Styx* SSM.
26 large patrol craft.
12 MTB (9 *Wisla*-, 3 P-6-class).
24 *Krogulec*-, T-43-class ocean minesweepers, 20
K-8-class minesweeping boats.
30 *Polnocny*-class landing ships and 20 landing
craft.
1 Naval Aviation Regt (60 combat aircraft):
1 lt bbr/recce sqn with 10 Il-28.
4 fighter sqns with 12 MiG-15, 38 MiG-17.
2 hel sqns with some 25 Mi-1/-2/-4.

RESERVES: 45,000.

Air Force: 62,000 (18,000 conscripts); 745 combat
aircraft.
1 lt bbr sqn with 6 Il-28.
15 FGA sqns: 14 with 160 MiG-17 and 30 Su-7, 1
with 28 Su-20.
33 interceptor sqns with 100 MiG-17, 340 MiG-21.
6 recce sqns with 72 MiG-15/-21, 5 Il-28, 4 Il-14.
Some 60 tpts, incl An-12/-24/-26, Il-14/-18/-62,
Tu-134, Yak-40.
165 Mi-1/-2, 19 Mi-4, 26 Mi-8 hel.
385 trainers, incl *Iskra*, MiG-15/-17/-21UTI, Il-28.
36 SA-2, 12 SA-3 SAM bns.

RESERVES: 60,000.

Para-Military Forces: 97,000: 18,000 Border
Troops, 58,000 Internal Security and Territorial
Defence, some tanks, AFV, ATK guns; 34 small
boats operated by coastguard; 21,000 Construction troops; 350,000 Citizens' Militia.

---

* See note on p. 13.

ROMANIA

Population: 21,600,000.
Military service: Army and Air Force 16 months,
Navy 2 years.
Total regular forces: 180,000 (110,000 conscripts).
Estimated GNP 1976: $45.3 bn.
Defence expenditure 1977: 11.3 bn lei ($824 m).
$1 = 13.7 lei.

Army: 140,000 (95,000 conscripts).
2 tk divs.*
8 motor rifle divs.*
3 mountain regts.
1 AB regt.
2 SSM bdes with *Scud*.
2 arty bdes.
4 arty regts.
2 ATK regts.
2 AA arty regts.
1,500 T-34, T-54/-55 med, PT-76 lt tks; 1,600 OT-65
scout cars and BTR-50/-60/-152, OT-62/-64/-810,
TAB-70/-72 (BTR-60) APC; 50 76mm, 50 85mm,
600 122mm, 150 152mm guns/how; 1,000 82mm,
120mm mor; 122mm, 150 130mm RL; 30 *FROG*,
20 *Scud* SSM; 57mm ATK guns; 260 76mm and
82mm RCL; 120 *Sagger*, *Snapper*, *Swatter* ATGW;
300 30mm, 37mm, 57mm, 85mm, 100mm towed,
ZSU-57-2 SP AA guns.

RESERVES: 300,000.

Navy: 10,000 (5,000 conscripts).
6 coastal escorts (3 *Poti*-, 3 *Kronstadt*-class).
5 *Osa*-class FPBG with *Styx* SSM.
19 MTB (13 P-4-class, 6 *Hu Chwan*-class hydrofoils).
14 *Shanghai*-class MGB.
26 patrol craft (16 coastal, 10 river).
22 MCM craft (4 coastal, 10 inshore, 8 river).
4 Mi-4 helicopters.

RESERVES: 20,500.

Air Force: 30,000 (10,000 conscripts); 327 combat
aircraft.
5 FGA sqns with 75 MiG-15/-17.
12 interceptor sqns with 27 MiG-15/-19, 210 MiG-
21.
1 recce sqn with 15 Il-28.
2 tpt sqns with some 20 Il-14, 4 Il-18, 1 Il-62, 10
An-24, 2 An-26, 12 Li-2, 1 Boeing 707.
6 Mi-4, 20 Mi-8, 20 *Alouette* III hel.
Trainers incl 60 L-29, 55 MiG-15, 18 MiG-21.
108 SA-2 *Guideline* at about 18 SAM sites.

RESERVES: 25,000.

Para-Military Forces: 37,000: 17,000 border,
20,000 security troops with AFV, ATK guns.
About 700,000 Patriotic Guard.

THE NORTH ATLANTIC TREATY

Treaties

The North Atlantic Treaty was signed in 1949 by Belgium, Britain, Canada, Denmark, France, Iceland, Italy, Luxembourg, the Netherlands, Norway, Portugal and the United States; Greece and Turkey joined in 1952, and West Germany in 1955. The Treaty unites Western Europe and North America in a commitment to consult together if the security of any one member is threatened, and to consider an armed attack against one as an attack against all, to be met by such action as each of them deems necessary, 'including the use of armed force, to restore and maintain the security of the North Atlantic area'.

The Paris Agreements of 1954 added a Protocol to the Treaty aimed at strengthening the structure of NATO and revised the Brussels Treaty of 1948, which now includes Italy and West Germany in addition to its original members (Benelux countries, Britain and France). The Brussels Treaty signatories are committed to give one another 'all the military and other aid and assistance in their power' if one is the subject of 'armed aggression in Europe'.

Since 1969 members of the Atlantic Alliance can withdraw on one year's notice; the Brussels Treaty was signed for 50 years.

Organization

The Organization of the North Atlantic Treaty is known as NATO. The governing body of the Alliance, the North Atlantic Council, which has its headquarters in Brussels, consists of Ministers from the fifteen member countries, who normally meet twice a year, and of ambassadors representing each government, who are in permanent session.

In 1966 France left the integrated military organization, and the 14-nation Defence Planning Committee (DPC) was formed, on which France does not sit. It meets at the same level as the Council and deals with questions related to NATO integrated military planning and other matters in which France does not participate. Greece has announced her intention to leave the integrated military organization; her status is under discussion, but she left the DPC in autumn 1974.

Two permanent bodies for nuclear planning were established in 1966. The first, the Nuclear Defence Affairs Committee (NDAC), is open to all NATO members (France, Iceland and Luxembourg do not take part); it normally meets at Defence Minister level once a year to associate non-nuclear members in the nuclear affairs of the alliance. The Secretary-General is Chairman of the NDAC.

The second, the Nuclear Planning Group (NPG), derived from and subordinate to the NDAC, has seven or eight members and is intended to go further into the details of topics raised there. The composition consists, in practice, of Britain, Germany, Italy and the United States, plus three or four other member countries serving in rotation, each for a term of 18 months. On 1 July 1977 there were four such members: Canada, Greece, the Netherlands and Norway. The Secretary-General also chairs the NPG.

The Eurogroup, which was set up by West European member states of the Alliance (with the exception of France, Portugal and Iceland) in 1968, is an informal consultative body acting to co-ordinate and improve the West European military contribution to the Alliance. Its activities have included the European Defence Improvement Programme (1970) and agreement on principles of co-operation in the fields of armaments (1972), training (1973) and logistics (1975).*

The Council and its Committees are advised on politico-military, financial, economic and scientific aspects of defence planning by the Secretary-General and an international staff. The Council's military advisers are the Military Committee, which gives policy direction to NATO military commands. The Military Committee consists of the Chiefs-of-Staff of all member countries except France, which maintains a liaison staff, and Iceland, which is not represented; in permanent session the Chiefs-of-Staff are represented by Military Representatives, who are located in Brussels

---

* Discussion in Eurogroup of the need to extend European armaments co-operation led to the formation in 1976 of the European Programme Group, open to all European members of the Alliance but independent of it. Its membership now includes France and ten member countries of Eurogroup.

together with the Council. The Military Committee has an independent Chairman and is served by an integrated international military staff. The major NATO commanders are responsible to the Committee, although they also have direct access to the Council and heads of Governments.

The principal military commands of NATO are Allied Command Europe (ACE), Allied Command Atlantic (ACLANT) and Allied Command Channel (ACCHAN).

The NATO European and Atlantic Commands participate in the Joint Strategic Planning System at Omaha, Nebraska, but there is no Alliance command specifically covering strategic nuclear forces. The United States has, however, committed a small number of ballistic-missile submarines (and Britain all hers) to the planning control of SACEUR and a larger number to SACLANT.

The Supreme Allied Commander Europe (SACEUR) and the Supreme Allied Commander Atlantic (SACLANT) have always been American officers and the Commander-in-Chief Channel (CINCCHAN), Deputy SACEUR and Deputy SACLANT British (a second Deputy SACEUR is to be appointed, who will be German). SACEUR is also Commander-in-Chief of the United States Forces in Europe.

(i) ALLIED COMMAND EUROPE (ACE) has its headquarters, known as SHAPE (Supreme Headquarters, Allied Powers in Europe), at Casteau, near Mons, in Belgium. It is responsible for the defence of all NATO territory in Europe except Britain, France, Iceland and Portugal, and for that of all Turkey. It also has general responsibility for the air defence of Britain.

The European Command has some 7,000 tactical nuclear warheads in its area. The number of delivery vehicles (aircraft, missiles and howitzers) is over 3,000, spread among all countries excluding Luxembourg. The nuclear explosives, however, are maintained in American custody, with the exception of certain British weapons (there are also French nuclear weapons in France). There is a large number of low-yield weapons, but the average yield of bombs is about 100 kilotons, and of missile warheads, 20 kilotons.

About 66 division equivalents are available to SACEUR in peacetime. The Command has some 3,100 tactical aircraft, based on about 200 standard NATO airfields, backed up by a system of jointly financed storage depots, fuel pipelines and signal communications. Most land and air forces stationed in the Command are assigned to SACEUR, while naval forces are normally earmarked.

The 2nd French Corps of two divisions (which is not integrated in NATO forces) is stationed in Germany under a status agreement reached between the French and German Governments. Co-operation with NATO forces and commands has been agreed between the commanders concerned.

The following Commands are subordinate to Allied Command Europe:

(a) *Allied Forces Central Europe* (AFCENT) has command of both the land forces and the air forces in the Central European Sector. Its headquarters are at Brunssum in the Netherlands, and its Commander (CINCENT) is a German general.

The forces of the Central European Command include 26 divisions, assigned by Belgium, Britain, Canada, West Germany, the Netherlands and the United States, and about 1,400 tactical aircraft.

The Command is sub-divided into Northern Army Group (NORTHAG) and Central Army Group (CENTAG). NORTHAG, responsible for the defence of the sector north of the Göttingen–Liege axis, includes the Belgian, British and Dutch divisions and four German divisions and is supported by 2nd Allied Tactical Air Force (ATAF), composed of Belgian, British, Dutch and German units. (One newly-formed American brigade is being stationed in the NORTHAG area.) American forces, seven German divisions and the Canadian battle group are under CENTAG, supported by the 4th ATAF, which includes American, German and Canadian units and an American Army Air Defense Command. Allied Air Force, Central Europe (AIRCENT) was set up in 1974 to provide centralized control of air forces in the sector.

(b) *Allied Forces Northern Europe* (AFNORTH) has its headquarters at Kolsaas, Norway, and is responsible for the defence of Denmark, Norway, Schleswig-Holstein and the Baltic Approaches. The commander (CINCNORTH) has always been a British general. Most of the Danish and Norwegian land, sea and tactical air forces are earmarked for it, and most of their active reserves assigned to it. Germany has assigned one division, two combat air wings and her Baltic fleet. Apart from exercises and some small units, US naval forces do not normally operate in this area.

(c) *Allied Forces Southern Europe* (AFSOUTH) has its headquarters at Naples, and its commander (CINCSOUTH) has always been an American admiral. It is responsible for the defence of Italy,

Greece and Turkey and for safeguarding communications in the Mediterranean and the Turkish territorial waters of the Black Sea. The formations in the area include 22 divisions from Turkey, 13 from Greece and 8 from Italy, as well as the tactical air forces of these countries. Other formations have been earmarked for AFSOUTH, as have the United States Sixth Fleet and naval forces from Italy. The ground-defence system is based upon two separate commands: the Southern, comprising Italy and the approaches to it, under an Italian commander and the South-Eastern, comprising Greece and Turkey, under an American commander. There is, however, an overall air command (AIRSOUTH), and there are two naval commands (NAVSOUTH and STRIKEFORSOUTH), responsible to AFSOUTH, all with headquarters in Naples.

A maritime air patrol unit with aircraft from Southern Region nations, Britain and the United States operates in the Mediterranean, co-ordinated by Maritime Air Forces Mediterranean (MARAIRMED), a functional command of NAVSOUTH. French aircraft participate. The MARAIRMED commander is an American rear-admiral.

The Allied Naval On-Call Force for the Mediterranean (NAVOCFORMED) has consisted of at least five destroyers, contributed by Southern Region nations, Britain and the United States, and three smaller ships provided according to the area of operation.

(*d*) *United Kingdom Air Forces* (UKAIR) has its headquarters at High Wycombe, England.

(*e*) *ACE Mobile Force* (AMF), with headquarters at Seckenheim, Germany, has been formed with particular reference to the northern and south-eastern flanks. Found by seven countries, it comprises seven infantry battalion groups, an armoured reconnaissance squadron, six artillery batteries, helicopter detachments and ground-support fighter squadrons, but has no air transport of its own.

(II) ALLIED COMMAND ATLANTIC (ACLANT) has its headquarters at Norfolk, Virginia, and is responsible for the North Atlantic area from the North Pole to the Tropic of Cancer, including Portuguese coastal waters. The commander is an American admiral.

In the event of war, its duties are to participate in the strategic strike and to protect sea communications. There are no forces assigned to the command in peacetime except Standing Naval Force Atlantic (STANAVFORLANT), which normally consists, at any one time, of four destroyer-type ships. However, for training purposes and in the event of war, forces which are predominantly naval are earmarked for assignment by Britain, Canada, Denmark, Germany, the Netherlands, Portugal and the United States. There are six subordinate commands: Western Atlantic, Eastern Atlantic, Iberian Atlantic, Striking Fleet Atlantic, Submarine Command and STANAVFORLANT. The nucleus of the Striking Fleet Atlantic has been provided by the United States 2nd Fleet with some five attack carriers; carrier-based aircraft share the nuclear strike role with missile-firing submarines.

(III) ALLIED COMMAND CHANNEL (ACCHAN) has its headquarters at Northwood, near London. The commander (CINCCHAN) is a British admiral. The wartime role of Channel Command is to exercise control of the English Channel and the southern North Sea. Many of the smaller warships of Belgium, Britain and the Netherlands are earmarked for this Command, as are some maritime aircraft. There are arrangements for co-operation with French naval forces. A Standing Naval Force, Channel (STANAVFORCHAN) was formed in 1973 to consist of mine counter-measures ships from Belgium, Germany, the Netherlands and Britain; other interested nations might participate on a temporary basis. Its operational command is vested in CINCCHAN.

BELGIUM

Population: 9,919,000.
Military service: 8 or 10 months.*
Total armed forces: 85,650 (26,850 conscripts).
Estimated GNP 1976: $66.5 bn.
Defence expenditure 1977: 66.47 bn francs
  ($1.82 bn).
  $1 = 36.6 francs (1977), 39.0 francs (1976).

Army: 62,050, incl Medical Service and 22,700
  conscripts.
1 armd bde.
3 mech inf bdes.
3 recce bns.
2 mot inf bns.
1 para-cdo regt.
3 arty bns.
2 SSM bns with 8 *Honest John*.
2 SAM bns with 24 *HAWK*.
5 engr bns (3 fd, 1 bridge, 1 eqpt).
4 aviation sqns.
334 *Leopard*, 74 M-47 med, 136 *Scorpion*, 60 M-41
  lt tks; 154 *Scimitar* AFV; 1,236 M-75, AMX and
  73 *Spartan* APC; 22 105mm, 15 203mm how; 96
  M-108 105mm, 25 M-44, 41 M-109 155mm,
  11 M-110 203mm SP how; 12 *Honest John* SSM
  (being replaced by *Lance*); 80 JPK C-80 SP ATK
  guns; *ENTAC*, *Milan* ATGW; 41 *Striker* AFV
  with *Swingfire* ATGW; 119 C20mm, 40mm, 57mm
  AA guns; 60 *HAWK* SAM; 6 Piper *Super Cub*, 12
  BN *Islander* ac, 74 *Alouette* II hel; 38 *Epervier*
  RPV. (193 *Spartan* APC, 55 *Gepard* SP AA guns, 5
  Lance SSM on order.)

DEPLOYMENT: *Germany*: 27,000; 1 corps HQ, 2 div
  HQ, 1 armd bde, 2 mech inf bdes.

RESERVES: 50,000: 10,000 train every year, 1 mech,
  1 mot inf bde train every two years.

Navy: 4,200 (950 conscripts).
2 frigates with *Sea Sparrow* SAM, *Exocet* SSM (2
  building).
6 ocean minesweepers, 2 minehunters (ex-US).
9 coastal minesweepers/minehunters.
12 inshore minesweepers.
2 log support and comd ships (for MCM).
6 river patrol boats.
1 HSS-1, 3 *Alouette* III hel.

RESERVES: 5,500.

Air Force: 19,400 (3,200 conscripts); 144 combat
  aircraft.
2 FB sqns with 36 F-104G.
3 FB sqns with 54 *Mirage* VBA/BD.
2 AWX sqns with 36 F-104G.
1 recce sqn with 18 *Mirage* VBR.

2 tpt sqns with 12 C-130H, 3 HS-748, 6 *Merlin*
  IIIAS, 2 *Falcon* 20, 2 Boeing 727QC.
1 SAR sqn with 4 HSS-1, 5 *Sea King* 48 hel.
18 *Magister*, 34 SF-260, 15 T-33 trainers.
8 SAM sqns with 21 *Nike Hercules*.
(116 F-16, 33 *AlphaJet* ac, 40 BDX APC on order.)

Para-Military Forces: 16,000 Gendarmerie with 62
  FN armd cars, 5 *Alouette* II, 3 *Puma* hel.

BRITAIN

Population: 56,600,000.
Military service: voluntary.
Total armed forces: 339,150 (14,500 women and
  8,800 enlisted outside Britain).
Estimated GNP 1976: $224.5 bn.
Defence expenditure 1977–78: £6.33 bn
  ($10.88 bn).
  $1 = £0.582 (1977), £0.544 (1976).

Strategic forces:
SLBM: 4 SSBN, each with 16 *Polaris* A-3 missiles.
Ballistic Missile Early Warning System (BMEWS)
  station at Fylingdales.

Army: 175,250 (5,800 women and 7,900 enlisted
  outside Britain).
14 armd regts (3 converting to armd recce).
5 armd recce regts.
47 inf bns.
3 para bns (1 in para role).
5 Gurkha bns.
1 special air service (SAS) regt.
1 msl regt with *Lance* SSM.
3 AD regts with *Rapier* SAM.
1 hy, 13 field, 1 GW, 1 cdo, 1 locating arty regts.
10 engr regts.
6 army aviation regts.
910 *Chieftain* med, 271 FV101 *Scorpion* lt tks; 243
  Saladin armd cars; 290 *Scimitar*, 178 FV438/
  FV712 AFV; 1,804 *Ferret*, 125 *Fox* scout cars;
  2,338 FV432, 600 *Saracen*, 60 *Spartan* APC; 92
  105mm pack how and lt guns; 155 *Abbot*
  105mm, 50 M-109 155mm, 31 M-107 175mm,
  16 M-110 203mm SP guns/how; *Lance* SSM;
  84mm *Carl Gustav*, 120mm RCL; *Vigilant*,
  Swingfire ATGW; FV102 *Striker* with ATGW;
  L/70 40mm AA guns; *Blowpipe*, *Rapier*/*Blindfire*, *Thunderbird* SAM; 30 *Beaver* lt ac; 113
  Scout, 8 *Alouette* II, 118 *Sioux*, 145 *Gazelle* hel.
  (*Lance* SSM, FH70 155mm guns, *Milan* ATGW,
  100 *Lynx*, 13 *Gazelle* hel on order.)

DEPLOYMENT AND ORGANIZATION:†
United Kingdom. (United Kingdom Land Forces
  (UKLF): United Kingdom Mobile Force (UKMF)

---

* Conscripts serve 8 months if posted to Germany,
10 months if serving in Belgium.

† The army organization is being changed, eliminating
the brigade. BAOR is to have 1 Corps HQ, 4 armd, 1 arty

– 1 div of 2 bdes (to become 6th Field Force with 5 inf bns by April 1978); 1 para bde (to become 7th Field Force, with regular and TAVR units, by April 1978); 8th Field Force (regular and TAVR for Home Defence); 1 bn gp (for ACE Mobile Force (Land)); 1 SAS regt less one sqn; 1 Gurkha inf bn. HQ Northern Ireland: 3 inf bde HQ, 1 armed recce regt and 3 sqns, a variable number of major units in inf role,* 1 SAS, 3 engr, 2 army aviation sqns.

Germany. British Army of the Rhine (BAOR): 55,000; 1 corps HQ, 1 armd div, 2 div HQ, 4 armd bdes, 1 field force, 2 arty bdes. Berlin: 3,000: Berlin Field Force.

Brunei: 1 Gurkha bn.

Hong Kong: 7,500; Gurkha Field Force with 1 British, 3 Gurkha inf bns, 1 engr sqn and support units.

Cyprus: 1 inf bn less 2 coys, 1 armd recce sqn, 1 flt of hel and log support with UNFICYP; 1 inf bn plus 2 inf coys, 1 armd recce sqn in garrison at Sovereign Base Areas.

Oman: Trg team and engr det.

Gibraltar: 1 inf bn.

Belize: 1 reinforced inf bn gp with hel.

RESERVES: 110,000 Regular reserves. 60,100 Territorial Army and Volunteer Reserve (TAVR): 2 armd recce regts, 38 inf bns, 2 SAS, 2 med, 3 lt AD, 7 engr regts. 7,600 Ulster Defence Regiment: 11 bns.

Navy: 76,700, incl Fleet Air Arm, Royal Marines, 3,950 women and 500 enlisted outside Britain; 75 major combat surface vessels.

Submarines, attack:
9 nuclear, 18 diesel.

Surface ships:
1 aircraft carrier (30 ac, 6 hel).
2 ASW carriers with *Seacat* SAM, 9 hel.
2 assault ships with *Seacat* SAM (1 trg).
2 cruisers each with 4 *Sea King* hel, *Seacat* SAM.
11 destroyers (7 County-class with *Seaslug*, *Seacat* SAM, ASW hel, 4 with *Exocet* SSM; 1 Type 82 with *Sea Dart* SAM, *Ikara* ASW; 3 Type 42 with *Sea Dart* SAM, ASW hel).
57 frigates: 48 GP (48 with 1 hel, most with *Seacat* SAM, 8 with *Ikara* ASW, 1 with *Exocet* SSM, 1 with *Seawolf* SAM), 3 ASW (1 trg), 2 AA, 3 aircraft direction (2 with *Seacat*), 1 trg.
38 coastal minesweepers/minehunters (4 trg).
5 inshore minesweepers (trg).
5 coastal patrol, 4 FPB, seaward defence boats (trg).
2 offshore patrol vessels.

divs and a new inf formation (5th Field Force). By April 1978 UKLF (excluding Northern Ireland) will consist of 6th, 7th and 8th Field Forces. Units in Hong Kong form the Gurkha Field Force and those in Berlin the Berlin Field Force.

* Some nine drawn from BAOR on short tours.

12 survey, 1 ice patrol, 1 Royal Yacht/hospital, 6 depot/support ships.
6 landing ships (log), 41 landing craft.
2 hovercraft (SRN-6, BH-N7).
Included above are 4 nuclear, 3 diesel subs, 1 ASW carrier, 1 assault ship, 2 destroyers, 13 frigates, 4 minesweepers in reserve or undergoing refit. (2 ASW cruisers, 3 SSN, 6 destroyers, 6 frigates, 1 FPB, 1 MCM, 3 offshore patrol vessels building; *Sub-Harpoon*, *Sea Skua* ASM on order.)

THE FLEET AIR ARM:
1 strike sqn with 14 *Buccaneer* S2 (*Martel* ASM).
1 FGA sqn with 12 *Phantom* FG1.
1 AEW sqn and 1 flt with 7 *Gannet* AEW3.
7 ASW hel sqns embarked: 5 with 29 *Sea King*, 1 of 40 *Wasp* flts, 1 of 7 *Wessex* 3 flts.
2 cdo assault sqns with 16 *Wessex* 5.
4 SAR flts with *Wessex* HAS-1.
1 utility hel sqn with *Wessex* 5.
4 trg sqns with *Sea King*, *Wasp*, *Wessex* 3/5, *Gazelle* and *Lynx*.
(25 *Sea Harrier* VTOL ac, 21 *Sea King*, 60 *Lynx* hel on order.)

THE ROYAL MARINES: 7,700.
1 cdo bde with 4 cdo gps, 1 lt hel sqn, spt units.
120mm RCL; SS-11 ATGW; *Scout*, *Gazelle* hel. (*Milan* ATGW, *Blowpipe* SAM on order.)

DEPLOYMENT:
Malta: 1 indep cdo coy gp (to be withdrawn by April 1979).
Falkland Islands: 1 det.

RESERVES (naval and Marines): 30,600 regular and 6,700 volunteers.

Air Force: 87,200 (4,750 women and 300 enlisted outside Britain); about 550 combat aircraft.
6 strike sqns with 50 *Vulcan* B2.
4 strike sqns with 56 *Buccaneer* S2.
3 close support sqns with 48 *Harrier* GR3.
6 attack and close support sqns with 72 *Jaguar* GR1.
9 interceptor sqns: 2 with 24 *Lightning* F6, 7 with 84 *Phantom* FG1/FGR2.
5 recce sqns: 1 with 10 *Vulcan* SR2, 2 with 24 *Jaguar* GR1, 2 with 24 *Canberra* PR7/9.
1 AEW sqn with 12 *Shackleton* (being replaced by *Nimrod*).
5 MR sqns with 43 *Nimrod* MR1.
1 ECM sqn with 3 *Nimrod* SR1, 4 *Canberra* B6.
2 tanker sqns with 24 *Victor* K2.
1 strategic tpt sqn with 11 VC-10.
4 tac tpt sqns with 45 C-130.
3 lt comms sqns with HS-125, *Andover*, *Pembroke*, *Devon*, *Whirlwind* hel.
Operational conversion units with some 90 combat aircraft, incl *Vulcan*, *Buccaneer*, *Canberra*, *Phantom*, *Jaguar*, *Lightning*, *Harrier*, *Nimrod*;

trg units with *Hunter, Hawk, Gnat, Bulldog, Jet Provost,* C-130 ac, *Wessex, Whirlwind, Puma, Gazelle* hel.

8 hel sqns: 2 tac tpt with 26 *Puma* HC-1, 3 with 45 *Wessex* HC-2, 3 SAR with *Whirlwind* HAR-10.

2 SAM sqns with *Bloodhound.*

(*Jaguar,* 24 *Harrier* FGA, 11 *Nimrod* AEW, 175 *Hawk, Bulldog* trg ac, *Sidewinder* AAM on order.)

ROYAL AIR FORCE REGIMENT:

7 fd and AD sqns: 5 with *Rapier* SAM, 2 with L/70 40mm AA guns.

1 flt with *Tigercat* SAM.

DEPLOYMENT:

The Royal Air Force includes an operational home command (Strike Command), responsible for the UK Air Defence Region and the Near and Far East, and 1 overseas command (RAF Germany: 8,600). Sqns are deployed overseas as follows:

Germany: 2 *Phantom* FGR2, 2 *Buccaneer,* 5 *Jaguar,* 2 *Harrier,* 1 *Wessex,* 1 *Bloodhound,* 4 *Rapier,* 1 fd sqn RAF Regt.

Gibraltar: Hunter det.

Cyprus: 1 *Whirlwind* (4 ac with UNFICYP); periodic dets of other ac; 1 sqn RAF Regt.

Malta: 1 *Nimrod,* 1 *Canberra* PR7 (to be withdrawn 1979).

Hong Kong: 1 *Wessex;* 1 RAF Regt det.

Belize: 6 *Harrier* FGA ac, *Puma* hel, RAF Regt det.

RESERVES: 33,300 regular; about 300 volunteer.

CANADA

Population: 23,370,000.
Military service: voluntary.
Total armed forces: 80,000 (2,700 women).
Estimated GNP 1976: $US 175.3 bn.
Defence Expenditure 1977–78: $Can 3.79 bn ($US 3.61 bn).
  $US1 = $Can 1.05 (1977), $Can 0.98 (1976).

Army (Land Forces): 28,500.*
Mobile Command (about 17,700 land and air).†
3 bde gps each comprising:
  3 inf bns.
  1 armd regt.
  1 lt arty regt of 2 close support, 1 AD btys.
  support units.

---

* The Canadian Armed Forces were unified in 1968; the strengths shown here for army, naval and air forces are only approximate.
† Mobile Command commands army combat forces, and Maritime Command all naval forces. Air Command commands all air forces but Maritime Command has operational control of maritime air forces, and HQ 4 ATAF in Europe operational control of 1 CAG; Air Defence Group is part of NORAD. There are also a Communications Command and a Canadian Forces Training System.

1 special service force comprising:
  1 armd regt.
  1 inf bn.
  1 AB regt.
  1 arty regt of 2 close support btys.
  support units.

1 sigs regt.

32 *Leopard,*‡ 223 *Centurion* med tks; 121 *Ferret* scout cars, 174 *Lynx* AFV; 827 M-113 APC; 58 105mm pack, 159 105mm how, 50 M-109 155mm SP how; 810 *Carl Gustav* RL; *TOW* ATGW; CL-89 drones; 57 40mm AA guns; 103 *Blowpipe* SAM. (128 *Leopard* med tks, 152 Mowag armd cars, 180 Mowag APC, *TOW* on order.)

DEPLOYMENT:

Europe: One mech bde gp of 2,800 with 32 *Leopard* A2 med tks, 375 M-113 APC/recce, 18 M-109 155mm SP how, 14 CH-136 (*Kiowa*) hel.

Cyprus (UNFICYP): 505.

Egypt (UNEF): 871.

Syria (UNDOF): 164.

Other UN: 33.

RESERVES: about 15,200 Militia; 99 combat arms units plus support units (all in Mobile Command).

Navy (Maritime); 13,400.*
Maritime Command (about 9,000).†
3 submarines (*Oberon*-class).
4 ASW hel destroyers each with 2 CH-124 (*Sea King*) hel and 2 *Sea Sparrow* SAM.
19 ASW frigates (8 with 1 CH-124 hel, 4 with *ASROC,* 3 in reserve).
3 support ships with 3 CH-124 hel.
6 coastal patrol trg ships.
5 reserve trg vessels.
1 hydrofoil (in reserve).

DEPLOYMENT:

Atlantic: 3 subs, 13 surface (1 in reserve), 2 spt ships.
Pacific: 10 surface (2 in reserve), 1 spt ship.

RESERVES: about 3,200.

Air Force (Air): 36,600;* some 210 combat aircraft.
Air Command (22,800).†

Air Defence Group:
  4 main, 17 auxiliary sites of Distant Early Warning (*DEW*) Line.
  24 long-range radar sites (*Pine Tree Line*).
  3 AWX sqns with 48 CF-101 *Voodoo.*
  1 ECM sqn with 9 CF-100 and 15 T-33.
  1 trg sqn with 8 CF-101.

Air Transport Group:
  4 tpt sqns: 2 with 24 C-130E/H, 1 with 5 CC-137 (Boeing 707), 1 with 7 *Cosmopolitan,* 7 *Falcon* 20.

---

‡ Leased until tanks on order are delivered.

4 tpt/SAR sqns with 14 CC-115 *Buffalo*, 8 CC-138 *Twin Otter* ac, 6 CH-113 *Labrador*, 8 CH-113A *Voyageur* hel.

Maritime Air Group:
4 maritime patrol sqns with 30 CP-107 *Argus*.
1 MR sqn with 26 CP-121 (*Tracker*).
2 ASW hel sqns with 26 CH-124 (*Sea King*).
2 sqns with 9 T-33, 3 CP-121 ac, 2 CH-135 (UH-1N) hel.
1 trg sqn with 2 CP-121 ac, 6 CH-124 hel.
1 proving and evaluation sqn with 2 CP-107.
(18 CP-140 (*Orion*) on order.)

10 Tactical Air Group (10 TAG):
2 fighter sqns with 24 CF-5 (plus 25 in storage).
5 hel sqns with 30 CH-135, 36 CH-136 (*Kiowa*).
1 tpt sqn with 7 CH-147 hel.

1 Canadian Air Group (1 CAG):
3 fighter sqns with 48 CF-104D.
1 hel sqn with 12 CH-136.

DEPLOYMENT:
Europe: 1 Canadian Air Group (1 CAG).

RESERVES: 700. Air Reserve Group: 4 wings with *Otter, Twin Otter* and *Dakota*.

DENMARK

Population: 5,091,000.
Military service: 9 months.
Total armed forces: 34,700 (12,270 conscripts).
Estimated GNP 1976: $34.2 bn.
Defence expenditure 1977–78: kr 6.32 bn ($1.08 bn).
$1 = 5.85 kroner (1977), 6.05 kroner (1976).

Army: 21,800 (9,000 conscripts).
3 mech inf bdes, each with 1 tk, 2 mech, 1 arty bn, 1 recce sqn, 1 engr coy, spt units.
2 mech inf bdes, each with 1 tk, 2 mech, 1 arty bn, 1 engr coy, spt units.
1 indep recce bn.
Some indep mot inf bns.
120 *Leopard* 1 (being delivered), 200 *Centurion* med, 48 M-41 lt tks; 630 M-113, 68 M-106 mortar-armed APC; 24 155mm guns; 144 105mm, 96 155mm, 12 203mm* how; 72 M-109 155mm SP how; 120mm mor; 252 106mm RCL; *TOW* ATGW; 224 L/60 and L/70 40mm AA guns; *Redeye* (*Hamlet*) SAM; 9 Saab T-17 lt ac; 12 Hughes OH-6A hel.

DEPLOYMENT: *Cyprus* (UNFICYP): 360.

RESERVES: 4,500 Augmentation Force, subject to immediate recall; 41,000 Field Army Reserve, comprising 12,000 Covering Force Reserve (to bring units to war strength and add 1 mech bn

to each bde) and 29,000 other reserve units to provide combat and log support; 24,000 Regional Defence Force, with 21 inf, 7 arty bns, ATK sqns, support units; 54,400 Army Home Guard.

Navy: 5,800 (1,900 conscripts).
6 coastal submarines.
2 frigates with *Sea Sparrow* SAM.
5 fishery-protection frigates, each with 1 hel.
3 coastal escorts (corvettes).
10 FPB, 4 FPBG.
6 minelayers (2 coastal, 1 coastal on order).
8 coastal minesweepers.
23 large patrol craft.
8 *Alouette* III hel.
(3 corvettes, 6 FPBG, *Harpoon* SSM on order.)

RESERVES: 4,500, Navy Home Guard 4,800.

Air Force: 7,100 (1,370 conscripts); 116 combat aircraft.
1 FB sqn with 20 F-35XD *Draken*.
2 FB sqns with 40 F-100D/F.
2 interceptor sqns with 40 F-104G.
1 recce sqn with 16 RF-35XD *Draken*.
1 tpt sqn with 8 C-47, 3 C-130H.
1 SAR sqn with 8 S-61A hel.
23 Saab T-17 trainers.
8 SAM sqns: 4 with 36 *Nike Hercules*, 4 with 24 *HAWK*.
(58 F-16, 5 TF-35 on order.)

RESERVES: 8,000; Air Force Home Guard 12,000.

FRANCE

Population: 53,777,000.
Military service: 12 months.
Total armed forces: 502,100 (273,600 conscripts).
Estimated GNP 1976: $353.2 bn.
Defence expenditure 1977: fr 58.41 bn ($11.72 bn).
$1 = 4.98 francs (1977), 4.69 francs (1976).

Strategic forces:
SLBM: 4 SSBN: 2 with 32 MSBS M-1, 1 with 16 M-2, 1 with 16 M-20 msls.
IRBM: 2 sqns, each with 9 SSBS S-2 msls.
Aircraft:
Bombers: 6 sqns with 32 *Mirage* IVA.
Tankers: 3 sqns with 11 KC-135F.
Reserve: 18 *Mirage* IVA bombers.
Reconnaissance: 4 *Mirage* IVA.

Army: 330,000, incl Army Aviation and 214,300 conscripts.†
5 mech divs.

---

* Dual-capable; no nuclear warheads on Danish soil.

† The army is being reorganized to combine the *Force de Manoeuvre* and the DOT and to form 8 armd, 6 inf, 1 para and 1 Alpine divs, plus corps troops incl 5 SSM

2 inf divs.
1 alpine div.
1 air-portable mot div (Marines).
1 para div of 2 bdes.
10 armd car regts.
1 mot inf regt.
2 para bns.
8 inf bns.
4 SSM regts with 24 *Pluton*.
3 SAM regts with 54 *HAWK*.
1,060 AMX-30 med, 1,120 AMX-13 lt tks; some 950 AFV, incl 720 Panhard EBR hy and AML lt armd cars; 442 AMX-10, AMX-VCI APC; Model 56 105mm pack, 155mm how; AMX 105mm and 155mm SP how; *Pluton* SSM; 120mm mor; 105/6 mm RCL; SS-11/-12, *Milan*, *ENTAC* ATGW; 40mm towed, 30mm SP AA guns; *HAWK* SAM. (*HOT* ATGW, Roland SAM on order.)

ARMY AVIATION (ALAT): 5,500.
2 groups, 6 divisions and 7 regional commands.
200 light fixed-wing aircraft.
190 *Alouette* II, 72 *Alouette* III, 150 SA-330 *Puma*, 140 SA-341 *Gazelle* hel (40 *Gazelle* on order).

DEPLOYMENT AND ORGANIZATION (incl Navy and Air Force):
Manoeuvre Forces (Forces de Maneouvre):
  First Army: 140,000, 2 mech divs in Germany (48,000); 3 mech divs in support in France; Berlin: 2,000.
Territorial Defence Forces (Défense Operationnelle du Territoire – DOT): about 52,000, incl 2 inf, 1 alpine divs, 8 indep inf, 1 mot inf, 2 armd car regts.
Strategic Reserve (Force d'Intervention):
  1 para div (2 bdes); 1 air-portable mot div.
Overseas Commands:
There are six overseas commands (Antilles-Guyane, West Africa, Djibouti, South Indian Ocean, New Caledonia, Polynesia), an indep comd in the Ivory Coast and a naval comd. Some 22,000 from all services are deployed overseas (numbers can vary according to local circumstances); equipment includes: 130 AFV, 36 hel, 9 frigates, 2 FPB, 2 lt tpt ships, 12 combat and 16 tpt ac.

RESERVES: about 400,000.

Navy: 68,500, incl Naval Air and 18,500 conscripts; 53 major surface combat vessels.
21 submarines.
2 lt attack aircraft carriers (each with 40 ac).
2 cruisers: 1 with *Exocet* SSM and *Masurca* SAM, 1 with 4 hy ASW hel.
20 destroyers: 2 with *Masurca* SAM and *Malafon*

and 4 SAM regts. An additional 14 divs will be formed on mobilization. The divisions will be smaller than now, armd divs consisting of 8,200 men, 2 tk, 2 mech inf and 1 arty regts; inf divs having 6,500 men, 3 mot inf, 1 armd car and 1 arty regts.

ASW msls, 3 with *Exocet* SAM and *Malafon*, 6 ASW with *Malafon*, 4 with *Tartar* SAM, 5 GP (1 with *Exocet* and ASW hel, 3 building).
22 frigates (11 building).
26 patrol craft.
6 FPBG.
38 ocean and coastal MCM.
2 landing ships, 5 LCT, 46 landing craft.

NAVAL AIR FORCE: 13,000; 111 combat aircraft.
2 attack sqns with 24 *Etendard* IVM.
2 interceptor sqns with 20 F-8E(FN) *Crusader*.
2 ASW sqns with 24 *Alizé*.
4 MR sqns with 25 *Atlantic* and 10 SP-2H *Neptune*.
1 recce sqn with 8 *Etendard* IVP.
3 ASW hel sqns with 12 *Super Frelon*, 12 HSS-1, 8 *Alouette* III.
1 assault hel sqn with 12 HSS-1.
2 SAR sqns with 9 *Alouette* II, 11 *Alouette* III.
1 hel sqn with 4 *Alouette* II, 2 *Super Frelon*.
9 comms sqns with DC-6, C-47 ac, 16 HSS-1, *Alouette* II/III, *Super Frelon* hel.
3 trg sqns with Nord 262, C-47, Fouga CM-175, *Etendard*, *Alizé*, *Rallye*.
(36 *Super Etendard* fighters, 26 *Lynx* hel on order.)

MARINES: 1 bn.

RESERVES: about 50,000.

Air Force: 103,600 (40,800 conscripts); 557 combat aircraft.
Air Defence Command (CAFDA): 9,000.
  8 interceptor sqns, 1 with 15 *Mirage* IIIC, 6 with 90 *Mirage* F1, 1 with 15 *Super Mystère* B2 (re-equipping with *Mirage* F1).
  10 SAM bns with *Crotale*.
  Automatic *STRIDA II* air-defence system.
Tactical Air Force (FATAC): 14,200.
  16 FB sqns: 7 with 140 *Mirage* IIIE, 2 with 48 *Mirage* VF, 1 with 10 F-100D (to be replaced with *Jaguar* 1978), 6 with 120 *Jaguar* A/E.
  2 lt bbr sqns with 16 *Vautour* IIB/N (being withdrawn).
  3 recce sqns with 58 *Mirage* IIIR/RD.
  2 OCU: 1 with 30 *Mirage* IIIB/BE/C, 1 with 15 Jaguar A/E.
Air Transport Command (COTAM): 7,400.
  7 tac tpt sqns: 3 with 47 Transall C-160, 4 with 72 *Noratlas*.
  4 tpt sqns with 5 DC-8F, 18 *Frégate*, 8 *Mystère* 10/20, 1 *Caravelle* ac, 3 *Alouette* II, 2 *Puma* hel.
  1 liaison sqn with 24 *Paris*, 12 *Broussard*, 1 *Rallye*.
  6 hel sqns with 130 *Alouette* II/III, 20 *Puma* hel.
Training Command (CEAA): Some 700 aircraft, incl 300 *Magister*, T-33, *Mystère* IV, 34 *Flamant*, *Noratlas*.

Para-Military Forces: 76,200 Gendarmerie (4,700 conscripts).

GERMANY: FEDERAL REPUBLIC OF

Population: 63,160,000 (incl West Berlin).
Military service: 15 months.
Total armed forces: 489,000 (235,000 conscripts).
Estimated GDP 1976: $449.1 bn.
Defence expenditure 1977: DM 32.9 bn ($13.76 bn)
$1 = 2.39 (1977), DM 2.53 (1976).

Army: 341,000 (180,000 conscripts).*
16 armd bdes (2 tk, 1 armd inf, 1 armd arty bns).
12 armd inf bdes (1 tk, 2 armd inf, 1 armd arty bns).
3 mot inf bdes.
2 mountain bdes.
3 AB bdes.
(Organized in 3 corps: 12 divs (4 armd, 4 armd inf,
2 *Jäger*, 1 mountain, 1 AB)).
15 SSM bns: 11 with *Honest John*, 4 with *Lance*.
3 army aviation comds, each with 1 lt, 1 med tpt
regt.
Territorial Army: peacetime strength 63,000, incl
30,000 conscripts; mobilization strength 504,000.
3 Territorial Commands of 5 Military Districts;
6 Home Defence bde-sized units being formed.
In support are 4 service support comds, 1 sig bde,
2 sig, 2 engr regts. The Territorial Army provides
defensive, comms, police and service units on
mobilization.
1,400 M-48A2, 2,437 *Leopard* 1 med tks; 500 SPZ
HS-30, 1,100 *Hotchkiss*, 2,136 *Marder* MICV; 300
SPZ-2 recce; 3,700 M-113 APC; 280 105mm, 80
155mm how; 600 155mm, 150 175mm towed, 80
203mm SP gun/how; 210 *LARS* 110mm multiple
RL; 70 *Honest John*, 20 *Sergeant*, 26 *Lance* SSM;
770 JPZ 4-5 SP ATK guns; 106mm RCL; *Cobra,
Milan*, *TOW*, *HOT* ATGW; 350 RJPZ-2 SP
ATGW; 2,000 20mm, 800 40mm towed, 150
Gepard 30mm SP AA guns; 1,400 *Redeye* SAM; 18
Do-27, 35 OV-10Z ac; 200 UH-1D, 240 *Alouette*
II/III, 110 CH-53G hel; CL-89 drones. (1,000
Leopard 2 tks, 500 M-113 APC, 2,500 ATGW, 300
Gepard SP AA, 143 *Roland* II SAM on order.)

RESERVES: 1,056,000; 615,000 field army, 441,000
Territorial Army.

Navy: 38,000, incl Naval Air Arm and 11,000
conscripts.
24 coastal submarines.
3 GW destroyers.
14 destroyers/escorts.
5 ASW coastal escorts.
11 fast combat spt ships.
57 MCM ships (18 coastal, 21 fast, 18 inshore)
10 FPB, 30 FPBG with *Exocet* SSM.

18 landing craft.
(150 *Exocet* SSM on order.)

NAVAL AIR ARM: 6,000; 139 combat aircraft.
3 FB sqns with 96 F-104G.
1 recce sqn with 25 RF-104G.
2 MR sqns with 18 *Atlantic*.
1 SAR hel sqn with 21 *Sea King* Mk 41.
2 utility sqns with 27 Do-28 ac, 15 H-34G hel.

RESERVES: 23,500.

Air Force: 110,000 (44,000 conscripts); 509 combat aircraft.
16 FGA sqns: 4 with 60 F-4F, 8 with 144 F-104G;
4 with 84 G-91 (to be replaced by *AlphaJet*).
4 AWX sqns with 60 F-4F.
4 recce sqns with 88 RF-4E.
2 OCU with 18 TF-104G, 55 G-91T.
5 tpt sqns with 89 Transall C-160.
4 hel sqns with 117 UH-1D.
8 SSM sqns with 72 *Pershing*.
24 SAM btys with 216 *Nike Hercules*.
36 SAM btys with 216 *HAWK*.
4 aircraft control and warning regts.
Other ac: 4 Boeing 707, 3 C-140, 9 HFB-320, 3
VFW-614, 9 *Pembroke*, 2 C-47, 5 *Noratlas*, 121
Do-28D. (10 F-4F, 175 *AlphaJet* FGA, 3 AB-212
hel on order.)

RESERVES: 100,000.

Para-Military Forces: 20,000 Border Police.

GREECE

Population: 9,095,000.
Military service: 28–30 months.
Total armed forces: 200,000 (148,000 conscripts).
Estimated GNP 1976: $22.76 bn.
Defence expenditure 1977: 41.05 bn drachmas
($1.10 bn).
$1 = 37.3 drachmas (1977), 36.5 drachmas (1976).

Army: 160,000 (123,000 conscripts).
1 armd div.
11 inf divs.
1 armd bde.
1 para-cdo bde.
1 marine inf bde.
2 SSM bns with 8 *Honest John*.
1 SAM bn with 12 *HAWK*.
12 arty bns.
14 army aviation coys.
275 M-47, 650 M-48, 75 AMX-30 med, 170 M-24 lt
tks; 180 M-8 armd cars; 450 M-59, 500 M-113,
Mowag APC; 100 75mm pack, 80 105mm, 240
155mm how; 105mm, 155mm, 175mm, 203mm
SP gun/how; *Honest John* SSM; 550 106mm RCL;

---

* The army is being reorganized to form 16 armd bdes
(each with 3 tk, 1 armd inf, 1 armd arty bns), 17 armd
inf/*Jäger* bdes (each with 2 tk, 2 armd inf, 1 *Jäger*, 1
armd arty bns) and 3 AB bdes.

SS-11, *TOW*, 7 *Milan* ATGW; 40mm, 75mm, 90mm AA guns; *HAWK* SAM; 2 Aero *Commander*, 25 U-17, 28 L-21 ac; 5 Bell 47B, 25 UH-1D, 42 AB-204/-205 hel. (95 AMX-30 med tks on order.)

RESERVES: about 270,000.

Navy: 17,500 (11,000 conscripts).
6 submarines (2 ex-US *Guppy*, 4 Type 209, 3 on order).
11 destroyers.
4 destroyer escorts.
9 FPBG, 7 with *Exocet* SSM (1 more on order), 2 with SS-12 SSM (6 with *Penguin* SSM on order).
9 fast torpedo boats.
2 large, 4 small patrol craft.
2 coastal minelayers.
14 coastal minesweepers.
14 landing ships (8 LST, 5 med, 1 dock).
6 landing craft.
1 sqn with 5 *Alouette* III hel.
(7 destroyers, 2 LST, *Exocet* SSM on order.)

RESERVES: about 20,000.

Air Force: 22,500 (14,000 conscripts); 235 combat aircraft.
6 FGA sqns: 2 with 37 F-4E, 3 with 60 A-7H, 1 with 15 F-104G.
5 interceptor sqns: 2 with 40 F-5A, 1 with 15 F/TF-104G, 2 with 40 *Mirage* F1CG.
1 recce sqn with 20 RF-5A.
1 MR sqn with 8 HU-16B *Albatross*.
2 tpt sqns with 28 C-47, 12 C-130H, 1 *Gulfstream*, 5 CL-215.
3 hel sqns with 14 AB-205, 2 AB-206, 10 Bell 47G, 12 SH-19D.
Trainers incl 60 T-33A, 20 T-41D, 18 T-37B, 8 F-5B, 40 T-2E.
1 SAM bn with *Nike Hercules*.
(18 F-4E FGA, 300 *Sidewinder* AAM on order.)

RESERVES: about 20,000.

Para-Military Forces: 28,000 Gendarmerie, 90,000 National Guard.

ITALY

Population: 56,700,000.
Military service: Army and Air Force 12 months, Navy 18 months.
Total armed forces: 330,000 (211,000 conscripts).
Estimated GNP 1976: $161.6 bn.
Defence expenditure 1977: 4,117 bn lire ($4.64 bn). $1 = 888 lire (1977), 852 lire (1976).

Army: 218,000 (163,000 conscripts).
3 corps, each of 1 armd, 3 mech divs.
1 indep mech bde.
5 indep mot bdes.
5 alpine bdes.
1 AB bde.
2 amph bns.
1 msl bde with 1 *Lance* SSM, 4 *HAWK* SAM bns.
700 M-47, 200 M-60, 600 *Leopard* med tks; 30 Fiat 6616 armd cars; 4,000 M-106, M-113, M-548, M-577 APC; 1,500 guns/how, incl 105mm (incl Model 56 pack), 155mm, 203mm; 369 SP guns/how, incl M-109 155mm, M-107 175mm; 120mm mor; *Lance* SSM; 57mm, 106mm RCL; *Mosquito*, *Cobra*, SS-11, *TOW* ATGW; 40mm AA guns; *Indigo*, *HAWK* SAM. (267 M-113, 208 M-548 APC, 36 M-109 SP how, CL-89 drones on order.)

ARMY AVIATION: 20 units with 40 L-19, 39 L-21, 80 SM-1019 lt ac; hel incl 70 AB-47G/J, 36 AB-204B, 99 AB-205A, 141 AB-206A/A-1, 26 CH-47C. (5 A-109 hel on order.)

RESERVES: 550,000.

Navy: 42,000, incl air arm, 1,700 Marines and 24,000 conscripts.
8 submarines (4 more building).
1 hel cruiser with 9 AB-204B ASW hel, 1 *Terrier/ ASROC*.
6 GW destroyers (2 with 4 ASW hel, *Terrier* SAM; 2 with 2 ASW hel, *Tartar* SAM; 2 with 1 ASW hel, *Tartar* SAM).
12 destroyers/escorts.
8 coastal escorts.
4 ocean, 30 coastal, 10 inshore minesweepers.
5 FPBG, 1 hydrofoil with *Otomat* SSM (6 hydrofoils building).
2 landing ships, 57 landing craft.
1 Marine inf bn with LVTP-7 APC.

NAVAL AIR ARM:
2 ASW hel sqns with 24 SH-3D, 30 AB-204/-212, 2 S-61.

RESERVES: 115,800.

Air Force: 70,000 (24,000 conscripts); 336 combat aircraft.
6 FGA sqns: 1 with 18 F-104G, 3 with 54 F/RF-104S/G, 2 with 36 G-91Y.
3 lt attack/recce sqns with 54 G-91R.
6 AWX sqns with 72 F-104S.
3 recce sqns with 54 F/RF-104S/G.
3 MR sqns: 2 with 14 *Atlantic*, 1 with 8 S-2 *Tracker*.
1 ECM recce sqn with 6 PD-808.
3 tpt sqns: 2 with 28 C-119 (being replaced by G-222), 1 with 12 C-130H.
5 comms sqns with 50 P-166M, 40 SIAI-208M, 8 PD-808, 2 DC-9.
2 SAR sqns with 11 HU-16 ac, 15 AB-204 hel.
1 OCU with 20 TF-104G.
9 trg sqns with 75 G-91T, 100 MB-326, 51 P-166M ac, AB-47, AB-204 hel.

Hel incl 40 AB-204B, 65 AB-47J.
8 SAM groups with *Nike Hercules*.
(44 G-222, 20 SF-260 ac, 20 HH-3F, 2 S-61 hel
on order.)

RESERVES: 29,000.

Para-Military Forces: 90,000 *Carabinieri*, incl 1 AB
bn, with M-47 tks, M-113 APC, 72 hel; 72,000
Public Security Guard; 5,000 Finance Guards.

LUXEMBOURG

Population: 358,000.
Military service: voluntary.
Total armed forces: 625.
Estimated GDP 1976: $2.42 bn.
Defence expenditure 1977: 921 m francs ($25.16 m).
$1 = 36.6 francs (1977), 39.0 francs (1976).

Army: 625.
1 lt inf bn.
1 indep coy.
TOW ATGW.

Para-Military Forces: 430 Gendarmerie.

NETHERLANDS

Population: 13,948,000.
Military service: Army 14 months, Navy and Air
Force 14–17 months.
Total armed forces: 109,700 (49,100 conscripts).
Estimated GNP 1976: $85.1 bn.
Defence expenditure 1977: 8.37 bn guilders
($3.36 bn).
$1 = 2.49 guilders (1977), 2.71 guilders (1976).

Army: 75,000 (43,000 conscripts).
2 armd bdes.
4 mech inf bdes.
2 SSM bns with *Honest John*.
3 army aviation sqns (Air Force crews).
340 *Centurion*, 470 *Leopard* med, AMX-13 lt tks;
2,000 AMX-VCI, YP-408 and M-113 APC; 105
mm, 155mm, 203mm how; AMX 105mm,
M-109 155mm, 24 M-107 175mm, M-110 203mm
SP gun/how; 107mm, 120mm mor; *Honest John*
SSM; *LAW*, *Carl Gustav* 84mm, 106mm RCL;
TOW ATGW; L/70 40mm AA guns; 60 *Alouette*
III, 30 BO-105 hel. (2,000 YPR-765 APC, twin
35mm SP AA guns, *Lance* SSM on order.)

DEPLOYMENT: *Germany:* 1 armd bde, 1 recce bn.

RESERVES: 145,000; 1 armd, 2 inf bdes and corps
troops, incl 1 indep inf bde, would be completed
by call-up of reservists. A number of inf bdes
could be mobilized for territorial defence.

Navy: 17,000 (2,900 Marines, 1,900 naval air arm,
2,000 conscripts).
6 submarines.
2 GW destroyers with *Tartar/Sea Sparrow* SAM,
Harpoon SSM, 1 lt ASW hel.
6 frigates with *Seacat* SAM and 1 lt ASW hel.
9 destroyers/escorts.
6 coastal escorts.
5 patrol vessels.
37 MCM ships (3 spt, 18 coastal, 16 inshore).
2 fast combat spt ships.
(12 frigates on order.)

MARINES:
2 amph combat gps.
1 mountain/arctic warfare coy.

NAVAL AIR ARM:
2 MR sqns with 8 *Atlantic*, 15 P-2 *Neptune*.
2 ASW hel sqns with 7 *Lynx*, 12 *Wasp*.
(10 *Lynx* on order.)

DEPLOYMENT: *Netherlands Antilles:* 1 destroyer, 1
amph combat det, 1 MR det (3 ac).

RESERVES: about 20,000; 9,000 on immediate recall.

Air Force: 17,700 (4,100 conscripts); 162 combat
aircraft.
2 FB sqns with 36 F-104G.
3 FB sqns with 54 NF-5A/B.
1 FB/trg sqn with 18 NF-5B.
2 interceptor sqns with 36 F-104G.
1 recce sqn with 18 RF-104G.
1 tpt sqn with 12 F-27.
4 SAM sqns with 16 *Nike Hercules*.
11 SAM sqns with 66 *HAWK*.
(84 F-16 fighters, 840 *Sidewinder* AAM on order.)

RESERVES: about 11,500.

Para-Military Forces: 3,700 Gendarmerie; 4,000
Home Guard.

NORWAY

Population: 4,068,000.
Military service: Army 12 months, Navy and Air
Force 15 months.
Total armed forces: 39,000 (25,000 conscripts).
Estimated GNP 1976: $31.1 bn.
Defence expenditure 1977: 5.85 bn kroner ($1.12
bn).
$1 = 5.24 kroner (1977), 5.47 kroner (1976).

Army: 20,000 (16,000 conscripts).
1 bde gp of 3 inf bns in North Norway.
Indep armd sqns, inf bns and arty regts.
78 *Leopard*, 38 M-48 med, 70 NM-116 lt tks
(M-24/-90); M-113 APC; 250 105mm, 155mm
how, 130 M-109 SP how; 107mm mor; 75mm,

Carl Gustav 84mm, 106mm RCL; *ENTAC, TOW* ATGW; Rh-202 20mm, L/60 and L/70 40mm AA guns; 40 O-1E, L-18 lt ac.

RESERVES: 120,000. 11 Regimental Combat Teams (bdes) of about 5,000 men each, supporting units and territorial forces; 21 days' refresher training each 3rd/4th year. Home Guard (all services) 80,000, mobilizable in 4 hours (all have done full initial service).

Navy: 9,000, incl 1,600 coastal artillery and 5,000 conscripts.
15 coastal submarines.
5 frigates/escorts with *Sea Sparrow* SAM and *Penguin* SSM.
2 coastal escorts.
20 FPB, 26 FPBG with *Penguin* SSM (14 on order).
10 coastal minesweepers, 5 minelayers (2 on order).
1 spt ship.
7 landing craft.
6 patrol ships (fishery protection, 7 on order).
36 coastal arty btys.

RESERVES: 22,000. Coastguard will be established as part of navy.

Air Force: 10,000 (4,000 conscripts); 145 combat aircraft.
3 FGA sqns with 75 F-5A.
1 FGA sqn with 22 CF-104G.
1 AWX sqn with 16 F-104G.
1 recce sqn with 13 RF-5A.
1 MR sqn with 5 P-3B.
1 OCU with 14 F-5B.
2 tpt sqns: 1 with 6 C-130H, 1 with 5 DHC-6, 2 *Falcon* 20 ECM ac.
1 SAR sqn with 10 *Sea King* Mk 43 hel.
2 hel sqns with 32 UH-1B.
17 Saab *Safir* trainers.
4 lt AA bns with L/70 40mm guns.
4 SAM btys with *Nike Hercules*.
(72 F-16 fighters, 40 *Roland* II SAM on order.)

RESERVES: 18,000. 7 lt AA bns for airfield defence with L/60 40mm guns.

PORTUGAL

Population: 8,787,000.
Military service: Army 15–24 months.
Total armed forces: 58,800.*
Estimated GNP 1976: $15.8 bn.
Defence expenditure 1977: 17.86 bn escudos ($461 m).
$1 = 38.7 escudos (1977), 30.0 escudos (1976).

Army: 36,000.*
5 cav regts.
16 inf regts.
6 arty regts.
2 engr regts.
2 sigs regts.
100 M-47, 5 M-48 med, 10 M-24 lt tks; Panhard EBR armd cars; 40 *Chaimite* (*Commando*) APC; 10 25-pdr, 30 5.5-in. guns, 50 105mm guns/how; 105mm SP guns/how; 18 106mm RCL; SS-11 ATGW; coast and 40mm AA arty.

Navy: 12,800 (2,500 Marines).*
3 submarines (*Daphne*-class).
7 frigates.
10 corvettes.
10 large, 8 coastal patrol craft.
7 coastal minesweepers (3 in reserve).
2 LCT, 8 landing craft.

Air Force: 10,000;* 52 combat aircraft.
1 FGA sqn with 18 G-91.
1 interceptor sqn with 20 F-86F.
1 MR sqn with 8 P-2V5 *Neptune* (being phased out).
1 recce sqn with 6 CASA C-212 *Aviocar*.
20 CASA C-212 *Aviocar*, 2C-130H, DC-6 tpt ac.
5 G-91T, 14 T-33, 24 T-37, 16 Do-27, 28 *Chipmunk*, 35 Reims-Cessna FTB 337G, 10 T-38 trainers.
34 *Alouette* III, 12 SA-330 *Puma* hel.
1 para regt of 1,200.

Para-Military Forces: 9,700 National Republican Guard, 13,700 Public Security Police, 6,500 Fiscal Guard.

TURKEY

Population: 41,093,000.
Military service: 20 months.
Total armed forces: 465,000 (310,000 conscripts).
Estimated GNP 1976: $40.2 bn.
Defence expenditure 1977–78: 46.42 bn liras ($2.65 bn).
$1 = 17.5 liras (1977), 16.0 liras (1976).

Army: 375,000 (250,000 conscripts).†
1 armd div.
2 mech inf divs.
14 inf divs.
5 armd bdes.
4 mech inf bdes.
5 inf bdes.
1 para bde.
1 cdo bde.
4 SSM bns with *Honest John*.
2,800 M-47 and M-48 med tks; 1,650 M-113, M-59, *Commando* APC; 1,500 75mm, 105mm, 155mm

---

* The three services are being reduced, the army to 26,000, the navy and air force to 8,000 each.

† About half the divs and bdes are below strength.

and 203mm how; 265 105mm, 190 155mm, 36 175mm SP guns; 1,750 60mm, 81mm, 4.2-in. mor; 18 *Honest John* SSM; 1,200 57mm, 390 75mm, 800 106mm RCL; 85 *Cobra* ATGW; 900 40mm AA guns; 10 *Beaver*, 95 U-17, 3 Cessna 421, 7 Do-27, 18 Do-28 D-1, 20 Beech *Baron* ac; 100 AB-205/ -206, 20 Bell 47G, 48 UH-1D hel. (193 *Leopard* tks; *TOW*, *Milan* ATGW; 56 AB-205 hel on order.)

DEPLOYMENT: *Cyprus:* 2 inf divs.

RESERVES: 700,000.

Navy: 43,000 (31,000 conscripts).
14 submarines (2 on order).
12 destroyers (5 ex-US *Gearing*, 5 *Fletcher*, 1 *Sumner*, 1 *R. H. Smith*-class).
2 frigates (with 1 hel.)
14 FPB (14 on order), 6 FPBG (3 on order).
41 large, 4 coastal patrol craft.
21 coastal, 4 inshore minesweepers.
9 minelayers (6 coastal).
2 LST, 20 LCT, 36 landing craft.
1 MR sqn with 10 S-2E *Tracker* (2 trainers).

3 AB-205, 12 AB-212 ASW hel.
(6 AB-212 hel, 33 *Harpoon* SMM on order.)

RESERVES: 25,000.

Air Force: 47,000 (29,000 conscripts); 319 combat aircraft.
14 FGA sqns: 2 with 40 F-4E, 4 with 70 F-5A, 2 with 34 F-104G, 2 with 40 F-104S, 3 with 54 F-100D/F, 1 with 20 F-100C.
1 interceptor sqn with 25 F/TF-102A.
2 recce sqns with 36 RF-5A.
4 tpt sqns with 7 C-130E, 20 Transall C-160, 30 C-47, 3 C-54, 3 *Viscount* 794, 2 *Islander*.
Hel incl 10 AB-204, 10 UH-1D, 10 H-19.
8 SAM sqns with *Nike Ajax/Hercules*.
Trainers incl 20 T-33A, 35 T-37, 18 T-34, 25 T-41, 35 F-100C, 13 F-5B, TF-102A, TF-104G, Beech AT-11, Cessna 421B.
(56 *AlphaJet* trainers on order.)

Para-Military Forces: 75,000 Gendarmerie (incl 3 mobile bdes).

OTHER EUROPEAN COUNTRIES

ALBANIA

Population: 2,650,000.
Military service: Army 2 years; Air Force, Navy and special units 3 years.
Total armed forces: 45,000 (22,500 conscripts).
Estimated GNP 1974: $1.1 bn.
Defence expenditure 1977: 805 m leks ($137 m).
  $1 = 5.88 leks.

Army: 34,000 (20,000 conscripts).
1 tk bde.
9 inf bdes.
2 tk bns.
1 arty regt.
2 AD regts.
8 lt coastal arty bns.
70 T-34, 15 T-54, 15 T-59 med tks; 20 BA-64, BTR-50/-152, K-63 APC; 76mm, 85mm, 122mm, 152mm guns/how; SU-76, SU-100 SP guns; 120mm mor; 107mm RCL; 57mm, 76mm, 85mm ATK guns; 37mm, 57mm, 85mm, 100mm AA guns; SA-2 SAM.

Navy: 3,000 (1,000 conscripts).
4 submarines (Soviet W-class, 1 trg).
4 coastal escorts (*Kronstadt*-class).
42 MTB (12 Soviet P-4, 30 *Hu Chwan* hydrofoils).
4 *Shanghai*-class MGB.
8 MCM ships (2 Soviet T-43-, 6 T-301-class).
10 patrol boats (Soviet PO-2).

Air Force: 8,000 (1,500 conscripts); 103 combat aircraft.
2 AWX sqns with 10 MiG-17/F-4, 13 MiG-19/F-6.
6 interceptor sqns with 26 MiG-15/F-2, 10 MiG-17/F-4, 32 MiG-19/F-6, 12 MiG-21/F-8 (Chinese).
1 tpt sqn with 4 Il-14.
2 hel sqns with 30 Mi-4.
Trainers incl 10 MiG-15UTI.

RESERVES (all services): 100,000.

Para-Military Forces: 13,000: Internal security force 5,000; frontier guard 8,000.

AUSTRIA

Population: 7,880,000.
Military service: 6 months, followed by 60 days' reservist training for 12 years.
Total armed forces: 37,300 (25,000 conscripts).
Estimated GNP 1976: $39.8 bn.
Defence expenditure 1977: 9.05 bn schilling ($534 m).
  $1 = 16.95 schilling (1977), 18.3 schilling (1976).

Army: 33,000 (23,000 conscripts).
1 mech div of 3 mech bdes, each with 1 tk, 1 mech inf, 1 armd arty bns and/or 1 armd ATK bn.
3 inf bdes, each with 3 inf, 1 arty bns.
3 arty bns.
1 cdo bn.
3 engr bns.
5 sigs bns.
150 M-47, 120 M-60 med tks; 460 Saurer 4K4F APC; 132 M-2 105mm, M-1 155mm how, 38 M-109 155mm SP how; 18 Steyr 680 M3 130mm multiple RL; 300 81mm, 100 M-2 107mm, 82 M-30 120mm mor; 150 M-18 57mm, 45 M-20 75mm, 390 M-40 106mm RCL; 240 M52/M55 85mm towed, 120 *Kuerassier* SP ATK guns; 50 *Pinzgauer* 712 20mm AA guns.

DEPLOYMENT: *Cyprus* (UNFICYP): 1 inf coy, fd hospital (312); *Syria* (UNDOF): 1 bn (520); other Middle East (UNTSO): 12.

RESERVES: 112,000; 3 reserve bdes (each of 3 inf, 1 arty bns), 16 regts and 4 bns *Landwehr* distributed among 8 regional military comds. 650,000 have a reserve commitment.

Air Force: 4,300 (2,000 conscripts); 30 combat aircraft.*
3 FB sqns with 30 Saab 105Ö.
1 tpt sqn with 3 *Beaver*, 2 *Skyvan*, 12 *Turbo-Porter*.
6 hel sqns with 22 AB-204B, 10 AB-206A, 24 *Alouette* III, 12 OH-58B, 2 S-65Oe (HH-53), 4 Bell 47G.
2 trg sqns with 20 Saab 91D, 5 Saab 105Ö.
Other ac incl 20 Cessna L-19.
4 indep AD bns.
300 20mm Oerlikon, 70 35mm Z/65, Z/75, 60 Types 55 and 60 40mm Bofors AA guns; *Super-Bat* and *Skyguard* AD system.

RESERVES: 700.

Para-Military Forces: 11,250 Gendarmerie.

EIRE

Population: 3,200,000.
Military service: voluntary.
Total armed forces: 14,650.
Estimated GNP 1976: $8.1 bn.
Defence budget 1977: £85.2 m ($146 m).
  $1 = £0.584 (1977), £0.544 (1976).

Army: 13,370.
10 inf bns.
4 recce sqns.

* Austrian air units, an integral part of the Army, are listed separately for purposes of comparison.

3 fd arty btys.
1 AA arty bty.
7 engr coys.
10 AML H90, 32 AML H60 AFV; 50 Panhard VTT/M3, 10 *Unimog* APC; 48 25-pdr gun/how; 72 m/41C 120mm mor; 477 *Carl Gustav* 84mm, 96 IIIO 90mm RCL; 26 Bofors 40mm AA guns.

Navy (Naval Service): 570.
2 patrol vessels (1 on order).
3 coastal minesweepers (ex-British *Ton*-class).
1 training/supply vessel.

Air Force (Air Corps): 710; 16 combat aircraft.
1 COIN sqn with 6 *Super Magister*, 10 SF-260W.
4 *Chipmunk*, 8 Cessna FR-172H trainers; 1 *King Air*, 1 *Dove* lt tpts; 8 *Alouette* III hel.

RESERVES: 18,665 (1st line 490, 2nd line 18,175).

FINLAND

Population: 4,739,000.
Military service: 8–11 months (11 months for officers and NCOs).
Total armed forces: 39,900 (32,000 conscripts; total mobilizable strength 700,000 within days).
Estimated GNP 1976: $32.4 bn.
Defence expenditure 1977: 1.62 bn markka ($426 m).
   $1 = 3.8 markka (1977), 3.9 markka (1976).

Army: 34,400.
1 armd bde.
6 inf bdes.
8 indep inf bns.
3 fd arty regts.
2 indep fd arty bns.
2 coast arty regts.
3 indep coast arty bns.
1 AA arty regt.
4 indep AA arty bns.
T-54, T-55 med, PT-76 lt tks; BTR-50P/-60 APC; 76mm, 105mm, 122mm, 130mm, 150mm, 152mm, 155mm guns/how; 60mm, 81mm, 120mm, 160mm mor; 55mm, 95mm RCL; SS-11 ATGW; 23mm, 30mm, 35mm, 40mm, 57mm towed, ZSU-57-2 SP AA guns.

DEPLOYMENT: *Cyprus* (UNFICYP): 290; *Egypt* (UNEF): 640.

Navy: 2,500 (incl 500 coastguard).
2 *Riga*-class frigates.
2 corvettes.
15 MGB, 4 *Osa*-II class FPBG with *Styx* SSM.
5 large, 12 coastguard patrol craft.
1 coastal minelayer, 6 inshore minesweepers.
17 small landing craft/tpts.

Air Force: 3,000; 48 combat aircraft.
2 fighter sqns with 24 MiG-21F, 24 J-35S *Draken*.
Tpts incl 8 C-47, 1 Cessna 402, 5 *Cherokee Arrow*.
Trainers incl 60 *Magister*, 30 Saab *Safir*, 3 MiG-15UTI, 4 MiG-21UTI, 3 J-35C.
1 hel flt with 3 Mi-4, 4 Mi-8, 2 Hughes 500, 1 AB-206A.
(6 J-35F fighters on order.)

RESERVES (all services): 690,000 (30,000 a year do training).

Para-Military Forces: 4,000 frontier guards.

SPAIN

Population: 36,396,000.
Military service: 18 months.
Total armed forces: 309,000 (217,000 conscripts).
Estimated GNP 1976: $101.7 bn.
Defence expenditure 1976: 147.8 bn pesetas ($2.15 bn).
   $1 = 68.6 pesetas (1977), 67.5 pesetas (1976).

Army: 220,000 (178,000 conscripts).
1 armd div ⎫
1 mech inf div ⎪
1 mot inf div ⎪ (about
2 mountain divs ⎬ 70 per cent
1 armd cav bde ⎪ strength).
10 indep inf bdes ⎭
1 mountain bde.
1 airportable bde.
1 para bde.
2 arty bdes.
10 mixed AA/coast arty regts.
3 Foreign Legion regts.
3 *Regulares* regts (local forces in Ceuta/Melilla).
1 SAM bn with *Nike Hercules* and *HAWK*.
200 AMX-30, 475 M-47/-48 med, 200 M-41 lt tks; 75 AML-60/-90 armd cars; 400 M-113 APC; 500 105mm, 122mm, 155mm, 203mm guns/how; 75 105mm, 155mm and 175mm SP guns/how; 216mm, 300mm multiple RL; 60mm, 81mm, 120mm mor; 90mm, 106mm RCL; *Milan, Cobra* ATGW; 400 40mm, 88mm, 90mm AA guns; 88mm, 6-in, 15-in coast arty guns; *Nike Hercules* and *HAWK* SAM; 20 *Cessna* O-1, 20 Do-27 lt ac; 20 UH-1B/H, 16 AB-206A, 6 CH-47C, 1 *Alouette* III, 13 Bell 47G, 3 *Puma* hel.
(180 AMX-30; 8-in how; 12 *Skyguard* AD systems on order.)

DEPLOYMENT: *Balearics:* 6,000. *Canaries:* 16,000. *Ceuta/Melilla:* 18,000.

Navy: 48,000 (8,000 Marines, 30,000 conscripts).
10 submarines (4 *Daphne*-class, 4 US, 2 midget).
1 helicopter carrier (capacity 20 hel).

13 destroyers (10 ex-US *Gearing-*, *Fletcher-*class).

14 frigates/corvettes (5 with *Standard* SAM and *ASROC*, 8 more on order).

2 motor torpedo boats.

22 minesweepers.

23 patrol craft (11 coastal).

8 large landing ships, 8 tank landing craft.

1 FGA sqn with 5 AV-8A *Matador* (*Harrier*), 2 TAV-8A.

1 comms sqn with 4 *Commanche*.

5 hel sqns with 10 SH-3D, 11 AB-204/212AS, 12 Bell 47G, 10 Hughes 500HM, 6 AH-1G.

4 Marine lt inf regts and 2 indep gps.

(2 subs, 5 AV-8A FGA, 6 *Sea King* hel on order.)

Air Force: 41,000 (9,000 conscripts); 157 combat aircraft.

5 FGA sqns with 35 F-4C(S), 24 *Mirage* IIIE, 6 IIIDE, 15 *Mirage* F1CE.

2 FGA/recce sqns with 40 F/RF-5A.

1 COIN sqn with 25 HA-220 *Saeta*.

1 MR sqn with 9 HU-16B *Albatross* and 3 P-3A *Orion*.

3 SAR sqns with 17 AB-205/-206, 5 SA-16.

8 tpt sqns with 7 C-130H, 12 CASA-207, 30 CASA-212, 12 DHC-4.

Other ac incl 3 Convair C-440, 1 *Falcon* 20, 36 Do-27, 8 *King Air*, 3 *Baron*, 3 KC-97 tankers.

7 trg sqns with 24 F-5B, 40 T-33, 25 T-34, 10 Piper and Beechcraft, 80 T-6G, 40 HA-200A/B, 42 *Bonanza*; 28 AB-47, 3 AB-205 hel.

(5 C-103H tpts on order.)

Para-Military Forces: 65,000 *Guardia Civil*, 38,000 *Policia Armada*.

SWEDEN

Population: 8,263,000.

Military service: Army and Navy 7½–15 months, Air Force 8–12 months.

Total armed forces: 68,550 (49,300 conscripts;* total mobilizable strength about 750,000 within 72 hours).

Estimated GNP 1976: $76.5 bn.

Defence expenditure 1977–78: Kr. 11.93 bn ($2.83 bn)

$1 = 4.21 kronor (1977), 4.39 kronor (1976).

Army: 46,000 (36,500 conscripts).*

Peace establishment:

49 non-operational armd, inf and arty trg regts for basic conscript trg.

War establishment:

5 armd bdes.

20 inf bdes.

4 *Norrland* bdes.

50 indep inf, arty and AA arty bns.

23 Local Defence Districts with 100 indep bns and 400–500 indep coys.

350 Strv 101, 102 (*Centurion*), 300 103B (S-tank) med, Strv 74, Ikv 91 lt tks; Pbv 302A APC; 105 mm, 150mm, 155mm how; Ikv 102/103 105mm, Bk 1A (L/50) 155mm SP guns; 81mm, 120mm mor; 90mm ATK guns; *Carl Gustav* 84mm, *Miniman* RCL; SS-11, *Bantam* ATGW; 20mm, 40mm, 57mm AA guns; *Redeye*, RBS-70, *HAWK* SAM; 20 Sk-61 (*Bulldog*), 12 *Super Cub*, 5 Do-27; 15 HKP-3 (AB-204B), 19 HKP-6 (*JetRanger*) hel. (Ikv 91 lt tanks, FH77 155mm how on order.)

DEPLOYMENT: *Cyprus* (UNFICYP): 425; *Egypt* (UNEF/UNDOF): 687.

Navy: 12,000 (7,100 conscripts).*

17 submarines (3 building).

6 destroyers (2 with Rb-08 SSM, 4 with *Seacat* SAM).

6 frigates (2 with lt hel).

1 FPBG with *Penguin* SSM (16 on order).

29 large torpedo boats.

12 MTB, 22 patrol launches (under 100 tons).

12 minelayers (9 coastal, 1 command ship).

12 inshore minesweepers (8 under 100 tons).

86 landing craft (under 100 tons).

25 mobile, 45 static coastal arty btys with 75mm, 105mm, 120mm, 152mm, 210mm guns, Rb-08, Rb-52 (SS-11) SSM.

5 HKP-2 (*Alouette* II), 3 HKP-4B (Vertol 107), 7 HKP-4 (KV-107/II), 10 HKP-6 (*JetRanger*) hel.

Air Force: 10,550 (5,700 conscripts);* 504 combat aircraft.†

7 FGA sqns: 2 with 36 A-32A *Lansen* (with Rb-04E ASM), 4 with 72 AJ-37 *Viggen*, 1 with 18 SK-60C (Saab 105).

17 AWX sqns: 13 with 234 J-35F *Draken*, 4 with 72 J-35D.

4 recce sqns: 1 with 18 S-32C *Lansen*, 2 with 36 S-35E *Draken*, 1 with 18 SH-37 *Viggen*.

2 tpt sqns with 3 C-130E/H, 3 *Caravelle*, 7 C-47, 6 *Pembroke*.

5 comms sqns with 110 SK-60A/B (Saab 105), 57 SK-61 (*Bulldog*).

Trainers incl 150 SK-60, 78 SK-61, 20 SK-35C *Draken*, 40 SK-50 *Safir*, 17 SK-37 *Viggen*.

5 hel gps (3–4 ac each) with 1 HKP-2 (*Alouette* II), 6 HKP-3 (AB-204B), 10 HKP-4B (Vertol 107).

2 SAM sqns with *Bloodhound* II.

A fully computerized, fully automatic control and air surveillance system, *Stril* 60, co-ordinates all air defence components.

(30 JA-37 interceptors, *Maverick* ASM, *Skyflash* AAM, 100 *Improved HAWK* SAM on order.)

---

* There are some 120,200 more conscripts (105,000 army, 9,400 navy, 5,800 air force) plus 15,000 officer and NCO reservists doing 18–40 days refresher training at some time in the year.

† Further aircraft in storage, including 110 A-32A.

RESERVES: voluntary defence organizations (all services) 500,000.

SWITZERLAND

Population: 6,720,000.
Military service: 17 weeks recruit training followed by reservist refresher training of 3 weeks for 8 out of 12 years for *Auszug* (age 20–32), 2 weeks for 3 years for *Landwehr* (33–42), 1 week for 2 years for *Landsturm* (43–50).
Total armed forces: about 3,500 regular and 15,000 recruits* (total mobilizable strength 625,000 within 48 hours).
Estimated GNP 1976: $58.9 bn.
Defence expenditure 1977: fr 3.25 bn ($1.28 bn).
$1 = 2.53 francs (1977), 2.49 francs (1976).

Army: 580,000 on mobilization.†
War establishment:
3 fd corps, each of 1 mech, 2 inf divs.
1 mountain corps of 3 mountain inf divs.
Some indep inf and fortress bdes.
320 *Centurion*, 150 Pz-61, 170 Pz-68 med, 200 AMX-13 lt tks; 1,250 M-113 APC; 105mm guns; 105mm, 155mm, 150 M-109U 155mm SP how; 120mm mor; 80mm multiple RL; 75mm, 90mm, 105mm ATK guns; 83mm, 106mm RCL; *Bantam* ATGW; 10 patrol boats. (110 Pz-68 med tks on order.)

Air Force:‡ 45,000 on mobilization (maintenance by civilians); 345 combat aircraft.
9 FGA sqns with 140 *Hunter* F58.
9 FGA sqns with 150 *Venom* FB50 (to be replaced by F-5E).
2 interceptor sqns with 39 *Mirage* IIIS.
1 recce sqn with 16 *Mirage* IIIRS.
1 tpt sqn with 3 Ju-52/3m.
7 lt ac sqns with 6 Do-27, 12 *Porter*, 6 *Turbo-Porter*, 3 *Bonanza*.
2 hel sqns with 30 *Alouette* II/III.
Other ac incl 49 Pilatus P-2, 70 P-3, 65 *Vampire* FB6, 35 T55, 2 *Mirage* IIIBS, 23 FFA C-3605; 70 *Alouette* II/III hel.
1 para coy.
3 air-base regts.
1 AD bde with 1 SAM regt of 2 bns, each with 32 *Bloodhound*, and 7 arty regts (22 bns) with 176 20mm, 35mm and 40mm AA guns.
(66 F-5E, 6 F-5F FGA, 45 *Skyguard* AA systems on order.)

RESERVES: Militia 621,500.

---

* There are two recruit intakes per year (Jan/Jun) each of 15,000. In addition, some 300,000 reservists are called up for refresher training at some time during the year.
† Excluding Aviation Brigade (Air Force).
‡ Aviation Brigade, part of the Army.

YUGOSLAVIA

Population: 21,734,000.
Military service: Army and Air Force 15 months; Navy 18 months.
Total armed forces: 260,000 (145,000 conscripts).
Estimated GDP 1975: $30.2 bn.
Defence expenditure 1977: 30 bn dinars ($1.64 bn).
$1 = 18.28 dinars (1977), 17.3 dinars (1975).

Army: 193,000 (130,000 conscripts).
9 inf divs.
7 indep tk bdes.
11 indep inf bdes.
3 mountain bdes.
1 AB bn.
9 arty, 5 ATK regts.
12 AA arty regts.
1,500 T-34, T-54/-55, M-47, about 650 M-4 med, some PT-76 lt tks; M-3, M-8, BTR-40/-50/-60P/-152, M-60, APC; M-980 MICV; 76mm, 105mm, 122mm, 150mm, 152mm, 155mm guns/how; SU-76, SU-100, 105mm SP how; 120mm mor; 130mm multiple RL; *FROG*-7 SSM; 57mm, 75mm, 100mm towed; M-18 76mm, M-36 90mm, ASU-57 SP ATK guns; 57mm, 75mm, 82mm, 105mm RCL; *Snapper, Sagger* ATGW; 20mm, 30mm, 37mm, 40mm, 57mm, 85mm, 88mm towed, ZSU-57-2 SP AA guns.

Navy: 27,000, incl Marines (8,000 conscripts).
5 submarines (2 building).
1 destroyer.
3 corvettes.
10 *Osa*-class FPBG with *Styx* SSM.
14 *Shershen*-class MTB.
20 FPB, 23 large patrol craft.
4 coastal, 10 inshore, 14 river minesweepers.
31 landing craft.
25 coast arty btys.
Mi-8, Ka-25 hel.
1 marine bde.
(10 FPBG on order).

Air Force: 40,000 (7,000 conscripts); 287 combat aircraft.
12 FGA sqns with 9 F-84G, 12 *Kraguj*, 110 *Galeb/Jastreb*.
8 fighter sqns with 110 MiG-21F/PF.
3 recce sqns with 21 RT-33A, 25 *Galeb/Jastreb*.
60 tpts, incl 38 C-47, 2 Il-18, 4 Yak-40, 1 *Caravelle*, 2 An-12, 9 An-26, 4 Li-2, 1 Boeing 727-200.
120 *Galeb/Jastreb*, 3 T-33, 18 MiG-21UTI trainers.
14 Mi-1, 11 Mi-4, 48 Mi-8, 30 *Gazelle*, 20 *Alouette* III, some Ka-25 ASW hel. (102 *Gazelle* on order.)
8 SA-2, 4 SA-3 SAM btys.

Para-Military Forces and Reserves: 500,000 Reservists, 16,000 Frontier Guards, 600,000 Territorial Defence Force, 300,000 Youth units.

The Middle East and the Mediterranean

Bilateral Agreements with External Powers

The Soviet Union has a fifteen-year treaty of friendship and co-operation with Iraq which was signed in April 1972. A similar but more comprehensive treaty with Egypt, signed in May 1971, was abrogated by Egypt in March 1976. Before May 1975 the Soviet Union was a major arms supplier to Egypt but no significant quantities of arms or spare parts have been delivered since then. The Soviet Union continues to deliver arms to Iraq, Syria and Libya, and military assistance has also been provided from time to time to Algeria, Morocco, Sudan and the People's Democratic Republic of Yemen.

The United States has varying types of security assistance agreements and has been providing military aid on either a grant or credit basis to Greece, Turkey, Spain, Morocco, Tunisia, Lebanon, Jordan, Saudi Arabia and Israel. She provides, in addition, a significant amount of military equipment on a cash-sales basis to many countries, notably Greece, Spain, Israel, Iran, Kuwait, Saudi Arabia and Jordan.

There are US military facilities in Greece and Turkey, recently the subject of renegotiation. A treaty with Spain extending the use of military bases in Spain for five years was signed on 24 January 1976 and ratified in June 1976. (There is also an agreement with Portugal for the use of the Azores.) The United States has had limited base rights in Bahrain, terminated on 30 June 1976, and maintains communications facilities in Morocco under informal arrangements.

Britain has an agreement with the Republic of Malta, signed on 26 March 1972, which permits her to base forces on the island for British and for NATO purposes.* Britain concluded treaties of friendship with Bahrain, Qatar and the United Arab Emirates in August 1971 and is also an arms supplier to Iran, Kuwait, Bahrain, Qatar, the United Arab Emirates, Saudi Arabia, Oman, Jordan and Egypt. Some British troops have been aiding government forces in Oman and providing training and technical assistance.

Britain – a signatory, with Greece and Turkey, of the 1959 Treaty of Guarantee which guarantees the independence, territorial integrity and security of the Republic of Cyprus – maintains a garrison in two Sovereign Base Areas in Cyprus. Greece and Turkey are each entitled to maintain a contingent in the island under an associated Treaty of Alliance with the Republic.†

The People's Republic of China has supplied arms to Albania, Sudan and the People's Democratic Republic of Yemen.

France has a military mission in Morocco and supplies arms to a number of countries, including Egypt, Greece, Libya, Morocco, Abu Dhabi, Iraq, Kuwait and Saudi Arabia.

Multilateral Agreements including External Powers

A number of Mediterranean countries are members of the North Atlantic Treaty Organization (see pp. 16–28).

The members of the Central Treaty Organization (CENTO) are Britain, Iran, Pakistan and Turkey, with the United States as an associate. All sit on the Military, Economic and Counter-Subversion Committees and on the Permanent Military Deputies Group. The Treaty provides for mutual co-operation for security and defence but has no central command structure for forces allocated to it. For the local powers, the economic organization of Regional Co-operation for Development (RCD), which has evolved independently out of CENTO, is a basis for more concrete co-operation.

There are United Nations forces stationed in Cyprus (UNFICYP), Syria (UNDOF) and Egypt (UNEF).

Arrangements within the Region

Algeria, Bahrain, Iraq, Jordan, Kuwait, Lebanon, Libya, Morocco, Oman, Qatar, Saudi Arabia, Sudan, Syria, Tunisia, the United Arab Emirates, the Yemen Arab Republic and the People's

---

* This expires on 31 March 1979, and British forces are to leave by then.
† Turkish forces in Cyprus were very substantially increased in July 1974, and the constitutional provisions of the 1959 agreement are now under review.

Democratic Republic of Yemen are members of the League of Arab States. Among its subsidiary bodies are the Arab Defence Council, set up in 1959, and the Unified Arab Command, organized in 1964.

Defence agreements were concluded by Egypt with Syria in November 1966 and Jordan in May 1967, to which Iraq later acceded. These arrangements provided for the establishment of a Defence Council and Joint Command. The loosely associated Eastern Front Command, comprising Iraq, Jordan, the Palestine Liberation Army and Syria, was reorganized in December 1970 into separate Jordanian and Syrian commands. Iraq and Syria concluded defence pacts in May 1968 and July 1969, but friction between the two countries casts some doubt on their application. Jordan and Syria have set up a joint committee to co-ordinate economic and political planning and a Syrian–Jordanian consultative body to co-ordinate military policy. The Federation of Arab Republics, formed by Libya, Syria and Egypt in April 1971, provided for a common defence policy and a Federal Defence Council, and in January 1973 an Egyptian Commander-in-Chief was appointed to command all Federation forces. The present status of this agreement is unclear. Algeria and Libya signed a defence agreement in December 1975, and Egypt signed one with Sudan in January 1977.

Iran has provided military assistance to Oman, and Iranian and Jordanian troops have been assisting government forces there.

ALGERIA

Population: 17,885,000.
Military service: 6 months.
Total armed forces: 75,800.
Estimated GNP 1976: $14.5 bn.
Defence expenditure 1977: 1.6 bn dinars ($387 m).
  $1 = 4.13 dinars (1977), 4.13 dinars (1976).

Army: 67,000.
1 armd bde.
4 mot inf bdes.
3 indep tk bns.
50 indep inf bns.
1 para bn.
12 coys of desert troops.
10 indep arty bns.
5 AA arty bns.
3 engr bns.
100 T-34, 300 T-54/-55 med, 50 AMX-13 lt tks; AML armd cars; 440 BTR-40/-50/-60/-152, *Walid* APC; 600 85mm, 122mm, 152mm guns and how; 5 SU-85, 85 SU-100, ISU-122/-152 SP guns; 240 120mm and 240mm mor; 14 *FROG*-4 SSM; 20 140mm, 40 240mm RL; *Sagger* ATGW; 85mm, 100mm AA guns.

RESERVES: up to 100,000.

Navy: 3,800.
6 ex-Soviet SO-1 submarine chasers.
6 *Komar*, 3 *Osa* I, 2 *Osa* II-class FPBG with *Styx* SSM.
12 ex-Soviet P-6 torpedo boats.
2 fleet minesweepers (ex-Soviet T-43 class).
1 LST (*Polnocny*-class).

Air Force: 5,000; 177 combat aircraft.
2 lt bbr sqns with 24 Il-28.
3 interceptor sqns with 35 MiG-21.
7 FGA sqns: 2 with 20 Su-7BM, 4 with 50 MiG-17, 1 with 20 MiG-15.
2 COIN sqns with 28 *Magister*.
2 tpt sqns with 8 An-12, 7 F-27, 4 Il-18, 12 Il-14.
4 hel sqns with 4 Mi-6, 42 Mi-4, 5 Mi-8, 6 Hughes 269A, 5 *Puma*.
Tpts incl 1 *King Air*, 3 *Super King Air*, 2 CL-215.
Trainers incl MiG-15/-17/-21UTI, Su-7U, Yak-11/ -18.
SA-2 SAM.

Para-Military Forces: 10,000 Gendarmerie.

BAHRAIN

Population: 270,000.
Estimated GNP 1976: $1.6 bn.
Total armed forces: 2,300.

Army: 2,300.
1 inf bn.
1 armd car sqn.
8 *Saladin* armd cars; 8 *Ferret* scout cars; 6 81mm mor; 6 120mm RCL.

Navy (Police):
9 patrol launches.

Air Force (Police):
2 *Scout* hel.

EGYPT

Population: 38,880,000.
Military service: 3 years.
Total armed forces: 345,000.
Estimated GNP 1976: $12.9 bn.
Defence expenditure 1977–78: £E 1.72 bn
 ($4.37 bn).
 $1 = £E 0.394 (1977), £E 0.391 (1976).

Army: 300,000, incl Air Defence Command.
2 armd divs (each with 1 armd, 2 mech bdes).
3 mech inf divs.
5 inf divs (each with 2 inf bdes).
1 Republican Guard Brigade (div).
3 indep armd bdes.
7 indep inf bdes.
2 airmobile bdes.
1 para bde.
6 cdo gps.
6 arty, 2 hy mor bdes.
1 ATGW bde.
2 SSM regts (up to 24 Scud).
1,100 T-54/-55, 750 T-62 med, 80 PT-76 lt tks;
 2,500 OT-62/-64, BTR-40/-50/-60/-152, Walid
 APC; 200 BMP-76PB AFV; 1,300 76mm, 100mm,
 122mm, 130mm, 152mm and 180mm, 40 203mm
 guns and how; about 200 SU-100 and ISU-152
 SP guns; 300 120mm, 160mm, 240mm mor; 300
 140mm, 240mm RL; 30 FROG-3/-7, 24 Scud,
 Samlet SSM; 900 57mm, 85mm and 100mm ATK
 guns; 900 82mm, 107mm RCL; 1,000 Sagger,
 Snapper, Swatter ATGW; 350 ZSU-23-4, ZSU-57-
 2 AA guns; SA-6/-7/-9 SAM; 6 Fournier RF-4 ac.*
 (Beeswing ATGW on order.)

AIR DEFENCE COMMAND (75,000): 108 combat ac.
9 interceptor sqns with 108 MiG-21MF interceptors; 360 SA-2, 200 SA-3, 75 SA-6 SAM; 2,500
 20mm, 23mm, 37mm, 40mm, 57mm, 85mm and
 100mm AA guns; missile radars incl Fan Song,
 Low Blow, Flat Face, Straight Flush and Long
 Track; gun radars Fire Can, Fire Wheel and
 Whiff; EW radars Knife Rest and Spoon Rest.*
 (Crotale SAM on order.)

RESERVES: about 500,000.

Navy: 20,000.
12 submarines (6 W- and 6 R-class, ex-Soviet).
5 destroyers (4 Skory, 1 ex-British Z-class).
3 escorts (ex-British).
12 SO-1 submarine chasers (ex-Soviet).
12 FPBG (6 Osa, 6 Komar) with Styx SSM (6 building).
30 MTB (6 Shershen, 20 P-6, 4 P-4).
3 large patrol craft.
14 ex-Soviet MCM (6 T-43, 4 Yurka, 2 T-301, 2 K8).
16 landing craft (9 Vydra, 4 SMB-1, 3 Polnocny).
3 SRN-6 hovercraft
10 Sea King hel.
(2 submarines, 30 Otomat SSM on order.)

* There is a shortage of spares for Soviet equipment.

RESERVES: about 15,000.

Air Force: 25,000; about 365 combat aircraft.*
25 Tu-16D/G medium bbrs (some with Kelt ASM).
5 Il-28 lt bbrs.
3 FB regts with 80 MiG-21, 90 MiG-17.
4 FGA/strike regts, 3 with 60 Su-7, 1 with 38 Mirage
 IIIE, also some 25 Su-20, 18 MiG-27 Flogger D.
24 MiG-23 Flogger B interceptors.
4 C-130, 2 EC-130H, 30 Il-14, 19 An-12, 1
 Falcon, 1 Boeing 707 tpts.
12 Mi-4, 32 Mi-6, 70 Mi-8, 6 Sea King, 30
 Commando, 42 Gazelle hel.
150 MiG-15/-21/-23, Su-7, L-29 and 40 Gomhouria
 trainers.
(44 Mirage F-1 on order.)

Para-Military Forces: about 50,000; National
 Guard 6,000, Frontier Corps 6,000, Defence and
 Security 30,000, Coast Guard 7,000.

IRAN

Population: 34,756,000.
Military service: 2 years.
Total armed forces: 342,000.
Estimated GDP 1975: $56.8 bn.
Defence expenditure 1977–78: 562.48 bn rials
 ($7.9 bn).
$1 = 71.2 rials (1977), 66.6 rials (1975).

Army: 220,000.
3 armd divs.
4 inf divs.
4 indep bdes (2 inf, 1 AB, 1 special force).
1 SAM bn with HAWK.
Army Aviation Command.
760 Chieftain, 400 M-47/-48, 460 M-60A1 med tks;
 250 Scorpion lt tks; Fox, Ferret scout cars; about
 2,000 M-113, BTR-40/-50/-60/-152 APC; 650
 guns and how, incl 75mm, 330 105mm, 130mm,
 100 155mm, 175mm SP, 203mm towed and SP;
 64 BM-21 RL; 106mm RCL; ENTAC, SS-11, SS-12,
 Dragon, TOW ATGW; 650 23mm, 35mm, 40mm,
 57mm, 85mm towed, ZSU-23-4, ZSU-57-2 SP
 AA guns; HAWK SAM. (1,220 Chieftain med, 110
 Scorpion lt tks, BMP MICV, ASU-85 SP ATK,
 ZSU-23-4 SP AA guns, Rapier, Improved HAWK,
 SA-7/-9 SAM on order.)
Aircraft include 45 Cessna 185, 10 O-2A, 6 Cessna
 310, 3 F-27, 5 Shrike Commander.
120 AH-1J, 100 Bell 214A, 20 Huskie, 52 AB-205A,
 40 CH-47C hel. (193 Bell 214A, 82 AH-1J on
 order.)

DEPLOYMENT: Oman: 1,000: 2 coys, 1 hel sqn.
 Syria (UNDOF): 388.

RESERVES: 300,000.

Navy: 22,000.
3 destroyers (1 with *Seacat*, all with *Standard* SAM).
4 frigates with Mk 2 *Seakiller* SSM and *Seacat* SAM.
4 corvettes (ex-US patrol frigates).
20 patrol boats (9 under 100 tons).
5 minesweepers (3 coastal, 2 inshore).
2 landing ships, 2 landing craft.
2 logistic support ships.
8 SRN-6 and 6 *Wellington* BH-7 hovercraft.
(3 *Tang*-class submarines, 4 *Spruance*-class destroyers, 12 FBPG with *Exocet* SSM, 2 landing craft on order.)

NAVAL AIR:
1 MR sqn with 6 P-3F *Orion*.
1 ASW sqn with 6 S-65A.
1 tpt sqn with 6 *Shrike Commander*, 4 F-27.
Hel incl 5 AB-205A, 14 AB-206A, 6 AB-212, 20 SH-3D, 3 RH-53D.
3 Marine bns.
(3 P-3C MR ac, 3 RH-53D hel on order.)

Air Force: 100,000; 341 combat aircraft.
10 FB sqns with 32 F-4D, 141 F-4E with *Sidewinder* and *Sparrow* AAM, *Maverick* ASM.
10 FGA sqns with 12 F-5A, 100 F-5E.
2 fighter sqns with 40 F-14A *Tomcat*.
1 recce sqn with 16 RF-4E.
1 tanker sqn with 10 Boeing 707-320L.
4 med tpt sqns with 57 C-130E/H, 5 Boeing 747.
4 lt tpt sqns with 23 F-27, 3 *Aero Commander* 690, 4 *Falcon* 20.
10 *Huskie*, 6 AB-205, 4 AB-206A, 5 AB-212, 5 Bell 214C, 2 CH-47C, 16 *Super Frelon* hel.
Trainers include 9 T-33, 18 F-5B/F, 30 *Bonanza* F33A/C.
5 SAM sqns with *Rapier* and 25 *Tigercat*.
(69 F-5E/F, 40 F-14, 160 F-16 fighters; 4 Boeing 747, 2 F-27 tpts; 1 Boeing 707-320C tanker; 19 F-33A/C *Bonanza* trainers; 50 CH-47, 2 AS-61A, 38 Bell 214C hel; *Blindfire* SAM radar; *Phoenix*, *Sparrow*, *Sidewinder* AAM on order.)

Para-Military Forces: 70,000 Gendarmerie with lt ac and hel; 40 patrol boats.

IRAQ

Population: 11,800,000.
Military service: 2 years.
Total armed forces: 188,000.
Estimated GNP 1976: $14.2 bn.
Defence expenditure 1977–78: 491.5 m dinars ($1.66 bn).
$1 = 0.296 dinars (1977), 0.299 dinars (1976).

Army: 160,000.
4 armd divs (each with 2 armd, 1 mech bde).
2 mech divs.

4 inf divs (each with 1 mech, 2 mot bdes).
1 indep armd bde.
1 Republican Guard mech bde.
2 indep inf bdes.
1 special forces bde.
1,350 T-62, T-54/-55, 50 T-34, AMX-30 med, 100 PT-76 lt tks; about 1,800 AFV incl BTR-40/-50/-60/-152, OT-62, 100 BMP; 700 75mm, 85mm, 100mm, 122mm, 130mm, 152mm guns/how; 50 SU-100, 40 ISU-122 SP guns; 120mm, 160mm mor; BM-21 RL; *Sagger*, SS-11 ATGW; 20 FROG-7, *Scud*-B SSM; 800 23mm, 37mm, 57mm, 85mm, 100mm AA guns; ZSU-23-4, ZSU-57-2; SA-7 SAM. (T-62 med tks, *Scud* SSM on order.)

RESERVES: 250,000.

Navy: 3,000.
3 SO-1 submarine chasers.
10 *Osa*-class FPBG with *Styx* SSM.
12 P-6 torpedo boats.
4 patrol boats (under 100 tons).
2 minesweepers.

Air Force: 25,000 (10,000 AD personnel); about 369 combat aircraft.
1 bbr sqn with 4 Tu-16.
1 lt bbr sqn with 10 Il-28.
12 FGA/interceptor sqns: 4 with 90 MiG-23B, 3 with 60 SU-7B, 3 with 30 MiG-17, 2 with 20 *Hunter* FB59/FR10.
5 interceptor sqns with 115 MiG-21, 20 MiG-19.
1 COIN sqn with 20 *Jet Provost* T52.
2 tpt sqns with 12 An-2, 6 An-12, 10-An-24, 2 Tu-124, 13 Il-14, 2 *Heron*, 2 *Islander*.
7 hel sqns with 4 Mi-1, 35 Mi-4, 16 Mi-6, 30 Mi-8, 40 *Alouette* III, 10 *Super Frelon*.
Trainers incl 30 MiG-15/-21/-23UTI, Su-7U, *Hunter* T69, Yak-11, L-29.
SA-2, SA-3 and 25 SA-6 SAM.
(L-39 trainers, 20 *Alouette* III hel on order.)

Para-Military Forces: 4,800 security troops, 50,000 People's Army.

ISRAEL

Population: 3,622,000.
Military service: men 36 months, women 24 months (Jews and Druses only; Muslims and Christians may volunteer). Annual training for reservists thereafter up to age 54 for men, up to 25 for women.
Total armed forces: 164,000 (123,000 conscripts), mobilization to 400,000 in 72 hours.
Estimated GNP 1976: $12.6 bn.
Defence expenditure 1977–78: £I 40.2 bn ($4.27 bn).
$1 = £I 9.42 (1977), £I 7.67 (1976).

Army: 138,000 (120,000 conscripts, male and female), 375,000 on mobilization.
20 armd bdes.*
9 mech bdes.*
9 inf bdes.*
5 para bdes.*
3,000 med tks, incl 1,000 *Centurion*, 650 M-48, 810 M-60, 400 T-54/-55, 150 T-62, *Chariot*; 65 PT-76 lt tks; about 3,600 AFV, incl AML-60, 15 AML-90, RBY *Ramta* armd cars; about 4,000 M-2/-3/-113, BRDM, BTR-40/-50P(OT-62)/-60P/-152 APC; 500 105mm, L-354, M-109 and 155mm, 60 175mm, some 203mm SP how; 450 120mm, 122mm, 130mm and 155mm guns/how; *Lance*, *Ze'ev* (*Wolf*) SSM; 122mm, 135mm, 240mm RL; 900 81mm, 120mm and 160mm mor (some SP); 106mm RCL; *TOW, Cobra, Dragon*, SS-11, *Sagger* ATGW; about 900 *Vulcan/Chaparral* 20mm msl/gun systems and 30mm and 40mm AA guns; *Redeye* SAM.
(125 M-60 med tks; 700 M-113 APC; 94 155mm how; 175mm gun; *TOW; Lance* on order.)

Navy: 5,000 (1,000 conscripts), 6,000 on mobilization.
1 Type 206 submarine (2 building).
6 *Reshef*-class FPBG with *Gabriel* SSM.
12 *Saar*-class FPBG with *Gabriel* SSM.
About 40 small patrol boats (under 100 tons).
12 landing craft (3 under 100 tons).
3 *Westwind* 1124N MR ac.
Naval cdo: 300.
(7 *Reshef*-class FPBG and *Harpoon* SSM on order.)

Air Force: 21,000 (2,000 conscripts, AD only), 25,000 on mobilization; 549 combat aircraft.†
12 FGA/interceptor sqns: 1 with 5 F-15, 6 with 165 F-4E, 3 with 30 *Mirage* IIICJ/BJ, 2 with 100 *Kfir/Kfir* C2.
6 FGA sqns with 235 A-4E/H/M/N *Skyhawk*.
1 recce sqn with 12 RF-4E, 2 EV-1.
Tpts incl 10 Boeing 707, 24 C-130E/H, 12 C-97, 20 *Noratlas*, 10 C-47, 2 KC-130H, 14 *Arava*, 15 Do-28, 10 *Islander*.
10 Do-27, 25 Cessna U206, 2 *Turbo-Porter* lt ac.
Trainers incl 24 TA-4H, 80 *Magister, Mystère* IV, *Super Mystère*, 20 *Queen Air*, 20 *Super Cub*.
Hel incl 12 *Super Frelon*, 28 CH-53G, 6 AH-1G, 40 AB-205A, 25 AB-206, 30 UH-1D, 15 S-65, 30 *Alouette* II/III.
15 SAM btys with 90 *HAWK*.
(20 F/TF-15A interceptors, 35 F-4 FGA, 4 E-2C AEW ac, *Sidewinder* AAM on order).

RESERVES (all services): 460,000.

---

* 11 bdes (5 armd, 4 inf, 2 para) normally kept near full strength; 6 (1 armd, 4 mech, 1 para) between 50 per cent and full strength; the rest at cadre strength.
† In addition there are combat aircraft in reserve, incl 25 *Mystère* IVA.

Para-Military Forces: 4,500 Border Guards and 5,000 *Nahal* Militia.

JORDAN

Population: 2,886,000.
Military service: 24 months.
Total armed forces: 67,810.
Estimated GNP 1976: $1.3 bn.
Defence expenditure 1977: 67 m dinars ($200.6 m).
$1 = 0.334 dinars (1977), 0.330 dinars (1976).

Army: 61,000.
2 armd divs.
2 mech divs.
2 inf divs.
4 special forces bns.
2 AA bdes.
320 M-47/-48/-60, 200 *Centurion* med tks; 140 *Ferret* scout cars; 600 M-113, 120 *Saracen* APC; 110 25-pdr, 90 105mm, 155mm, 203mm how; 35 M-52 105mm, 20 M-44 155mm SP how; 16 155mm guns; 81mm, 107mm, 120mm mor; 106mm and 120mm RCL; *TOW, Dragon* ATGW; 200 M-42 40mm SP AA guns; *Redeye* SAM. (100 *Vulcan* 20mm AA guns, *Improved HAWK* SAM on order.)

DEPLOYMENT: *Oman:* engr det.

Navy: 160.
10 small patrol craft.

Air Force: 6,650; 78 combat aircraft.
3 FGA sqns with 60 F-5A/E.
1 interceptor sqn with 18 F-104A.
4 C-130B, 1 *Falcon* 20, 4 CASA 212A *Aviocar*, 2 *Dove* tpts.
18 *Alouette* III hel.
4 F-5B, 1 *Hunter*, 2 F-104B, 10 T-37 and 12 *Bulldog* trainers.
(4 S-76 hel on order.)

RESERVES: 30,000.

Para-Military Forces: 10,000; 3,000 Mobile Police Force, 7,000 Civil Militia.

KUWAIT

Population: 1,090,000.
Military service: 18 months.
Total armed forces: 10,000.
Estimated GNP 1976: $12.6 bn.
Defence expenditure 1976: 592.2 m dinars ($2.06 bn).
$1 = 0.288 dinars (1976), 0.286 dinars (1975).

Army: 8,500.
1 armd bde.
2 inf bdes.
12 *Chieftain*, 50 Vickers, 50 *Centurion* med tks; 90
   Saladin armd, 20 *Ferret* scout cars; 130 *Saracen*
   APC; 10 25-pdr guns; 20 AMX 155mm how;
   SS-11, *HOT*, *TOW*, *Vigilant* ATGW. (153 *Chieftain*
   med tks; APC; arty; SA-7 SAM on order.)

Navy: 500 (Coastguard).
12 inshore patrol boats.
16 patrol launches.
3 landing craft.

Air Force: 1,000;* 49 combat aircraft.
2 FB sqns (forming) with 4 A-4M.
1 FGA sqn with 4 *Hunter* FGA57, 5 T67.
1 interceptor sqn with 10 *Lightning* F53, 2 T55, 12
   Mirage F-1CK.
1 COIN sqn with 12 BAC-167 *Strikemaster* Mk 83.
2 DC-9, 2 DHC-4, 1 *Argosy*, 2 *Hercules* tpts.
1 hel sqn with 6 AB-204B, 4 AB-205, 2 *Whirlwind*,
   24 *Gazelle*, 12 *Puma*.
6 *Jet Provost* T51 trainers (in store).
50 *Improved HAWK* SAM.
(8 *Mirage* F-1BK/CK interceptors, 26 A-4KU, 6
   TA-4KU FGA on order.)

LEBANON

Population: 2,980,000.
Estimated GNP 1974: $3.7 bn.
Defence expenditure 1977: £L 211.7 m ($69.9 m).
   $1 = £L 3.03 (1977), £2.65 (1976).

Army: The Lebanese army no longer exists as a
   cohesive organization, being split into a number
   of factions. Formerly its strength was some
   17,000, organized into 20 tk, inf and arty bns.
   The eqpt available to it included the following:
   25 AMX-13, 18 M-41 lt tks; 100 Panhard,
   AEC ,*Chaimite* armd cars; 80 M-113, 16 M-59,
   Panhard M-3 APC; 6 75mm guns, 24 122mm,
   20 155mm mor; 25 120mm mor; 106mm RCL;
   60 *Charioteer* 84mm SP ATK guns; *ENTAC*,
   SS-11, 20 *TOW* ATGW; 60 20mm and 30mm,
   15 M-42 40mm SP AA guns.

Navy: 250.
4 large, 2 coastal patrol craft.
1 landing craft.

Air Force: 1,000; 21 combat aircraft.
1 FGA sqn with 10 *Hunter* F70 and 2 T66.
1 interceptor sqn with 9 *Mirage* IIIEL/BL with
   R.530 AAM.
1 hel sqn with 10 *Alouette* II/III, 6 AB-212.

* Excluding expatriate personnel.

6 SA *Bulldog*, 8 *Magister* and 3 *Vampire* trainers.
1 *Dove*, 1 *Turbo-Commander* 690A tpts.
Some French EW/ground-control radars.

Para-Military Forces: formerly 5,000 Gendarmerie
   (now being reformed after having disintegrated).

LIBYA

Population: 2,630,000.
Military service: voluntary.
Total armed forces: 29,200.
Estimated GNP 1975: $12.2 bn.
Defence expenditure 1976: 67.9m Libyan dinars
   ($229 m).
   $1 = 0.296 dinars (1976), 0.296 dinars (1975).

Army: 22,000.
1 armd bde.
2 mech inf bdes.
1 National Guard bde.
1 special forces bde.
3 arty, 2 AA arty bns.
200 T-62, 1,000 T-54/-55 med tks; 100 *Saladin*, 75
   EE-9 *Cascavel* armd cars; 100 *Ferret* scout cars;
   220 BTR-40/-50/-60, 110 OT-62/-64, 60 *Saracen*,
   250 M-113A1, BMP APC; 75 105mm, 70 122mm,
   155mm how; 300 *Vigilant*, *Sagger* ATGW; *Scud*
   SSM; 120 23mm, L40/70, 57mm AA guns; 6 AB-
   47, 5 AB-206, 4 *Alouette* III hel; some Cessna
   O-1 lt ac. (400 *Cascavel/Urutu* AFV on order.)

Navy: 2,700.
1 frigate (with *Seacat* SAM).
2 corvettes (3 more building).
3 FPBG with SS-12M SSM.
11 patrol craft (10 large, 1 coastal).
1 log support ship.
(10 FPBG, 80 *Otomat* SSM, 1 LST on order.)

Air Force: 4,500;† 162 combat aircraft.‡
1 bbr sqn with 12 Tu-22.
4 interceptor sqns: 2 with 30 *Mirage* IIIE, 2 with
   30 MiG-23 *Flogger* E.
4 FGA sqns with 50 *Mirage* V.
2 COIN sqns with 30 *Galeb*.
1 recce sqn with 10 *Mirage* IIIER.
2 tpt sqns with 8 C-130E, 9 C-47, 2 *Falcon*, 1
   Jetstar.
10 *Mirage* IIIB, 2 *Mystère* 20, 5 MiG-23U, 12
   Magister, 3 T-33 trainers.
4 hel sqns with 13 *Alouette* II/III, 3 AB-47, 9 *Super
   Frelon*, 8 CH-47C, 12 Mi-8.
3 SAM regts with 60 *Crotale* and 8 btys with 60 SA-2,
   SA-3 and SA-6 SAM.
(38 *Mirage* F-1, 16 CH-47C hel on order.)

† Including expatriate personnel.
‡ Some may be in storage.

MOROCCO

Population: 18,200,000.
Military service: 18 months.
Total armed forces: 84,650.
Estimated GNP 1976: $7.85 bn.
Defence expenditure 1977: 1.56 bn dirham
($345.9 m).
$1 = 4.51 dirham (1977), 4.37 dirham (1976).

Army: 75,000.
1 lt security bde.
1 para bde.
5 armd bns.
2 mot inf bns.
18 inf bns.
9 Royal Guard bns.
7 camel corps bns.
2 desert cav bns.
7 arty gps.
2 engr bns.
50 M-48, 50 T-54 med, 120 AMX-13 lt tks; 36 EBR,
50 AML and M-8 armd cars; 40 M-3 half-track,
95 OT-62/-64, 30 UR-416 APC; 30 AMX-105,
150 76mm, 85mm and 105mm guns; 18 M-114
155mm how; 82mm, 120mm mor; 105mm RCL;
ENTAC, TOW ATGW; 50 37mm, 57mm, 100mm
AA guns, Chaparral SAM. (100 M-48 med tks;
334 M-113 APC on order.)

Navy: 4,000 (600 Marines).
3 corvettes.
1 coastal minesweeper.
3 large, 6 coastal patrol craft (14 building).
1 landing ship log (2 building).
1 landing craft.
1 naval inf bn.
(5 frigates, 1 corvette on order.)

Air Force: 5,650; 45 combat aircraft.*
2 FGA sqns with 24 Magister.
2 interceptor sqns with 17 F-5A and 4 F-5B.
2 tpt sqns with 8 C-47, 8 C-119G, 8 C-130H, 6
King Air, 12 Broussard, 1 Do-28D.
40 AB-205A, 8 AB-206, 5 AB-212, 4 Alouette II,
6 Gazelle and 20 Puma hel.
25 T-6, 18 T-28, 2 SF-260M trainers.
(50 Mirage F-1 fighters, 12 T-34C, 20 T-2E, 28
SF-260M trainers, 20 Puma hel on order.)

Para-Military Forces: 30,000, incl 11,000 Sureté
Nationale.

OMAN

Population: 806,000.
Military service: voluntary.

---

* Some ac, incl 2 MiG-15, 12 MiG-17 FGA in storage.

Total armed forces: 13,000.†
Defence expenditure 1977: 158 m rial omani
($457 m).
$1 = 0.345 rial omani (1976), 0.346 rial omani
(1977).

Army: 11,800.
2 bde HQ.
8 inf bns.
1 Royal Guard regt.
1 arty regt.
1 sigs regt.
1 armd car sqn.
1 para sqn.
1 engr sqn.
36 Saladin armd cars; 24 75mm pack how; 25-pdr,
36 105mm, 3 5.5-in guns; 120mm mor; 10 TOW
ATGW.

Navy: 450.
3 patrol vessels (1 Royal Yacht, 2 ex-Dutch MCM).
1 trg ship (ex-1,500-ton log ship).
4 FPB.
4 small landing craft.
(2 minesweepers, 3 FPB, 1 log support ship on order.)

Air Force: 750;* 36 combat aircraft.
1 FGA/recce sqn with 16 Hunter.
1 FGA sqn with 12 Jaguar.
1 COIN/trg sqn with 8 BAC-167.
1 tac tpt sqn with 15 Skyvan.
2 tpt sqns: 1 with 3 BAC-111 and 2 Viscount, 1 with
7 BN Defender, 1 Falcon.
1 hel sqn with 20 AB-205, 3 AB-206, 1 AB-212,
5 AB-214 hel.
1 SAM sqn with 28 Rapier SAM.

Para-Military Forces: 3,000 tribal Home Guard
(Firqats).

QATAR

Population: 200,000.
Total armed forces: 4,200.‡
Estimated GNP 1975: $425 m.

Army: 3,500.
2 armd car regts.
1 Guards inf bn.
1 mobile regt.
30 Saladin armed cars; 10 Ferret scout cars;
8 Saracen APC; 4 25-pdr guns; 81mm mor.

Navy: 400.
6 patrol craft.
5 coastal patrol craft.

---

† Excluding expatriate personnel.
‡ All services form part of the Army.

Air Force: 300.
4 *Hunter* FGA.
1 *Islander* tpt.
2 *Whirlwind*, 4 *Commando*, 2 *Gazelle* hel.
Tigercat SAM.
(3 *Lynx* hel on order.)

SAUDI ARABIA

Population: 7,500,000.
Military service: voluntary.
Total armed forces: 61,500.
Estimated GNP 1975: $37.2 bn.
Defence expenditure 1977–78: 26.69 bn Saudi riyals
   ($7.53 bn).
   $1 = 3.54 riyals (1977), 3.53 riyals (1975).

Army: 45,000.
1 mech div.
1 armd bde.
2 inf bns.
1 para bn.
1 Royal Guard bn.
3 arty bns.
6 AA arty bns.
10 SAM btys with *HAWK*.
400 AMX-30, 75 M-47/-60 med, 60 M-41, 150
   Scorpion, AMX-13 lt tks; 200 AML-60/-90, some
   Staghound and *Greyhound* armd cars; *Ferret*
   scout cars; M-113, Panhard M-3, *Commando*
   APC; 105mm guns; 75mm RCL; SS-11, *Dragon*,
   Vigilant, *Harpon* ATGW; AA guns; *Rapier*, *HAWK*
   SAM. (200 M-60 med, 100 *Scorpion* lt tks; 250
   AMX-10P AFV; 250 APC; guns/how; AMX-
   30SA SP AA guns; *Shahine* (*Crotale*) and 6 btys
   Improved HAWK SAM on order.)

DEPLOYMENT:
Lebanon (Arab Peace-keeping Force): 700.

Navy: 1,500.
1 FPBG.
3 FPB (*Jaguar*-class).
1 large patrol craft (ex-US coastguard cutter).
(6 FPBG, 4 MCM, 4 landing craft, *Harpoon* SSM on
   order.)

Air Force: 15,000; 137 combat aircraft.
2 FB sqns with 70 F-5E.
2 COIN/trg sqns with 30 BAC-167.
2 interceptor sqns with 37 *Lightning* F52/F53.
2 tpt sqns with 39 C-130E/H.
2 hel sqns with 16 AB-206 and 24 AB-205.
Other ac incl 4 KC-130 tankers, 1 Boeing 707, 2
   Falcon 20, 2 *Jetstar* tpts; 12 *Alouette* III, 1 AB-
   204 hel.
Trainers incl 20 F-5B, 7 *Lightning* T54/55, 6 *Cessna*
   T-41A.
(20 F-5F FB, 11 BAC-167 COIN ac, *Maverick* ASM,
   Sidewinder AAM on order.)

Para-Military Forces: 35,000 National Guard in
   regular and semi-regular bns; 6,500 Frontier
   Force and Coastguard with 50 small patrol boats
   and 8 SRN-6 hovercraft.

SUDAN

Population: 18,650,000.
Military service: voluntary.
Total armed forces: 52,100.
Estimated GNP 1974: $2.8 bn.
Defence expenditure 1975–76: £S 46 m ($131.4 m).
   $1 = £S 0.35 (1975), £S 0.35 (1974).

Army: 50,000.
2 armd bdes.
7 inf bdes.
1 para bde.
3 arty regts.
3 AD arty regts.
1 engr regt.
70 T-54, 60 T-55 med tks; 30 T-62 lt tks (Chinese);
   50 *Saladin*, 45 *Commando* armd cars; 60 *Ferret*
   scout cars; 100 BTR-40/-50/-152, 60 OT-64, 49
   Saracen APC; 55 25-pdr, 40 100mm, 20 105mm,
   18 122mm guns and how; 30 120mm mor; 30
   85mm ATK guns; 80 Bofors 40mm, 80 Soviet
   37mm, 85mm AA guns. (AMX-10 APC on order.)

DEPLOYMENT:
Lebanon (Arab Peace-keeping Force): 1,000.

Navy: 600.
3 patrol boats (ex-Iranian).
6 large patrol boats.
6 small patrol craft (ex-Yugoslav).
2 landing craft.

Air Force: 1,500; 27 combat aircraft.
1 interceptor sqn with 10 MiG-21MF.
1 FGA sqn with 17 MiG-17 (ex-Chinese).
5 BAC-145 and 6 *Jet Provost* Mk 55, 3 *Pembroke*
   (in storage).
1 tpt sqn with 5 An-24, 4 F-27, 1 DHC-6.
1 hel sqn with 10 Mi-8.
(15 *Mirage* fighters, 6 C-130H, 4 DHC-5D tpts, 10
   Puma hel on order.)

Para-Military Forces: 3,500: 500 National Guard,
   500 Republican Guard, 2,500 Border Guard.

SYRIA

Population: 7,750,000.
Military service: 30 months.
Total armed forces: 227,500.
Estimated GDP 1975: $4.7 bn.
Defence expenditure 1977: £Syr 3.93 bn ($1.07 bn).
   $1 = £Syr 3.68 (1977), £Syr 3.68 (1976).

Army: 200,000, incl AD Comd.
2 armd divs (each 2 armd, 1 mech bde).
3 mech divs (each 1 armd, 2 mech bdes).
3 armd bdes.
1 mech bde.
3 inf bdes.
2 arty bdes.
6 cdo, 4 para bns.
1 SSM bn with *Scud*, 2 btys with *FROG*.
48 SAM btys with SA-2/-3/-6.
200 T-34, 1,500 T-54/-55, 800 T-62 med, 100 PT-76 lt tks; 1,600 BTR-40/-50/-60/-152, BMP, OT-64 APC; 800 122mm, 130mm, 152mm and 180mm guns/how; ISU-122/-152, 75 SU-100 SP guns, 140mm and 240mm RL; 30 *FROG*-7, 36 *Scud* SSM; 120mm, 160mm mor; 85mm, 100mm ATK guns; *Snapper*, *Sagger*, *Swatter* ATGW; 23mm, 37mm, 57mm, 85mm, 100mm towed, ZSU-23-4, ZSU-57-2 SP AA guns; SA-2/-3/-6/-7/-9 SAM. (*Milan* ATGW, *Gazelle* hel on order.)

DEPLOYMENT:
Lebanon: (Arab Peace-keeping Force): 30,000.

RESERVES: 100,000.

AIR DEFENCE COMMAND.*
24 SAM btys with SA-2/-3, 14 with SA-6, AA arty, interceptor ac and radar.

Navy: 2,500.
2 *Petya*-class frigates.
6 *Komar*- and 6 *Osa*-class FPBG with *Styx* SSM.
1 T-43-class, 2 coastal minesweepers.
8 MTB (ex-Soviet P-4).

RESERVES: 2,500.

Air Force: 25,000; about 395 combat ac.†
4 FGA sqns with 80 MiG-17.
3 FGA sqns with 50 Su-7.
2 FGA sqns with 45 MiG-23.
About 220 MiG-21 interceptors.
Tpts incl 8 Il-14, 2 An-24, 4 An-26.
Trainers incl Yak-11/-18, L-29, MiG-15UTI and 32 MBB 223 *Flamingo*.
Hel incl 4 Mi-2, 8 Mi-4, 50 Mi-8 and 9 Ka-25.
(15 *Super Frelon*, 6 CH-47C hel on order.)

Para-Military Forces: 9,500. 8,000 Gendarmerie; 1,500 Desert Guard (Frontier Force).

TUNISIA

Population: 6,062,000.
Military service: 12 months selective.
Total armed forces: 22,200 (13,000 conscripts).
Estimated GNP 1975: $4.8 bn.

---

* Under Army Command, with Army and Air Force manpower.
† Some aircraft believed to be in storage.

Defence expenditure 1977–78: 68.65 m dinars ($156 m).
$1 = 0.44 dinars (1977), 0.43 dinars (1976).

Army: 18,000, (12,000 conscripts).
2 combined arms regts.
1 Sahara regt.
1 para-cdo bn.
1 arty bn.
1 engr bn.
30 AMX-13, 20 M-41 lt tks; 20 *Saladin*, 15 EBR armd cars; 10 155mm, 10 105mm SP guns; 40mm AA guns. (*Chaparral* SAM, 40 *Kuerassier* SP ATK guns on order.)

Navy: 2,500 (500 conscripts).
1 destroyer escort (ex-US radar picket).
1 corvette (ex-French *Fougeux*-type, 1 building).
1 coastal minesweeper.
3 patrol boats with SS-12M SSM (1 on order).
10 coastal patrol boats (less than 100 tons).

Air Force: 1,700 (500 conscripts); 18 combat aircraft.
1 fighter sqn with 10 F-86F.
1 COIN sqn with 8 MB-326B.
3 G-222 tpts.
12 SF-260W, 12 T-6 trainers.
6 *Alouette* II, 6 *Alouette* III, 1 *Puma* hel.
(12 MB-326G/K COIN ac on order.)

Para-Military Forces: 9,000; 5,000 Gendarmerie (6 bns), 4,000 National Guard.

UNITED ARAB EMIRATES (UAE)

Population: 690,000.
Military service: voluntary.
Total armed forces: 26,100.‡
Estimated GNP 1976: $8.5 bn.
Defence expenditure 1977–78: 392.3 m dirhams ($100.6 m).
$1 = 3.90 dirhams (1977), 3.94 dirhams (1976).

Army: 23,500.
1 Royal Guard bde.
3 armd/armd car bns.
7 inf bns.
3 arty bns.
3 AD bns.
80 *Scorpion* lt tks; 125 *Saladin*, 6 *Shorland*, Panhard armd cars; 60 *Ferret* scout cars; Panhard M-3, 30 *Saracen* APC; 22 25-pdr, 105mm guns; 16 AMX 155mm SP how; 81mm mor; 120mm RCL; *Vigilant* ATGW; *Rapier* SAM.

---

‡ The Union Defence Force and the armed forces of the United Arab Emirates (Abu Dhabi, Dubai, Ras Al Khaimah and Sharjah) were formally merged in May 1976.

DEPLOYMENT:
Lebanon (Arab Peace-keeping Force): 700.

Navy: 800.
6 large, 9 small patrol craft.
14 coastal patrol craft (police).

Air Force: 1,800; 38 combat aircraft.
2 sqns with 24 Mirage V, 8 Hunter FGA.
1 sqn with 6 MB-326 COIN.
Tpts incl 2 C-130H, 1 G-222, 4 Islander, 3 DHC-4,
   1 Cessna 182.
Hel incl 8 AB-205, 6 AB-206, 3 AB-212, 10
   Alouette III, 5 Puma.
2G-222, 4 DHC-5D tpts on order.)

YEMEN ARAB REPUBLIC (NORTH)

Population: 6,995,000.
Military service: 3 years.
Total armed forces: 39,850.
Estimated GNP 1973: $830 m.
Defence expenditure 1975–76: 261.7 m riyals
   ($60 m).
   $1 = 4.33 riyals (1975), 4.62 riyals (1973).

Army: 37,600.
3 inf divs (10 inf bdes, incl 3 reserve).
1 para bde.
3 cdo bdes.
2 armd bns.
2 arty bns.
1 AA arty bn.
30 T-34, T-54 med tks; 30 Saladin armd, Ferret
   scout cars; 120 BTR-40/-152, Walid APC;
   50 76mm, some 122mm guns; 50 SU-100 SP
   guns; 82mm, 120mm mor; 75mm RCL; Vigilant
   ATGW; 37mm guns. (How, AA guns on order.)

DEPLOYMENT:
Lebanon (Arab Peace-keeping Force): 500.

Navy: 750.
5 large patrol craft (ex-Soviet Poluchat-class).
3 MTB (ex-Soviet P-4 class).

Air Force: 1,500; some 22 combat aircraft.*
1 lt bbr sqn with 14 Il-28.
1 fighter sqn with 8 MiG-17, some MiG-21.

C-47, 2 Skyvan, some Il-14 tpts.
4 MiG-15UTI, 18 Yak-11 trainers.
Mi-4, AB-205 hel.

Para-Military Forces: 20,000 tribal levies.

YEMEN: PEOPLE'S DEMOCRATIC REPUBLIC (SOUTH)

Population: 1,790,000.
Military service: conscription, term unknown.
Total armed forces: 21,300.
Estimated GNP 1972: $500 m.
Defence expenditure 1977: 15.3 m South Yemeni
   dinars ($43.7 m).
   $1 = 0.35 dinars (1977), 0.383 dinars (1972).

Army: 19,000.
10 inf bdes, each of 3 bns.
2 armd bns.
1 arty bde.
1 sigs unit.
1 trg bn.
200 T-34, T-54 med tks; 10 Saladin armd cars; 10
   Ferret scout cars; 25-pdr, 105mm pack, 122mm,
   130mm how; mor; 122mm RCL; 23mm SP, 37mm,
   57mm, 85mm AA guns; SA-7 SAM.

DEPLOYMENT:
Lebanon (Arab Peace-keeping Force): 500.

Navy: 300 (subordinate to Army).
2 submarine chasers (ex-Soviet SO-1 class).
2 MTB (ex-Soviet P-6 class).
3 minesweepers (ex-British Ham-class).
6 small patrol craft.
2 landing craft (ex-Soviet Polnocny-class).

Air Force: 2,000; 33 combat aircraft.*
1 bbr sqn with 6 Il-28.
1 fighter sqn with 12 MiG-21.
1 FB sqn with 15 MiG-17.
1 tpt sqn with 4 Il-14, 3 An-24, some C-47.
1 hel sqn with 8 Mi-8, Mi-4.
3 MiG-15UTI trainers.

Para-Military Forces: Popular Militia; 1,500 Public
   Security Force.

---

* Some aircraft are believed to be in storage.

Sub-Saharan Africa

Multilateral Agreements

The Organization of African Unity (OAU), constituted in May 1963, includes all internationally recognized independent African states except South Africa. It has a Defence Commission which is responsible for defence and security co-operation and the defence of the sovereignty, territorial integrity and independence of its members; however, this has rarely met.

Bilateral Agreements

The US has security assistance agreements with Ghana, Kenya, Liberia, Senegal and Zaire.

The Soviet Union signed Treaties of Friendship with Somalia in July 1974, with Angola in October 1976 and with Mozambique in March 1977. Military aid has been given to Angola, Ethiopia, Guinea, Guinea-Bissau, Mali, Mozambique, Nigeria, Somalia and Uganda. Soviet naval facilities have been constructed in Somalia.

China has military assistance agreements with Cameroon, Equatorial Guinea, Guinea, Mali and Tanzania and has given aid to Mozambique.

Britain maintains overflying, training and defence arrangements with Kenya.

France has agreements on defence and military co-operation with the Central African Empire, Gabon, Ivory Coast, Niger and Upper Volta. The military agreement with the Malagasy Republic has been terminated but military co-operation between the two countries maintained. Since March 1974 France has had a co-operation agreement for defence with Senegal, and since February 1974 a co-operation agreement including military clauses with Cameroon. The defence agreements between France and Benin, Chad and Togo have been terminated but replaced by agreements on technical military co-operation. Similarly, a defence agreement with the People's Republic of Congo has been terminated and replaced by an agreement on training and equipment for the Congolese armed forces. An agreement has been concluded with Djibouti for the continued stationing of French forces there. Military assistance has been given to Zaire.

Cuba has given military aid to the People's Republic of Congo, Guinea and Somalia, and has some 15,000 men in Angola, now engaged in training Angola's armed forces and assisting with internal security. Cuban advisers are present in a number of other African countries.

Egypt, Morocco and South Africa have given military assistance to Zaire.

Arrangements within the Region

Kenya and Ethiopia signed a defence agreement in 1963.

Military links have existed in practice between South Africa and Rhodesia, with South Africa giving certain defence assistance. There is, however, no known formal agreement.

ANGOLA: PEOPLE'S REPUBLIC OF

Population: 6,100,000.
Military service: conscription, term unknown.
Total armed forces: 31,500.
Defence expenditure 1975: 2.5 bn escudos ($98.0 m).
$1 = 25.5 escudos (1975).

Army: 30,000.
1 armd regt.
9 inf regts.
1 cdo regt.
1 AD regt.
85 T-34, 50 T-54 med, some 70 PT-76 lt tks; 100 BRDM-2 armd cars; 165 BTR-40/-152, OT-62 APC; 120 guns, incl 105mm, 122mm; 110 BM-21 122mm multiple RL; 1,000 82mm, 120mm mor; 2,000 75mm, 82mm, 107mm RCL; ZIS-3 76mm ATK guns; *Sagger* ATGW; 23mm, 37mm AA guns; SA-7 SAM.*

Navy: 700.
5 *Argos*-class patrol boats.
1 *Zhuk*-class patrol boat (under 100 tons).
7 small coastal patrol boats.
5 landing craft.

* Eqpt totals uncertain. Some 15,000 Cubans serve with the Angolan forces and operate ac and hy eqpt. Some Portuguese also serve; several hundred Soviet advisers and technicians are reported in Angola.

Air Force: 800; 33 combat aircraft.
12 MiG-17, 17 MiG-21, 4 G-91 fighters.
Tpts incl 6 *Noratlas*, 2 C-45, 1 C-47, 10 Do-27,
　5 An-26, 2 *Turbo-Porter*, 27 *Auster*.
Some 4 Mi-8, 11 *Alouette*, 2 Bell 47 hel.

PEOPLE'S REPUBLIC OF CONGO

Population: 1,440,000.
Military service: voluntary.
Total armed forces: 7,000.
Estimated GNP 1976: $600 m.
Defence expenditure 1976: 8.89 bn CFA francs
　($37.2 m).
　$1 = 239 CFA francs (1976).

Army: 6,500.
1 armd bn (5 sqns).
1 inf bn.
1 para-cdo bn.
1 arty gp.
1 engr bn.
14 Chinese T-62, 3 PT-76 lt tks; 10 BRDM scout
　cars; 44 BTR-152 APC; 6 75mm, 10 100mm guns;
　8 122mm how; 82mm, 10 120mm mor; 57mm,
　76mm, 100mm ATK guns; 10 14.5mm, 37mm,
　57mm AA guns.

Navy: 200.
7 coastal patrol craft (3 *Shanghai*-class).
9 river patrol boats.

Air Force: 300; 8 combat aircraft.
8 MiG-15/-17 fighters.
3 C-47, 4 An-24, 1 F-28, 1 *Frégate*, 5 Il-14, 3
　Broussard tpts.
4 *Alouette* II/III hel.

Para-Military Forces: 1,400 Gendarmerie; 2,500
　militia.

ETHIOPIA

Population: 29,330,000.
Military service: voluntary.
Total armed forces: 53,500.
Estimated GNP 1975: $2.9 bn.
Defence expenditure 1976: 215 m birr ($103.4 m).
　$US 1 = 2.08 birr (1976), 2.07 birr (1975).

Army: 50,000.*
4 inf divs: 3 with 3 inf bdes; 1 with 1 mech, 1 mot,
　1 inf bde.
1 COIN div.
1 lt inf bn (bde).
1 AB inf bn.

---

* Augmented by 75,000 People's Militia. The Territorial
Army has now been incorporated in the army and reservists called up, largely for guard duties.

5 arty bns.
2 engr bns.
35 M-60, 35 T-34/-54 med, 70 M-41 lt tks; 56 AML-
　60 armd cars; about 90 M-113, *Commando*,
　M-59, 40 BTR-152 APC; 36 75mm pack, 52
　105mm, 12 155mm towed, 12 M-109 155mm SP
　how; 146 M-2 107mm, 140 M-30 4.2-in mor.

Navy: 1,500.
1 coastal minesweeper (ex-Netherlands).
1 training ship (ex-US seaplane tender).
3 large patrol craft (ex-US).
1 *Kraljevica*-class patrol boat.
4 FPB (ex-US *Swift* class).
4 coastal patrol craft (under 50 tons).
4 landing craft (ex-US, under 100 tons).

Air Force: 2,000; 35 combat aircraft.
1 lt bbr sqn with 2 *Canberra* B2.
3 FGA sqns: 2 with 20 F-5, 1 with 7 F-86F.
1 recce sqn with 6 T-28A.
1 tpt sqn with 6 C-47, 2 C-54, 7 C-119G, 3 *Dove*,
　1 Il-14, 1 *Otter*.
3 trg sqns with 20 *Safir*, 13 T-28A/D, 20 T-33A.
1 hel sqn with 10 AB-204, 5 *Alouette* III, 2 Mi-8,
　10 UH-1H.

RESERVES (all services): 20,000.

Para-Military Forces: 84,000: 9,000 mobile emer-
　gency police force; 75,000 People's Militia.

GHANA

Population: 10,400,000.
Military service: voluntary.
Total armed forces: 17,700.
Estimated GNP 1974: $3.6 bn.
Defence expenditure 1976–77: 113.5 m cedi
　($130.5 m).
　$1 = 0.87 cedi (1976), 1.15 cedi (1974).

Army: 15,000.
2 bdes (6 inf bns and support units).
1 recce bn.
1 mor bn.
1 fd engr bn.
1 sigs bn.
1 AB coy.
9 *Saladin* armd cars; 26 *Ferret* scout cars; 82mm,
　10 120mm mor.

DEPLOYMENT: *Egypt* (UNEF): 1 bn, 597 men.

Navy: 1,300.
2 ASW corvettes.
3 minesweeper (ex-British, 1 *Ton*-, 2 *Ham*-class).
4 patrol craft (2 ex-British *Ford*-class).
2 FPB (4 on order).
1 training vessel.

Air Force: 1,400; 6 combat aircraft.
1 COIN sqn with 6 MB-326F.
2 tpt sqns with 8 *Islander*, 6 *Skyvan* 3M.
1 comms and liaison sqn with 6 F-27, 1 F-28, 1 HS-125.
1 hel sqn with 2 Bell 212, 4 *Alouette* III, 3 Hughes 269, *Wessex* 53.
13 *Bulldog* trainers.
(6 MB-326K COIN ac on order.)

Para-Military Forces: 3,000, 3 Border Guard bns.

KENYA

Population: 14,360,000.
Military service: voluntary.
Total armed forces: 7,700.
Estimated GNP 1975: $2.8 bn.
Defence expenditure 1976: 294 m shillings ($35 m).
  $1 = 8.40 shillings (1976), 7.13 shillings (1975).

Army: 6,500.
4 inf bns.
1 spt gp.
1 engr bn.
3 *Saladin*, 14 *Ferret* armd cars; 15 UR-416, 10 Panhard M3 APC; 8 105mm lt guns; 20 81mm, 8 120mm mor; 56 84mm *Carl Gustav* and 120mm RCL. (40 Vickers Mk 3 med tks on order.)

Navy: 400.
7 large patrol craft (with 2 40mm Bofors guns).

Air Force: 800; 21 combat aircraft.
1 FGA sqn with 4 Hunter FGA9, 12 F-5E/F.
1 COIN sqn with 5 BAC-167 *Strikemaster*.
1 trg sqn with 14 *Bulldog*.
2 lt tpt sqns: 1 with 6 DHC-4, 1 with 15 *Beaver*.
Other ac incl 1 *Turbo Commander*, 2 *Navajo*.
3 *Alouette* II, 2 Bell 47G hel.

Para-Military Forces: 1,800 police.

MOZAMBIQUE

Population: 9,650,000.
Military service: voluntary.
Total armed forces: 19,000.*
Defence expenditure 1975: 600 m escudos ($18 m).
  $1 = 33.3 escudos (1975).

Army: 19,000 (incl Air Force manpower).
1 tk bn.
9 inf bns.

---

* The aim is to have 20,000 trained troops by end-1977. There are 2 Tanzanian bns in Mozambique. Chinese, Cuban, East German and Soviet advisers are reported with Mozambique forces.

2–3 arty bns.
35 T-34/-54/-55 med, some PT-76 lt tks; BTR-40, BRDM armd cars; BTR-60/-152 APC; 76mm 85mm, 100mm, 122mm guns/how; BM-21 multiple RL; 60mm, 82mm, 120mm mor; 82mm, 107mm ATK guns; *Sagger* ATGW; 23mm, 37mm, 57mm AA guns; 24 SA-6, SA-7 SAM.

Air Force: 8 combat aircraft.†
8 MiG-21 fighters.
Tpts incl 8 *Noratlas*, 5 C-47, An-24.
Lt ac incl 7 Zlin.
15 *Harvard* trainers.
2 *Alouette* II/III, some Mi-8 hel.

NIGERIA

Population: 66,350,000.
Military service: voluntary.
Total armed forces: 230,500.‡
Estimated GNP 1975: $24.3 bn.
Defence expenditure 1976–77: 1.5 bn naira ($2.4 bn).
  $1 = 0.625 naira (1976), 0.615 naira (1975).

Army: 221,000.
4 inf divs.
4 engr bdes.
4 recce regts.
4 arty regts.
Scorpion lt tks; 45 *Saladin*, 15 AML-60/-90 armd cars; 25 *Ferret*, some *Fox* scout cars; 12 *Saracen* APC; 76mm, 25-pdr, 105mm, 122mm, 130mm guns/how; 20mm, 40mm AA guns. (*Scorpion* lt tks, *Fox* scout cars on order.)

Navy: 3,500.
1 ASW/AA frigate.
2 corvettes (2 building).
6 patrol craft (4 large, 2 ex-British *Ford*-class).
1 landing craft.
(2 large patrol craft, *Seacat* SAM on order.)

RESERVES: 2,000.

Air Force: 6,000; 36 combat aircraft.§
1 lt bbr sqn with 4 Il-28.
2 FGA/AD sqns: 1 with 12 MiG-17, 1 with 20 MiG-21J.
2 tpt sqns with 12 F-27, 1 F-28, 6 C-130H, 7 C-47, 1 DC-6, 6 *Noratlas*.
1 SAR hel sqn with 3 *Whirlwind*, 4 BO-105, 2 *Puma*.
3 trg/service sqns with 4 MiG-15, 20 *Bulldog*, 10 P-149D, 23 Do-27/-28, 3 *Navajo*, 8 L-29.
6 *Alouette* III hel.

---

† Not all the aircraft shown are necessarily airworthy.
‡ Large-scale demobilization has been planned.
§ There are additional unserviceable aircraft.

RHODESIA

Population: 6,750,000 (270,000 White).
Military service: 18 months (White, Asian and Coloured population; Blacks may volunteer).*
Total armed forces: 9,550.†
Estimated GNP 1976: $US 3.4 bn.
Defence expenditure 1977–78: $R 98.4 m‡ ($US 159 m).
  $US 1 = $R 0.617 (1977), $R 0.617 (1976).

Army: 8,250 (3,250 conscripts).†
3 inf bns.§
3 Special Air Service sqns.
Selous Scouts (Special Air Service-type unit).
Grey's Scouts, mounted inf (250).
1 arty bty.
1 engr sqn.
60 AML-90 *Eland* armd cars; *Ferret* scout cars; UR-416 lt armd APC, lt APC; 25-pdr, 105mm pack how, 5.5-in/how; 105mm RCL.

Air Force: 1,300; 48 combat aircraft.
1 lt bbr sqn with 5 *Canberra* B2 and 2 T4.
2 FGA sqns: 1 with 10 *Hunter* FGA9, 1 with 12 *Vampire* FB9.
1 trg/recce sqn with 8 *Provost* T-52, 11 *Vampire* T55.
1 tpt sqn with 9 C-47, 1 *Baron* 55, 6 *Islander*.
1 lt tpt sqn with 12 Al-60C4, 18 Cessna 337.
2 hel sqns with 55 *Alouette* II/III.

RESERVES:
All White, Asian and Coloured citizens completing conscript service are liable to full-time National Service between ages 17–25 inclusive. Men of 26–34 do 84 days' continuous training, then 5-week periods of active service in Territorial Force. Men of 35–50 do 5-week periods of active service with Police Reserve or Ministry of Internal Affairs. Ground personnel servicing Air Force units are reservists or civilians. The Territorial Force has been expanded to 55,000; it contains 8 bns, each with an establishment of 1,000 men, and support units. There is also a Reserve Holding Unit of 3,000 for men over 38.

Para-Military Forces: British South African Police (BSAP): 8,000 active, 35,000 reservists (the White population provides about a third of the active strength but nearly three-quarters of the reservist strength). Guard Force: establishment 1,000.

* Partial mobilization is in effect. All men of 17–25 who have completed conscript service are liable to indefinite retention in the forces.
† Plus about 15,000 Territorial Force called up for service at any one time.
‡ A further $R 47.5 m is in the Police vote.
§ 1 White bn (1,000), 2 Black bns (2,400); a third Black forming. There is an establishment for 3 bdes, to be brought up to strength by mobilizing Territorials.

SENEGAL

Population: 4,630,000.
Military service: 2 years selective.
Total armed forces: 5,950.
Estimated GNP 1974: $1.2 bn.
Defence expenditure 1976: 11.0 bn CFA francs ($47 m).
  $1 = 234 CFA francs (1976), 241 CFA francs (1974).

Army: 5,500.
4 inf bns.
1 engr bn.
1 recce sqn.
2 para coys.
2 cdo coys.
1 arty bty.
AML armd cars; 75mm pack how, 6 105mm how; 8 81mm mor; 30mm, 40mm AA guns.

Navy: 250.
3 large patrol craft with SS-12 SSM (1 on order).
14 small patrol craft.
1 LCT, 6 landing craft.

Air Force: 200; no combat aircraft.
6 C-47, 2 F-27, 4 *Broussard*, 1 *Cessna* 337 tpts.
2 *Alouette* II, 1 *Gazelle* hel.

Para-Military Forces: 1,600.

SOMALI DEMOCRATIC REPUBLIC

Population: 3,335,000.
Military service: voluntary.
Total armed forces: 31,500.
Estimated GNP 1972: $300 m.
Defence expenditure 1976: 165 m shillings ($25 m).
  $1 = 6.6 shillings (1976), 6.93 shillings (1972).

Army: 30,000.‖
7 tk bns.
8 mech inf bns.
14 mot inf bns.
2 cdo bns.
13 fd, 10 AA arty bns.
200 T-34, 100 T-54/-55 med tks; 100 BTR-40/-50, 250 BTR-152 APC; about 100 76mm and 85mm guns; 80 122mm how; 100mm ATK guns; 150 14.5mm, 37mm, 57mm and 100mm AA guns; SA-2/-3 SAM.

Navy: 500.‖
3 *Osa*-class FPBG with *Styx* SSM.
6 large patrol craft (ex-Soviet *Poluchat* class).
4 MTB (ex-Soviet P-6 class).
4 medium landing craft (ex-Soviet T-4 class).

‖ Spares are short and not all equipment is serviceable.

Air Force: 1,000; 55 combat aircraft.*
1 lt bbr sqn with 3 Il-28.
2 FGA sqns with 40 MiG-17 and MiG-15UTI.
1 fighter sqn with 12 MiG-21MF.
1 tpt sqn with 3 An-2, An-24/-26.
Other aircraft incl 3 C-47, 1 C-45, 6 P-148, 15 Yak-11, 2 Do-28.
1 hel sqn with 5 Mi-4, 5 Mi-8, 1 AB-204.

Para-Military Forces: 12,000: 8,000 Police; 1,500 border guards; 2,500 People's Militia.

SOUTH AFRICA

Population: 26,910,000.
Military service: 24 months.
Total armed forces: 55,000 (38,400 conscripts).
Estimated GNP 1976: $31.7 bn.
Defence expenditure 1977–78: 1.65 bn rand ($1.9 bn).
  $1 = 0.87 rand (1977), 0.87 rand (1976).

Army: 41,000 (34,000 conscripts, 2,100 women).
1 corps, 2 div HQ.
1 armd bde.*
1 mech bde (one forming).*
4 mot bdes.*
2 para bns.*
8 fd and 2 med arty regts.*
9 lt AA arty regts.*
9 fd engr sqns.*
5 sigs regts.*
Some 150 *Centurion*, 20 *Comet* med, M-41 lt tks; 1,600 *Eland* (AML-60/-90) armd cars; 230 scout cars incl *Ferret*, M-3A1; 280 *Saracen*, *Ratel* APC; 500 lt APC incl *Hippo*, *Rhino*; 25-pdr, 105mm SP how, 25-pdr, 105mm, 5.5-in, 155mm guns/how; 81mm, 120mm mor; 17-pdr, 90mm ATK guns; 105mm RCL; SS-11, *ENTAC* ATGW; 204GK 20mm, K-63 twin 35mm, L/70 40mm, 3.7-in AA guns; 18 *Cactus* (*Crotale*), 54 *Tigercat* SAM.

RESERVES: 130,000 Active Reserve (Citizen Force). Reservists serve 30 days per year for 8 years.

Navy: 5,500 (1,400 conscripts).
3 *Daphne*-class submarines.
1 destroyer with 2 *Wasp* ASW hel.
3 ASW frigates (3 with 1 *Wasp* hel).
1 escort minesweeper (training ship).
6 coastal minesweepers.
2 patrol craft (ex-British *Ford*-class).
(2 *Agosta*-class submarines, 2 Type A69 frigates, 6 FPBG, 6 corvettes with *Gabriel* II SSM, *Exocet* SSM on order.)

RESERVES: 10,500 Citizen Force with 1 destroyer, 2 frigates, 7 minesweepers.

---

* Cadre units, forming 2 divs when brought to full strength on mobilization of Citizen Force.

Air Force: 8,500 (3,000 conscripts); 362 combat aircraft.
2 lt bbr sqns: 1 with 6 *Canberra* B(I)12, 3 T4; 1 with 9 *Buccaneer* S50.
2 FGA sqns with 32 *Mirage* F-1A.
1 fighter/recce sqn with 27 *Mirage* IIICZ/BZ/RZ.
1 interceptor sqn with 16 *Mirage* F-1CZ.
2 MR sqns with 7 *Shackleton* MR3, 19 Piaggio P166S.
4 tpt sqns with 7 C-130B, 1 L-100-20, 15 L-100-30, 9 Transall C-160Z, 30 C-47, 5 DC-4, 1 *Viscount* 781, 7 HS-125, 7 Swearingen *Merlin* IVA.
4 hel sqns: 2 with 40 *Alouette* III, 1 with 25 SA-330 *Puma*, 1 with 15 SA-321L *Super Frelon*.
1 flt of 11 *Wasp* (naval assigned).
2 comms and liaison sqns (army assigned) with 22 Cessna 185A/D/E, 40 AM-3C *Bosbok*, 20 C-4M *Kudu*.
Operational trainers incl 29 *Mirage* IIIEZ/DZ/D2Z, 12 F-86, 150 MB-326 *Impala* I, 22 *Impala* II, 30 *Vampire*; other trg ac incl 100 *Harvard* (some armed), C-47 ac, *Alouette* II/III hel.
(50 *Impala* II, 20 *Kudu* on order.)

RESERVES: 25,000 Citizen Force. 6 sqns with 75 *Impala* I/II, 10 *Harvard*, T-6G.

Para-Military Forces: 90,000 Commandos (in inf bn-type units grouped in formations of 5 or more with local industrial and rural protection duties). Members do 12 months' initial and 19 days' annual training. There are 13 Air Cdo sqns with private aircraft. 35,500 South African Police (SAP) (19,500 Whites, 16,000 Non-Whites).

TANZANIA

Population: 15,990,000.
Military service: voluntary.
Total armed forces: 18,600.
Estimated GNP 1974: $1.9 bn.
Defence expenditure 1975: 520 m shillings ($70 m).
  $1 = 7.43 shillings (1975), 7.16 shillings (1974).

Army: 17,000.
1 tk bn.
10 inf bns.
2 arty bns.
1 engr bn.
20 Chinese T-59 med, T-60, 14 T-62 lt tks; BTR-40/-152, K-63 APC; 24 ex-Soviet 76mm guns, 30 ex-Chinese 122mm how; 82mm, 50 ex-Chinese 120mm mor; 14.5mm, 37mm AA guns.

DEPLOYMENT: *Mozambique:* 2 inf bns.

Navy: 600.
6 FPB (*Shanghai*-class).
11 MTB (4 *Hu Chwan* hydrofoils, 3 P-6, 3 P-4 class).
8 coastal patrol craft.

Air Force: 1,000; 29 combat aircraft.
3 fighter sqns with 11 MiG-21/F-8, 3 MiG-17/F-4, 15 MiG-19/F-6.
1 tpt sqn with 1 An-2, 12 DHC-4, 1 HS-748, 6 Cessna 310.
2 MiG-15UTI, 11 *Cherokee* trainers.
2 Bell 47G, 2 AB-206 hel.

Para-Military Forces: 1,400 Police Field Force and a police marine unit; 35,000 Citizen's Militia.

UGANDA

Population: 12,300,000.
Military service: voluntary.
Total armed forces: 21,000.
Estimated GNP 1974: $2.0 bn.
Defence expenditure 1974–75: 350 m shillings ($49 m).
     $1 = 7.16 shillings (1974).

Army: 20,000.*
2 bdes, each of 4 bns.
1 mech inf bn.
1 para/cdo, 1 marine/cdo bn.
1 trg bn.
1 arty regt.
10 T-34, 15 T-54/-55, 10 M-4 med tks; BRDM, *Saladin* armd, 15 *Ferret* scout cars; 250 BTR-40/-152, OT-64, *Saracen* APC; 76mm, 122mm guns; 82mm, 120mm mor; *Sagger* ATGW; 50 40mm AA guns.

Navy: A small lake patrol service being formed.

Air Force: 1,000;† 24 combat aircraft.*
2 fighter sqns with 12 MiG-21, 10 MiG-17, 2 MiG-15UTI.
1 tpt sqn with 6 C-47, 1 DHC-6.
1 hel sqn with 6 AB-205, 4 AB-206.
Trainers incl 12 L-29, 10 Piper. (6 AS 202 *Bravo* on order.)

ZAIRE REPUBLIC

Population: 26,310,000.
Military service: voluntary.
Total armed forces: 33,400.
Estimated GNP 1974: $3.5 bn.
Defence expenditure 1976: 62.2 m zaires ($76.8 m).
     $1 = 0.81 zaires (1976), 0.5 zaires (1974).

Army: 30,000.
1 tk bn (another forming).
2 armd bns.
1 mech bn.

*Not all eqpt and ac are likely to be serviceable.
† Excluding expatriate instructors and maintenance personnel.

14 inf bns.
5 para, 2 cdo bns.
4 'Guard' bns.
60 Type-62 lt tks (ex-Chinese); 44 AML-90, 122 AML-60 armed cars; M-3 scout cars; 70mm, 75mm, 122mm, 130mm guns/how; 82mm, 120mm mor; 107mm RL; 57mm ATK guns; 75mm, 106mm RCL; *Snapper* ATGW; 20mm, 37mm, 40mm AA guns.

Navy: 400.
2 FPB (*Shanghai*-class).
1 70-ton coastal patrol craft.
3 P4-class torpedo boats (ex-Korean).
11 river patrol boats (6 ex-US *Sewart* type).
6 patrol boats (ex-US *Swift* class), under 100 tons.

Air Force: 3,000; 54 combat aircraft.
1 fighter sqn with 14 *Mirage* VM, 3 VDM.
2 COIN sqns with 17 MB-326GB, 8 AT-6G, 12 AT-28D.
1 tpt wing with 8 C-130H, 2 DHC-4A, 3 DHC-5, 2 DC-6, 4 C-54, 8 C-47, 2 Mu-2.
1 hel sqn with 15 *Alouette* III, 23 *Puma*, 7 Bell 47.
Trg ac incl 24 SF-260MC, 15 T-6, 15 Cessna A150.
(12 *Mirage* V fighters, 3 DHC-5 tpts on order.)

Para-Military Forces: 30,000: 8 National Guard, 6 Gendarmerie bns.

ZAMBIA

Population: 5,235,000.
Military service: voluntary.
Total armed forces: 8,500.
Estimated GNP 1974: $2.5 bn.
Defence expenditure 1977: 246.3 m kwacha ($309.4 m).
     $1 = 0.796 kwacha (1977), 0.644 kwacha (1974).

Army: 7,000.
4 inf bns.
1 armd car sqn.
1 arty bty, 1 SAM bty.
1 engr, 1 sigs sqn.
28 *Ferret* scout cars; 8 M-56 105mm pack how; 24 20mm AA guns; 4 *Rapier* SAM.

Air Force: 1,500; 18 combat aircraft.
1 COIN sqn with 18 MB-326G.
2 tpt sqns: 1 with 5 DHC-4, 7 DHC-5, 2 DC-6, 1 HS-748; 1 with 4 *Beaver*, 10 Do-28, 1 Saab *Supporter*.
Trainers incl 6 *Chipmunk*, 8 SF-260MZ.
1 hel sqn with 4 AB-205, 4 AB-206, 1 AB-212, 3 Bell 47G, 2 Mi-8. (10 AB-47G on order.)

Para-Military Forces: Police Mobile Unit 700 (1 bn)·

ARMED FORCES OF OTHER AFRICAN STATES*

Country	Estimated population (000)	Estimated GNP 1976 ($m)	Total armed forces	Army Manpower and formations	Army Equipment	Navy Manpower and equipment	Air Force Manpower and equipment	Para-military forces
Benin	3,320	425	2,250	2,100 2 inf bns 1 engr bn 1 para/cdo coy 1 arty bty	7 M-8 armd cars; 105mm guns; 60mm, 81mm mor	—	150 3 med, 5 lt tpts; 1 Bell 47, 1 *Alouette* hel	1,000
Burundi	3,900	—	7,000†	3 inf bns 1 'para' bn 1 'cdo' bn 1 armd car coy	AML armd cars	—	3 DC-3 tpts, some hel	2,000
Cameroon	7,165	1,700	6,000	5,500 4 inf bns 1 armd car sqn 1 para coy engr/spt units	M-8, *Ferret* scout cars; 75mm, 105mm guns; 57mm ATK guns; 81mm mor; 106mm RCL	200 1 FPB; 1 large, 6 coastal patrol boats; 6 small landing craft	300 4 *Magister*; 4 C-47, 2 *Caribou*, 2 HS-748 tpts (2 C-130H ordered); 5 *Alouette* II/III, 1 *Puma* hel	7,000
Central African Empire	1,800	302	1,200	1,100 1 inf bn 1 engr coy 1 sigs coy	*Ferret* scout cars; 81mm mor; 106mm RCL	—	100 1 DC-4, 4 C-47, 1 *Caravelle*, 1 *Falcon* tpts; 2 *Alouette* II, 5 H-34 hel	1,400
Chad	4,206	330 (1972)	5,200	5,000 3 inf/para bns	AML armd cars; 81mm, 120mm mor	—	200 4 A-1; 3 DC-4, 9 C-47, 1 *Caravelle* tpts; 3 *Alouette* III, 4 *Puma* hel	6,000
Gabon	110	1,710	1,250	950 1 inf bn 2 cdo coys 1 engr coy 1 service coy	Scout cars; RCL; 81mm mor	100 3 patrol craft (3 on order)	200 2 *Hercules*, 3 C-47, 3 Nord 262 tpts; 4 *Alouette* III, 3 *Puma* hel (6 *Mirage* V fighters on order)	1,600
Guinea	4,630	410 (1972)	5,850	5,000 1 armd bn 4 inf bns 1 engr bn	30 T-34/-54 med, 10 PT-76 lt tks; 40 BTR-40/-152 APC; 76mm, 85mm, 105mm, 122mm guns/how; 57mm ATK, 37mm, 57mm, 100mm AA guns	350 4 *Shanghai*, 4 P-6, 2 *Poluchat* patrol craft; 2 small landing craft	500 10 MiG-17, 3 MiG-21, 2 Il-18, 4 Il-14, 4 An-4 tpts; 2 MiG-15, 7 Yak-18, 3 L-29 trainers; 1 Bell 47 hel	8,000

For notes see p. 51.

Armed Forces of Other African States (cont.

Country	Estimated population (000)	Estimated GNP 1976 ($m)	Total armed forces	Army — Manpower and formations	Army — Equipment	Navy — Manpower and equipment	Air Force — Manpower and equipment	Para-military forces
Ivory Coast	5,135	2,400	4,950	4,500 / 3 inf bns / 1 tk sqn / 3 para coys / 1 arty bty / 1 engr coy	5 AMX-13 lt tks; 16 AML-60/-90 armd cars; 4 105mm how; 81mm, 120mm mor; 10 40mm AA guns	250 / 2 coastal patrol boats with SS-12 SSM; 1 80-ton, 5 river patrol boats; 2 small landing craft (1 LST on order)	200 / 3 C-47, 2 F-27, 2 F-28 tpts; 5 Alouette II/III, 3 Puma hel	3,000
Liberia	1,790	436 (1972)	5,220†	5 inf bns / 1 Guard bn / 1 arty bn / 1 engr bn / 1 service bn / 1 recce coy	M-3A1 scout cars; 75mm, 105mm how; 60mm, 10 81mm mor	1 MGB, 5 patrol boats	2 C-47 tpts	21,300
Malagasy Republic	7,905	1,400	10,150	9,550 / 2 inf regts / 1 engr regt / 1 sigs regt	Ferret scout cars; M-3A1 APC; mor; 106mm RCL	250 / 1 large, 1 small patro craft; 1 tpt; 1 trg ship	350 / 1 C-53, 5 C-47 tpts; 3 Alouette II/III, 1 Bell 47, 2 Mi-8 hel	7,000
Malawi	5,280	640	2,400†	2 inf bns / 1 recce coy	10 Ferret scout cars; 81 mm mor	3 small lake patrol boats	4 C-47, 2 Pembroke, 2 Do-28, 1 Defender tpts	460
Mali	5,990	375 (1972)	4,200†	5 inf bns / 1 tk coy / 1 para coy / 1 arty bn / 1 engr coy	Some 20 T-34, 6 Type 62 lt tks; BTR-40/BRDM-2 armd cars; BTR-152 APC; 81mm, 120mm mor; 85mm, 100mm ATK guns; 57mm AA guns	3 river patrol craft	8 MiG-17, 2 MiG-15UTI; 2 C-47, 2 An-2, 2 Il-14 tpts; 6 Yak trainers; 2 Mi-4 hel	5,700
Mauritania	1,400	290	7,450	7,000 / 30 mot inf coys / 3 recce sqns / 1 AB coy / 1 para/cdo coy	15 EBR-75, AML armd cars (more AML ordered); 60mm, 81mm mor; 57mm, 75mm RCL	300 / 4 small patrol boats (2 more on order)	150 / 4 Defender COIN (2 more ordered); 1 DC-4, 4 C-47, 2 Skyvan tpts; 4 Reims F-337	6,000
Niger	4,890	489 (1972)	2,050	2,000 / 1 recce sqn / 5 inf coys / 1 para coy / 1 engr coy	Some 10 M-8, M-20 armd cars; 60mm, 81mm mor; 57mm, 75mm RCL	—	50 / 1 C-54, 3 Noratlas, 2 C-47 tpts	1,800

Rwanda	4,500		3,750†	1 recce sqn 8 inf coys 1 cdo coy	12 AML armd cars; 6 57mm guns; 8 81mm mor	—	3 *Magister* COIN; 2 C-47, 1 *Islander* tpts; 2 *Alouette* III hel	1,200
Sierra Leone	2,780	233 (1972)	2,200†	1 inf bn	10 Mowag armd cars; 60mm, 81mm mor	2 *Shanghai*-class FPB	2 Saab MFI-15 trainers; 3 Hughes 300/500 hel	2,500
Togo	2,350	600 (1974)	2,500†	1 mot inf bn 2 inf bns 2 para/cdo bns	5 M-8 armd cars; 30 UR-416 APC	2 patrol vessels, 1 river gunboat	5 *Magister*, 3 EMB- 326GB COIN; 2 C-47, 2 DHC-5, 1 F-28 tpts; 1 *Alouette* III, 1 *Puma* hel (5 *AlphaJet* ordered)	1,400
		605					
Upper Volta	6,310	504	8,070†	11 inf bns 1 armd sqn 1 para coy 1 arty bty	Panhard, M-8 armd cars; *Ferret* scout cars; 60mm, 10 81mm mor; 75mm RCL	—	2 C-47, 2 *Frégate* tpts	1,850

* For many developing nations, particularly the smaller ones, maintenance facilities and skills pose problems, and spare parts may not be readily available. The amounts of military equipment shown may not necessarily be those which can be used. Logistic and maintenance support may be by civilian or expatriate personnel.

† All services form part of the Army.

Asia and Australasia

CHINA

Chinese defence policy has for many years maintained a balance, at times uneasy, between the two extremes of nuclear deterrence and People's War. The former aims to deter strategic attack, the latter, by mass mobilization of the population, to deter or repel conventional land invasion. With Mao's death in September 1976 and the attack on the 'Gang of Four' thereafter, the strongest adherents of the strategic concept that men are more important than weapons were removed. There is now some indication of an effort to develop more modern general-purpose forces, to meet more limited military contingencies than the extremes of nuclear deterrence or mass war.

The People's Liberation Army (PLA) was probably the key factor in the accession to power of Hua Kuo-feng, despite some division within its leadership. The PLA can therefore be expected to have increased influence over military policy, and it has not hidden its desire for more modern weapons and for increased spending. Military conferences have covered air defence, aircraft and missiles, and planning, research and production. While this foreshadows efforts at modernization, there is continuing debate about its pace and nature. It is too early yet to see whether, or how soon, the money for it will be forthcoming (but see the note on defence expenditure on p. 54). It is also too early to foresee the effect of Teng Hsiao-ping's reappointment at the end of July 1977 to his three major positions, including Chief of the PLA General Staff. The picture that can be drawn of Chinese forces accordingly is not dissimilar from that of last year.

Nuclear Weapons

The testing programme continued, with three tests in the year: one in September 1976, one (the third underground test) in October and one (of four megatons) in November, bringing the total to twenty-one since testing started in 1964. A theatre nuclear force is operational, capable of reaching large parts of the Soviet Union and Asia. The stockpile of weapons, both fission and fusion, probably amounts to several hundreds and could continue to grow rapidly. Fighter aircraft could be used for tactical delivery, and for longer ranges there is the Tu-16 medium bomber, with a radius of action up to 2,000 miles. MRBM with a range of some 600–700 miles are operational but may be phased out and replaced by IRBM, also operational now, with a range of 1,500–1,750 miles. The missile force seems to be controlled by the Second Artillery, apparently the missile arm of the PLA.

A multi-stage ICBM with a limited range of 3,000–3,500 miles was first tested in 1976 and some may have been deployed. An ICBM thought to have a range of 8,000 miles has also been under development but is unlikely to become operational for some years yet. Full-range testing, which would require impact areas in the Indian or Pacific Oceans, has not yet been carried out, but the missile has been successfully used (and thus tested) as a launcher for satellites. China has one G-class submarine with missile launching tubes, but does not appear to have missiles for it. All the present missiles are liquid-fuelled, but solid propellants are being developed.

Conventional Forces

The PLA is organized in 11 Military Regions and divided into Main and Local Forces. Main Force (MF) divisions, administered by the Military Regions in which they are stationed but commanded by the Ministry of National Defence, are available for operations in any region and are better equipped. Local Forces (LF), which include Border Defence and Internal Defence units, are predominantly infantry and concentrate on the defence of their own localities in co-operation with para-military units.

The PLA is generally equipped and trained for the environment of People's War, but new efforts are being made to arm a proportion of the formations with modern weapons. Infantry units account for most of the manpower and 121 of the 136 Main Force divisions; there are only 12 armoured divisions. The naval and air elements of the PLA have only about one-seventh of the total manpower, compared with about a third for their counterparts in the Soviet Union, but naval strength is increasing, and the equipment for both arms is steadily being modernized. The PLA, essentially a defensive force, lacks facilities and logistic support for protracted large-scale operations outside China.

Major weapons systems produced include MiG-19 and F-9 fighters (the last Chinese-designed), SA-2 SAM, Type-59 medium and Type-60 amphibious tanks, and a Chinese-designed Type-62 light tank and APC. R- and W-class medium-range diesel submarines are being built in some numbers, together with SSM destroyers and fast patrol boats; a nuclear-powered attack submarine (armed with conventional torpedoes) has been under test for some years. Most military equipment is 10–20 years out of date, but China has shown increasing interest in acquiring Western military technology.

Bilateral Agreements

China has a 30-year Treaty of Alliance and Friendship with the Soviet Union, signed in 1950, which contains mutual defence obligations, but it is highly unlikely that this remains in force. There is a mutual defence agreement with North Korea, dating from 1961, and an agreement to provide free military aid. There are non-aggression pacts with Afghanistan, Burma and Cambodia. Chinese military equipment and logistic support has been offered to a number of countries. Major recipients of arms in the past have been Albania, Pakistan and Tanzania.

CHINA

Population: 900–950,000,000.
Military service: Army 2–4 years, Air Force 4 years, Navy 5 years.
Total regular forces: 3,950,000.
GNP and defence expenditure—see note on p. 54.

Strategic Forces
IRBM: 30–40 CSS-2.
MRBM: 30–40 CSS-1.
Aircraft: about 80 Tu-16 med bbrs.

Army: 3,250,000.
Main Forces:
  12 armd divs.
  121 inf divs.
  3 AB divs.
  40 arty divs (incl AA divs).
  15 railway and construction engr divs.
  150 indep regts.
Local Forces:
  70 inf divs.
  130 indep regts.

10,000 Soviet IS-2 hy, T-34 and Chinese-produced Type-59/-63 med, Type-60 (PT-76) amph and Type-62 lt tks; 3,500 M-1967, K-63 APC; 20,000 guns, how and RL to 203mm, incl SU-76, SU-100 and ISU-122/-152 SP arty; 82mm, 90mm, 120mm, 160mm, 240mm mor; 57mm, 75mm RCL; 57mm, 85mm, 100mm ATK guns; 37mm, 57mm, 85mm, 100mm AA guns.

DEPLOYMENT:
China is divided into 11 Military Regions (MR), in turn divided into Military Districts (MD), with usually two or three Districts to a Region. Divs

are grouped into some 40 armies, generally of 3 inf divs, 3 arty regts and, in some cases, 3 armd regts. Main Force (MF) divs are administered by Regions but are under central comd.

The distribution of divs, excluding arty and engrs, is believed to be:
North and North-East China (Shenyang and Peking MR*): 55 MF divs, 25 LF divs.
North and North-West China (Lanchow and Sinkiang MR): 20 MF divs, 8 LF divs.
East and South-East China (Tsinan, Nanking, Foochow and Canton† MR): 28 MF divs, 18 LF divs.
Central China (Wuhan MR): 15 MF divs (incl 3 AB), 11 LF divs.
West and South-West China (Chengtu and Kunming MR*): 18 MF divs, 8 LF divs.

Navy: 300,000, incl 30,000 Naval Air Force and 38,000 Marines; 22 major surface combat ships.
1 G-class submarine (with SLBM tubes).‡
66 fleet submarines (incl 36 Soviet R-, 21 W-, 2 *Ming*-class).§
6 *Luta*-class destroyers with *Styx* SSM (more building).
4 ex-Soviet *Gordy*-class destroyers with *Styx* SSM.
12 destroyer escorts (4 *Riga*-type with *Styx* SSM).
16 patrol escorts.

---

* Figures include the equivalent of 2–3 divs of border troops in each of these MR.
† Includes Hainan island.
‡ China is not known to have any missiles for this boat. There is also 1 *Han*-class boat, nuclear-powered, armed with conventional torpedoes, under test.
  § Incl trg vessels.

35 submarine chasers (Soviet *Kronstadt*-type).

90 *Osa*- and 70 *Komar*-type FPBG with *Styx* SSM (more building).

175 MTB (under 100 tons).

100 hydrofoils (under 100 tons).

400 MGB (*Shanghai*-, *Swatow*-, *Whampoa*-classes).

22 minesweepers (16 Soviet T-43 type).

15 LST, 16 med, 15 inf landing ships, some 450 landing craft.

300 coast and river defence vessels (most under 100 tons).

DEPLOYMENT:

North Sea Fleet: about 200 vessels deployed from the mouth of the Yalu river to south of Lienyunkang; major bases at Tsingtao, Lushun, Luta.

East Sea Fleet: about 500 vessels; deployed from south of Lienyunkang to Tangshan; major bases at Shanghai, Chou Shan, Ta Hsiehtao.

South Sea Fleet: about 200 vessels; deployed from Tangshan to the Vietnamese frontier; major bases at Huangpu, Chanchiang, Yulin.

NAVAL AIR FORCE: 30,000; about 700 shore-based combat aircraft, organized into 4 bbr and 5 fighter divs, incl about 130 Il-28 torpedo-carrying, Tu-16 med and Tu-2 lt bbrs and some 500 fighters, incl MiG-17, MiG-19/F-6 and some F-9; a few Be-6 *Madge* MR ac; 50 Mi-4 *Hound* hel and some lt tpt ac. Naval fighters are integrated into the AD system.

Air Force: 400,000, incl strategic forces and 120,000 AD personnel; about 5,200 combat aircraft.

About 80 Tu-16 and a few Tu-4 med bbrs.

About 400 Il-28 and 100 Tu-2 lt bbrs.

About 600 MiG-15 and F-9 FB.

About 4,000 MiG-17/-19, 120 MiG-21 and some F-9 fighters organized into air divs and regts.

About 450 fixed-wing tpt ac, incl some 300 An-2, about 100 Li-2, 50 Il-14 and Il-18, some An-12/-24/-26 and *Trident*. 350 hel, incl Mi-4, Mi-8 and 16 *Super Frelon*. These could be supplemented by about 500 ac from the Civil Aviation Administration, of which about 150 are major tpts.

There is an AD system, capable of providing a limited defence of key urban and industrial areas, military installations and weapon complexes. Up to 4,000 naval and air force fighters are assigned to this role, also about 100 CSA-1 (SA-2) SAM and over 10,000 AA guns.

Para-Military Forces: Public security force and a civilian militia with various elements: the Armed Militia, up to 7 million, organized into about 75 divs and an unknown number of regts; the Urban Militia, of several million; the Civilian Production and Construction Corps, about 4 million; and the Ordinary and Basic Militia, 75–100 million, who receive some basic training but are generally unarmed.

GROSS NATIONAL PRODUCT AND DEFENCE EXPENDITURE

Gross National Product

There are no official Chinese figures for GNP or National Income. Western estimates have varied greatly, and it is difficult to choose from a range of figures, variously defined and calculated. The United States Arms Control and Disarmament Agency (ACDA) has estimated GNP for 1975 to be $299 bn, while a recent British estimate for 1976 was $309 bn.

Defence Expenditure

China has not made public any budget figures since 1960, and there is no general agreement on the volume of resources devoted to defence. Such estimates as there are have been speculative. The Joint Economic Committee of the United States Congress suggested in 1976 that China spends 20–25 per cent of what the United States spends on defence, or $23–28 bn. A speech by the Chinese Defence Minister in May 1977, to the effect that China was in a race against time and had decided to step up the manufacture of modern weapons, suggests that defence expenditure may increase.

Other Asian Countries and Australasia

Bilateral Agreements

The United States has bilateral defence treaties with Japan, the Republic of China (Taiwan) and the Republic of Korea, and one (being renegotiated) with the Philippines. Under several other arrangements in the region, she provides military aid on either grant or credit basis to Taiwan, Indonesia, the Republic of Korea, Malaysia, the Philippines and Thailand, and sells military equipment to many countries, notably Australia, Japan, Korea and Taiwan. There are military facilities agreements with Australia, Japan, the Republic of Korea, the Philippines and Taiwan. There are major bases in the Philippines and on Guam. The 1973 Diego Garcia Agreement between the British and American governments provides for the development of the present limited US naval communications facility on Diego Garcia into a US naval support facility.

The Soviet Union has treaties of friendship, co-operation and mutual assistance with India, Bangladesh, Mongolia and the Democratic People's Republic of Korea. Military assistance agreements exist with Sri Lanka (Ceylon) and the Socialist Republic of Vietnam. Important Soviet military aid is also given to Afghanistan.

Australia has supplied a small amount of defence equipment to Malaysia and Singapore and is giving defence equipment and assistance to Indonesia, including the provision of training facilities. Vietnam and Laos signed in July 1977 a series of agreements which contained military provisions and a border pact and may have covered the stationing of Vietnamese troops in Laos.

Multilateral Agreements

In 1954 the United States, Australia, Britain, France, New Zealand, Pakistan, the Philippines and Thailand signed the South-East Asia Collective Defence Treaty, which came into force in 1955 and brought the Treaty Organization, SEATO, into being. Pakistan left SEATO in 1973. The SEATO Council decided in 1975 that the Organization should be phased out, and it was formally closed down on 30 June 1977.

Australia, New Zealand and the United States are members of a tripartite treaty known as ANZUS, which was signed in 1951 and is of indefinite duration. Under this treaty each agrees to 'act to meet the common danger' in the event of attack on either metropolitan or island territory of any one of them, or on armed forces, public vessels or aircraft in the Pacific.

Five-Power defence arrangements, relating to the defence of Malaysia and Singapore and involving Australia, Malaysia, New Zealand, Singapore and Britain, came into effect on 1 November 1971. These stated that, in the event of any externally organized or supported armed attack or threat of attack against Malaysia or Singapore, the five governments would consult together for the purpose of deciding what measures should be taken, jointly or separately. Britain withdrew her forces from Singapore, except for a small contribution to the integrated air-defence system, by 31 March 1976. New Zealand troops remained, as did Australian air forces in Malaysia.

AFGHANISTAN

Population: 20,100,000.
Military service: 2 years.
Total armed forces: 110,000.
Estimated GNP 1976: $1.3 bn.
Defence expenditure 1976–77: 2.5 bn afghanis ($47.8 m).
  $1 = 52.3 afghanis (1976).

Army: 100,000.
3 armd divs (under strength).
10 inf divs (under strength).
3 mountain inf bdes.

1 arty bde, 3 arty regts.
1 cdo regt.
200 T-34, 500 T-54/-55, T-62 med, 40 PT-76 lt tks; 400 BTR-40/-50/-60/-152 APC; 900 76mm, 100mm, 122mm and 152mm guns and how; 100 120mm mor; 50 132mm multiple RL; 350 37mm, 57mm, 85mm, 100mm and ZSU-23-4 SP AA guns; *Sagger, Snapper* ATGW.

RESERVES: 150,000.

Air Force: 10,000; 184 combat aircraft.
3 lt bbr sqns with 30 Il-28.
7 FGA sqns with 80 MiG-17, 24 Su-7.

3 interceptor sqns with 50 MiG-21.
2 tpt sqns with 10 An-2, 10 Il-14, 2 Il-18.
3 hel sqns with 18 Mi-4, 12 Mi-8.
Trainers incl 30 MiG-15UTI/-17UTI, Yak-11/-18.
1 AD div: 1 SAM bde (3 bns with SA-2), 1 AA bde
    (2 bns with 37mm, 85mm, 100mm guns), 1 radar
    bde (3 bns).

RESERVES: 12,000.

Para-Military Forces: 30,000 Gendarmerie.

AUSTRALIA

Population: 13,990,000.
Military service: voluntary.
Total armed forces: 69,650.
Estimated GNP 1976: $US 100.7 bn.
Defence expenditure 1976–77: $A 2.26 bn
    ($US 2.80 bn).
    $1 = $A 0.805 (1976).

Army: 31,800.
1 inf div HQ and 3 task force HQ.
1 armd regt.
2 recce/APC regts.
6 inf bns.
1 Special Air Service regt.
4 arty regts (1 med, 2 fd, 1 lt AA).
1 aviation regt.
3 fd engr, 1 fd survey regt.
2 sigs regts.
24 *Leopard*, 143 *Centurion* med tks; 750 M-113
    APC; 17 5.5-in guns; 250 105mm how; M-40
    106mm RCL; *ENTAC* ATGW; 40mm AA guns;
    Redeye SAM; 25 Bell 47, 54 Bell 206B-1 hel; 18
    Pilatus *Porter* ac, 136 watercraft.
(77 *Leopard* med tks, 69 M-113 APC, 20 *Rapier* SAM,
    10 *Blindfire* AD radar, 11 *Nomad* lt ac on order.)

DEPLOYMENT: *Egypt* (UNEF): 44.

RESERVES: 28,000, incl active Reserve of 20,000
    in combat, support, log and trg units.

Navy: 16,200.
4 *Oberon*-class submarines.
1 aircraft carrier (carries 8 A-4, 6 S-2, 10 hel).
3 ASW destroyers with *Tartar* SAM, *Ikara* ASW msls.
2 modified *Daring*-class destroyers.
6 destroyers with *Seacat* SAM/SSM, *Ikara* ASW msls.
1 trg ship.
1 coastal minesweeper, 2 coastal minehunters
    (modified British *Ton*-class).
12 *Attack*-class patrol boats.
1 oiler, 1 destroyer tender, 6 landing craft.
(2 submarines, 2 frigates, 15 patrol craft on order.)

FLEET AIR ARM: 32 combat aircraft.
1 FB sqn with 13 A-4G *Skyhawk*.
2 ASW sqns with 3 S-2E, 16 S-2G *Tracker*.

1 ASW hel sqn with 8 *Sea King*.
1 hel sqn with 4 Bell UH-1H, 2 Bell 206B, 4 *Wessex*.
1 trg sqn with 8 MB-326H, 3 TA-4G.
2 HS-748 ECM trg ac.

RESERVES: 4,236, incl active reserve of 833.

Air Force: 21,650; 120 combat aircraft.*
2 strike/recce sqns with 23 F-111C.
3 interceptor/FGA sqns with 48 *Mirage* IIIO.
1 recce sqn with 13 *Canberra* B20.
2 MR sqns: 1 with 10 P-3 *Orion*; 1 with 12 *Neptune*
    SP2H.
5 tpt sqns: 2 with 24 C-130A/E; 2 with 22 DHC-4;
    1 with 2 BAC-111, 10 HS-748, 3 *Mystère* 20, 17
    C-47.
1 Forward Air Controller flight with 6 CA-25.
1 OCU with 14 *Mirage* IIIO.
1 hel tpt sqn with 6 CH-47 *Chinook*.
2 utility hel sqns with 47 UH-1H *Iroquois*.
Trainers incl 80 MB-326, 33 CA-25 *Winjeel*, 37
    CT-4 *Airtrainer*.
(10 *Orion* MR, 12 C-130H tpts on order.)

DEPLOYMENT: *Malaysia/Singapore:* 2 sqns with
    Mirage IIIO.

RESERVES: 1,095: 450 Air Force Reserve, 5 Citizens
    Air Force sqns; 645 Emergency Reserve.

BANGLADESH

Population: 80,520,000.
Military service: voluntary.
Total armed forces: 71,000.
Estimated GNP 1972: $5.3 bn.
Defence expenditure 1976–77: 746 m taka ($51.5 m).
    $1 = 14.5 taka (1976), 7.30 taka (1972).

Army: 65,000.
1 inf div HQ.
7 inf bdes (25 inf bns).
1 tk regt.
4 arty, 2 hy mor regts.
3 engr bns.
30 T-54 med tks; 30 105mm, 5 25-pdr gun/how;
    81mm, 50 120mm mor; 106mm RCL.†

Navy: 3,000.
1 frigate (ex British Type 61).
5 patrol craft (2 *Kraljevica*-class).
3 armed river patrol boats.
1 support vessel.

Air Force: 3,000; 11 combat aircraft.†
1 fighter sqn with 11 MiG-21MF.
1 tpt sqn with 1 An-24, 2 An-26, 4 *Beaver*.

---

* A further 8 *Canberra* B20 bbrs, 28 *Mirage* IIID/O
FGA, 6 CH-47, 16 *Wessex* 31B, 1 UH-1B hel also held.
† Spares are short; some equipment is unserviceable.

1 hel sqn with 5 *Alouette* III, 2 *Wessex* HC, 6 AB-212, 8 Mi-8.
Trainers incl 2 MiG-21UTI, 1 T-33A, 8 F-86.

Para-Military Forces: 12,000 Bangladesh Rifles, 36,000 Armed Police Reserve.

BRUNEI

Population: 170,000.
Military service: voluntary.
Total armed forces: 2,600.*
Estimated GNP 1976: $381.7 m.
Defence expenditure 1977: $B 303 m
    ($US 123.1 m).
    $1 US = $B 2.46 (1977), $B 2.62 (1976).

Army: 2,600.
2 inf bns.
24 Sankey APC, 16 81mm mor. (16 *Scorpion* lt tks on order.)

Navy
6 coastal, 3 river patrol craft; 2 landing craft.

Air Force
1 HS-748 tpt ac.
3 Bell 205, 3 Bell 206, 4 Bell 212 hel.

Para-Military Forces: 1,700 Royal Brunei Police.

BURMA

Population: 32,445,000.
Military service: voluntary.
Total armed forces: 169,500.
Estimated GNP 1975: $2.7 bn.
Defence expenditure 1976: 787 m kyat
    ($113 m).
    $1 = 6.96 kyat (1976), 6.56 kyat (1975).

Army: 153,000.
3 inf divs each with 10 bns.
2 armd bns.
84 indep inf bns (in regional comds).
5 arty bns.
Comet lt tks: 40 Humber armd cars; 45 *Ferret* scout cars; 50 25-pdr, 5.5-in gun/how; 120 76mm, 80 105mm how; 120mm mor; 50 6-pdr and 17-pdr ATK guns; 10 40mm, 3.7-in AA guns.†

Navy: 9,000 (800 marines).†
2 frigates.
4 coastal escorts.
5 MGB/MTB (under 100 tons).
37 gunboats (17 under 100 tons).

35 river patrol boats (under 100 tons).
1 support ship.
9 landing craft (1 utility, 8 med).

Air Force: 7,500; 25 combat aircraft.†
1 COIN sqn with 15 AT-33, 10 SF-260M.
Tpts incl 4 C-45, 6 C-47, 2 Bristol 170, 6 DHC-3, 10 Cessna 180.
Hel incl 10 KB-47G, 12 HH-43B, 10 *Alouette* III, 18 UH-1.
Trainers incl 25 *Provost*, 8 T-33, 10 T-37C, 7 *Chipmunk*.

Para-Military Forces: 38,000 People's Police Force, 35,000 People's Militia.

CHINA: REPUBLIC OF (TAIWAN)

Population: 17,235,000.
Military service: 2 years.
Total armed forces: 460,000.
Estimated GNP 1975: $16.1 bn.
Defence expenditure 1975–76: 38.3 bn New Taiwan dollars ($1 bn).
    $US 1 = $NT 38.0 (1975).

Army: 320,000.
2 armd divs.
12 hy inf divs.
6 lt inf divs.
2 armd cav regts.
2 AB bdes.
4 special forces gps.
1 SSM bn with *Honest John*.
3 SAM bns: 2 with 72 *Nike Hercules*, 1 with 24 *HAWK*.
150 M-47/-48 med, 1,000 M-41 lt tks; 250 M-113 APC; 550 105mm, 300 155mm guns and how; 350 75mm M-116 pack, 90 203mm, 10 240mm how; 225 105mm SP how; 150 M-18 76mm SP ATK; 500 106mm RCL; 300 40mm AA guns (some SP); *Honest John* SSM; *Nike Hercules, Chaparral* SAM; 50 UH-1H, 60 Hughes 500 hel. (24 *Improved HAWK* SAM, 118 UH-1H hel on order.)

DEPLOYMENT: *Quemoy:* 60,000; *Matsu:* 20,000.

RESERVES: 1,000,000.

Navy: 35,000.
5 submarines (2 ex-US *Guppy*-II-class, 3 SX-404 midget).
18 destroyers.
10 frigates (12 ex-US armed transports).
3 patrol vessels (plus up to 14 small patrol boats).
6 MTB.
22 MCM craft (9 coastal minesweepers).
50 landing vessels: 2 dock, 2 comd, 20 LST, 4 med, 22 utility.
(*Gabriel* SSM on order.)

---

* All services form part of the Army.
† Spares are short; some equipment is unserviceable.

5

RESERVES: 45,000.

Marines: 35,000.
2 divs.
M-47 med tks; LVT-4 APC; 105mm, 155mm how;
    106mm RCL.

RESERVES: 35,000.

Air Force: 70,000; 296 combat aircraft.
13 fighter sqns with 90 F-100A/D, 110 F-5A/B/E,
    63 F-104G.
1 recce sqn with 8 RF-104G.
1 MR sqn with 25 S-2A *Tracker.*
1 SAR sqn with 10 HU-16A ac, 10 UH-1H hel.
30 C-46, 50 C-47, 40 C-119, 10 C-123, 1 Boeing
    720B tpts.
160 trainers, incl PL-1B *Chien Shou*, T-28, T-33,
    T-38, F-5B/F, TF-104G.
7 UH-19, 10 Bell 47G hel.
(60 F-5E fighters, *Shafrir* AAM on order.)

RESERVES: 90,000.

Para-Military Forces: 100,000 militia.

INDIA

Population: 622,375,000.
Military service: voluntary.
Total armed forces: 1,096,000.
Estimated GNP 1975: $89.7 bn.
Defence expenditure 1977–78: 30.42 bn rupees
    ($3.45 bn).
    $1 = 8.83 rupees (1977), 8.55 rupees (1975).

Army: 950,000.
2 armd divs.
17 inf divs.
10 mountain divs.
5 indep armd bdes.
1 indep inf bde.
1 para bde.
14 indep arty bdes, incl about 20 AA arty regts,
    4 arty observation sqns and indep flts.
180 *Centurion* Mk 5/7, 900 T-54/-55/-62, some 700
    Vijayanta med, 150 PT-76 lt tks; 700 BTR-50/-
    152, OT-62/-64(2A) APC; about 2,000 75mm,
    76mm and 25-pdr (mostly towed), about 300
    100mm, 105mm (incl pack how) and *Abbot*
    105mm SP, 550 130mm, 5.5-in, 155mm guns/
    how; 500 120mm, 160mm mor; 57mm, 106mm
    RCL; SS-11 and *ENTAC* ATGW; 100mm ATK
    guns; ZSU-23-4 SP, 30mm, 40mm AA guns; 40
    Tigercat SAM; 40 *Krishak*, 20 *Auster* AOP9 lt ac;
    some *Alouette* III, 38 SA-315 *Cheetah* hel (75
    more on order).

RESERVES: 200,000. Territorial Army 40,000.

Navy: 46,000, incl Naval Air Force.
8 submarines (Soviet F-class).
1 aircraft carrier (capacity 25 ac, incl 12 *Sea Hawk*,
    4 *Alizé*, 2 *Alouette* III).
2 cruisers.
3 destroyers.
25 frigates (4 *Leander*-class with 2 *Seacat* SAM, 10
    Petya-class, 9 GP, 2 trg).
8 *Osa*-class FPBG with *Styx* SSM.
8 patrol boats (incl 5 *Poluchat*-class).
8 minesweepers (4 inshore).
1 landing ship, 6 landing craft (*Polnocny*-class).
(2 *Leander* frigates, 8 *Nanuchka* msl patrol ships,
    3 landing craft on order.)

NAVAL AIR FORCE: 2,000.
1 attack sqn with 25 *Sea Hawk* (10 in carrier).
1 MR sqn with 12 *Alizé* (4 in carrier).
1 MR sqn with 9 *Super Constellation*, 3 Il-38.
2 hel sqns with 22 *Alouette* III.
2 ASW sqns with 12 *Sea King* hel.
2 *Devon*, 7 HJT-16 *Kiran*, 5 BN *Islander*, 4 *Vampire*
    T55 ac, 4 Hughes 300 hel.
(5 *Sea King* ASW hel on order.)

Air Force: 100,000; about 670 combat aircraft.
3 lt bbr sqns with 50 *Canberra* B(I)58, B(1)12.
13 FGA sqns: 4 with 100 Su-7B, 4 with 50 HF-24
    Marut 1A, 5 with 65 *Hunter* F56.
10 interceptor sqns with 270 MiG-21F/PFMA/FL/
    MF.
8 interceptor sqns with 130 *Gnat* Mk 1.
1 recce sqn with 6 *Canberra* PR57.
11 tpt sqns: 1 with 12 Il-14; 1 with 16 HS-748,
    3 Tu-124; 2 with 32 C-119G; 2 with 30 An-12;
    1 with 29 *Otter*; 3 with 50 C-47; 1 with 14
    Caribou.
12 hel sqns: 6 with 100 Mi-4; 3 with 35 Mi-8; 3 with
    174 *Chetek* (*Alouette* III); 12 AB-47, 2 S-62.
Trainers incl *Mystère* IV, 110 *Kiran*, HT-2, *Hunter*,
    Canberra, 24 T-66, 14 MiG-21U, Su-7U, 32
    HS-748, 50 *Iskra.*
20 SAM sites with 120 SA-2.
(110 MiG-21MF, 100 *Ajeet* (*Gnat*), 10 HS-748, 10
    Marut Mk 1T, 40 *Iskra* ac, 45 *Chetek* hel on
    order.)

Para-Military Forces: About 200,000 Border
Security Force, 100,000 in other organizations.

INDONESIA

Population: 135,770,000.
Military service: selective.
Total armed forces: 247,000.
Estimated GNP 1975: $29.2 bn.
Defence expenditure 1977–78: 560 bn rupiahs
    ($1.35 bn).
    $1 = 415 rupiahs (1977), 415 rupiahs (1975).

Army: 180,000.*
1 armd cav bde (1 tk bn, support units).†
14 inf bdes (90 inf, 14 arty, 13 AA, 10 engr bns; 1 in
  KOSTRAD).
2 AB inf bdes (6 bns).†
5 fd arty regts.
4 AA arty regts.
Stuart, 150 AMX-13, 75 PT-76 lt tks; 75 *Saladin*
  armd, 55 *Ferret* scout cars; *Saracen*, 130 BTR-40/
  -152 APC; 50 76mm, 40 105mm, 122mm guns/how;
  200 120mm mor; *ENTAC* ATGW; 20mm, 40mm,
  200 57mm AA guns; 1 *Beaver*, 1 Beech 18, 2 C-47,
  2 Aero *Commander* 680, Cessna 185, Piper L-4,
  18 PZL *Wilga* 32 ac; 7 *Alouette* III hel.‡ (16
  AB-205 hel on order.)

DEPLOYMENT: *Egypt* (UNEF): 1 battalion, 510.

Navy: 39,000, incl Naval Air and 12,000 Marines.‡
3 submarines (ex-Soviet W-class).
11 frigates (3 ex-Soviet *Riga*-, 4 ex-US *Jones*-class).
23 coastal escorts (8 ex-Soviet *Kronstadt*-class).
12 *Komar*-class FPBG with *Styx* SSM.
44 patrol craft (2 under 100 tons).
15 MCM (incl ex-Soviet T-43-class, 6 ex-US).
3 comd/support ships.
10 amph vessels.
1 marine bde.
(2 Type 206 submarines, 3 corvettes, 5 minesweepers, 4 FPBG, 6 patrol boats, *Exocet* SSM on
  order.)

NAVAL AIR: 1,000.
5 HU-16, 6 C-47, 6 *Nomad* MR ac; 4 Bell 47G, 6
  Alouette II/III hel. (6 *Nomad* on order.)

Air Force: 28,000; 39 combat aircraft.§
2 FGA sqns with 16 CA-27 *Avon-Sabre*, 7 F-51D
  Mustang.
1 COIN sqn with 16 OV-10F.
61 tpts: 8 C-130B, 3 *Super Constellation*, 12 C-47,
  1 *Skyvan*, 8 F-27, 1 C-140 *Jetstar*, 7 Cessna 207/
  401/402, 18 *Gelatik*, 10 *Otter*, 6 CASA C-212.
2 hel sqns with 12 UH-34D, 5 Bell 204B, 4 *Alouette*
  III, 1 S-61A.
Trainers incl 4 T-6, 16 T-33, 20 T-34, *Airtourer*.
(2 *King Air* A-100, 21 *Musketeer*, 16 T-34, 22 CASA
  C-212 ac; 3 Bell 47G, 2 Bell 206B hel on order.)

Para-Military Forces: 12,000 Police Mobile bde;
  about 100,000 Militia.

---

* About one-third of the army is engaged in civil and
administrative duties.
† In KOSTRAD (Strategic Reserve Command).
‡ Some equipment and ships non-operational for lack
of spares.
§ Some aircraft non-operational for lack of spares. In
addition to the aircraft shown above, some 22 Tu-16,
10 Il-28, 40 MiG-15/-17, 35 MiG-19, 15 MiG-21, 10
Il-14, 10 An-12 ac, 20 Mi-4, 9 Mi-6 hel are in store.

JAPAN

Population: 114,010,000.
Military service: voluntary.
Total armed forces: 238,000.
Estimated GNP 1976: $567 bn.
Defence expenditure 1977–78: 1,691 bn yen
  ($6.10 bn).
  $1 = 277 yen (1977), 299 yen (1976).

Army: 155,000.
1 mech div.
12 inf divs (7–9,000 men each).
1 tk bde.
1 AB bde.
1 composite bde.
1 arty bde.
2 AA arty bdes.
1 sigs and 5 engr bdes.
8 SAM gps (each of 4 btys) with 190 *HAWK*.
1 hel wing and 34 aviation sqns.
560 Type 61, 150 Type 74 med, 130 M-41 lt
  tks; 430 Type SU 60, 70 Type 73 APC; M-2
  155mm guns; 360 M-2 105mm, 220 M-1 155mm,
  30 M-52 105mm SP, 10 M-44 155mm SP, 70
  203mm how; 550 107mm mor (some SP); 1,500
  57mm, 75mm, 106mm, 106mm SP RCL; Type 30
  SSM; Type 64, KAM-9 ATGW; 400 35mm twin,
  37mm, 40mm, 75mm, 90mm AA guns; *HAWK*
  SAM; 30 L-19, 20 LM-1/2, 10 LR-1 ac; 50 KV-
  107, 40 UH-1H, 80 UH-1B, 100 OH-6J, 3 H-13
  hel.
(2 LR-1 ac, 3 KV-107, 13 UH-1H, 10 OH-6J, 1 AH-
  1S hel on order.)

RESERVES: 39,000.

Navy: 40,000 (including Naval Air).
15 submarines.
30 destroyers (2 with 3 hel and *ASROC*; 1 with
  Tartar SAM, *ASROC*; 4 with 2 hel, *ASROC*; 8
  with 2 hel or *ASROC*; 1 with *Standard* SAM,
  ASROC; 14 GP).
15 frigates (11 with *ASROC*, 4 GP).
15 coastal escorts.
5 MTB.
9 coastal patrol craft (all under 100 tons).
37 MCM (1 tender, 1 minelayer, 29 coastal, 6 inshore).
5 LST.
(1 LST, 5 destroyers, 1 frigate, 2 submarines, 6 MCM
  on order.)

NAVAL AIR: 14,000.
11 MR sqns: with 110 P-2J, P2V-7, S-2A, 17 PS-1
7 hel sqns with 70 S-61A, KV-107A, HSS-2.
1 tpt sqn with 4 YS-11M, 1 S-2A.
5 SAR sqns with 3 US-1 ac, 1 S-61A, 8 S-62A hel.
Trainers incl 6 YS-11T, 5 TC-90, 30 B-65, 8 T-34,
  30 KM-2 ac; 7 Bell 47, 4 OH-6J hel.
(5 PS-1, 13 KM-2, 11 P-2J, 1 TC-90 ac, 14 HSS-2,
  2 S-61A hel on order; 1 P2V-7, 6 S-2A in store.)

RESERVES: 600.

Air Force: 43,000; 364 combat aircraft.
3 FGA sqns with 100 F-86F.
10 interceptor sqns: 6 with 160 F-104J; 4 with 90 F-4EJ.
1 recce sqn with 14 RF-4E.
3 tpt sqns with 10 YS-11, 22 C-1A.
1 SAR wing with 20 MU-2 ac, 21 KV-107, 7 S-62 hel.
220 trainers: incl T-1A/B, 25 T-2A, T-33, T-34, F-104DJ, 4 C-46.
5 SAM gps with *Nike-J* (6th forming).
A Base Defence Ground Environment with 28 control and warning units.
(43 F-4EJ, 44 F-1, 10 T-2, 18 T-3, 7 C-1, 2 MU-2, 2 MU-2J ac, 3 V-107 hel on order.)

KAMPUCHEA (CAMBODIA)

Population: 8,570,000.
Estimated GNP 1971: $1.5 bn.
Total armed forces: 90,000.

Army: The former Khmer Liberation Army, which was organized into some 4 divs and 3 indep regts, appears still to have the same strength it had at the end of hostilities in 1975, and none of the former regime's troops seem to have been incorporated into the structure. The forces are deployed in small detachments on internal security duties throughout the country. Their equipment, a mixture of Soviet, Chinese and American arms, includes: 10 BTR-152, 200 M-113 APC; 300 105mm, 122mm, 20 155mm guns/how; 107mm mor; 107mm RCL, 40mm AA guns.

Navy:* Some 150 small patrol, river and 6 landing craft.

Air Force:* Aircraft are thought to include some 10 AU-24 COIN, 9 C-47 and C-123 tpts, 15 T-51, 20 T-28 trainers, 25 UH-1H hel gunships. However, their condition is not known.

KOREA: DEMOCRATIC PEOPLE'S REPUBLIC (NORTH)

Population: 16,720,000.
Military service: Army, Navy 5 years, Air Force 3–4 years.
Total armed forces: 500,000.
Estimated GNP 1976: $8.9 bn.
Defence expenditure 1976: 2.06 bn won ($1 bn).†
　$1 = 2.05 won.

---

* May be part of the Army.
† It is uncertain whether this covers all defence expenditure, and there is no consensus on a suitable exchange rate for the dollar conversion.

Army: 430,000.
2 tk divs.
3 mot inf divs.
20 inf divs.
3 recce bdes.
12 indep inf and lt inf bdes.
3 AA arty bdes.
5 indep tk regts.
5 AB bns.
3 SSM regts with *FROG*.
20 arty regts.
10 AA arty regts.
350 T-34, 1,400 T-54/-55 and Type 59 med, 150 PT-76, 50 T-62 lt tks; 750 BTR-40/-50/-152, M-1967 APC; 3,000 guns and how up to 152mm; 1,200 RL; 9,000 120mm and 160mm mor; 1,500 82mm RCL; 57mm to 100mm ATK guns; 24 *FROG*-5/-7 SSM; 5,000 AA guns, incl ZSU-57-2 SP, 37mm, 57mm, 85mm, 100mm

Navy: 25,000.
10 submarines (ex-Soviet W-, ex-Chinese R-class).
7 frigates (1 building).
19 submarine chasers/escorts (15 ex-Soviet SO-1 class).
10 *Komar* and 8 *Osa*-class FPBG with *Styx* SSM.
100 MGB (incl 8 ex-Chinese *Shanghai*- and 8 *Swatow*-class).
150 MTB (incl 4 ex-Soviet *Shershen*, 12 P-4 and 60 P-6 class).
4 large patrol craft, 90 landing craft.

Air Force: 45,000; 630 combat aircraft.
3 lt bbr sqns with 80 Il-28.
13 FGA sqns with 20 Su-7 and 300 MiG-15/-17.
10 fighter sqns with 130 MiG-21 and 100 MiG-19.
225 tpts, incl An-2, An-24, Il-14/-18, Tu-154.
Hel incl 30 Mi-4, 20 Mi-8.
Trainers incl Yak-11/-18, MiG-15/-21UTI, Il-28U.
3 SAM bdes with 250 SA-2.

Para-Military Forces: 40,000 security forces and border guards; civilian militia of 1,000,000 to 2,000,000 with small arms, some AA arty.

KOREA: REPUBLIC OF (SOUTH)

Population: 35,200,000.
Military service: Army and Marines 2½ years, Navy and Air Force 3 years.
Total armed forces: 635,000.
Estimated GNP 1975: $18.4 bn.
Defence expenditure 1977: 871 bn won ($1.8 bn).
　$1 = 484 won (1977), 491 won (1975).

Army: 560,000.
1 mech div.
19 inf divs.
2 armd bdes.

5 special forces bdes.
2 AD bdes.
7 tk bns.
30 arty bns.
1 SSM bn with *Honest John*.
2 SAM bdes with *HAWK* and *Nike Hercules*.
M-60, 880 M-47/-48 med tks; 500 M-113/-577 APC;
2,000 105mm, 155mm, 175mm, 203mm towed
and SP guns/how; 3,000 82mm, 107mm mor;
M-18 SP ATK guns; 57mm, 75mm, 106mm RCL;
TOW, LAW ATGW; *Honest John* SSM; 40mm AA
guns; 80 *HAWK*, 40 *Nike Hercules* SAM; 5 KH-4
hel. (100 OH-6A hel on order.)

RESERVES: 1,100,000.

Navy: 25,000.
7 destroyers (*Gearing-, Sumner-, Fletcher*-class).
9 destroyer escorts (6 escort transports).
14 coastal escorts.
44 patrol boats (under 100 tons).
1 FPBG.
12 coastal minesweepers.
21 landing ships (8 LST, 1 dock, 11 med, 1 utility).
70 amph craft.
(7 FPBG, 120 *Harpoon* SSM on order.)

RESERVES: 25,000.

Marines: 20,000; 1 div, 2 bdes.

RESERVES: 60,000.

Air Force: 30,000; 335 combat aircraft.
11 FB sqns with 33 F-4D/E, 270 F-5A/E, F-86D/F,
AT-33.
1 recce sqn with 12 RF-5A.
1 ASW sqn with 20 S-2F.
Tpts incl 20 C-46, 12 C-54, 12 C-123, 2 HS-748,
Aero *Commander*.
Trainers incl 20 T-28D, 30 T-33A, 20 T-41D, 35
F-5B.
6 UH-19, 5 UH-1D, 2 Bell 212 hel.
(24 OV-10G COIN ac, *Sidewinder* AAM on order.)

RESERVES: 55,000.

Para-Military Forces: A local defence militia,
1,000,000 Homeland Defence Reserve Force.

LAOS

Population: 3,500,000.
Military service: conscription, term unknown.
Total armed forces: 48,550.
Estimated GNP 1972: $211 m.
Defence expenditure 1974–75: 16 bn kip ($27 m).
$1 = 600 kip (1974), 500 kip (1972).

Army: (Lao People's Liberation Army): 46,000.*
100 inf bns (under Military Regions).
Supporting arms and services.
M-24, PT-76 lt tks; BTR-40, M-113 APC; 75mm,
85mm, 105mm, 155mm how; 81mm, 82mm,
4.2-in mor; 107mm RCL; 4 Cessna U-17A lt ac.

Navy: About 550.
20 river patrol craft.
14 landing craft/tpts (all under 100 tons).

Air Force: 2,000; 45 combat aircraft.†
40 T-28A/D COIN aircraft.
5 AC-47 gunships.
Tpts incl 10 C-47, 10 C-123, 6 An-24, 1 Aero
Commander, 1 *Beaver*.
6 T-41D trainers.
6 *Alouette* II/III, 42 UH-34, Mi-8 hel.

MALAYSIA

Population: 13,340,000.
Military service: voluntary.
Total armed forces: 64,000.
Estimated GNP 1976: $US 8.6 bn.
Defence expenditure 1977: $M 1.35 bn
($US 544 m).
$1 = $M 2.48 (1977), $M 2.55 (1976).

Army: 52,500.
2 div HQ.
9 inf bdes, consisting of:
29 inf bns.
3 recce regts.
3 arty regts, 2 AD btys.
1 special service unit.
5 engr, 4 sigs regts and administrative units.
200 *Commando*, 140 Panhard, M-3 armd, 60 *Ferret*
scout cars, 80 105mm how; 120mm RCL; 35
40mm AA guns. (132 *Commando*, 12 105mm how
on order.)

RESERVES: About 26,000.

Navy: 5,500.
2 frigates (1 ASW with *Seacat* SAM, 1 training).
8 FPBG (4 with SS-12, 4 with *Exocet* SSM.
27 patrol craft.
6 coastal minesweepers.
3 LST (2 on order).
(10 FPBG, 4 *Spica* MTB, *Exocet* SSM on order.)

RESERVES: 1,000.

Air Force: 6,000; 34 combat aircraft.
1 FB sqn with 14 F-5E.
2 COIN sqns with 20 CL-41G *Tebuan*.

---

* The Royal Lao Army has been disbanded; some men
may have been absorbed into the Liberation Army.
† Most aircraft inherited from the Royal Lao Air Force;
degree of serviceability unknown.

4 tpt, 1 liaison sqns with 6 C-130H, 17 DHC-4A, 5
 Dove, 3 *Heron,* 2 HS-125, 2 F-28-100, 12 Cessna
 402B.
4 hel sqns with 21 S-61A-4, 30 *Alouette* III, 12 Bell
 47G, 5 Bell 206B, AB-212.
1 trg sqn with 2 F-5B, 15 *Bulldog* 102, 4 Cessna
 402B.
(20 *Gazelle* hel on order.)

Para-Military Forces: Police Field Force of 13,000,
 17 bns, 40 patrol boats; People's Volunteer
 Corps over 200,000.

MONGOLIA

Population: 1,535,000.
Military service: 2 years.
Total armed forces: 30,000.
Estimated GNP 1974: $2.8 bn.
Defence expenditure 1977: 405 m tugrik ($120.5 m).
 $1 = 3.36 tugrik (1977), 4.00 tugrik (1974).

Army: 28,000.
2 inf bdes.
1 construction bde.
30 T-34, 100 T-54/-55 med tks; 40 BTR-60, 50 BTR-
 152 APC; 76mm, 100mm, 130mm, 152mm guns/
 how; 10 SU-100 SP guns; *Snapper* ATGW; 37mm,
 57mm AA guns.

RESERVES: 30,000.

Air Force: 2,000;* 10 combat aircraft.
1 fighter sqn with 10 MiG-15.
20 An-2, 6 Il-14, 4 An-24 tpts.
10 Mi-1 and Mi-4 hel.
Yak-11/-18 trainers.
1 SAM bn with SA-2.

Para-Military Forces: about 18,000 frontier guards
 and security police.

NEPAL

Population: 13,185,000.
Military service: voluntary.
Total armed forces: 20,000.
Estimated GNP 1972: $1.0 bn.
Defence expenditure 1975: 146 m rupees ($13.2 m).
 $1 = 11.05 rupees (1975), 10.1 rupees (1972).

Army: 20,000.†
5 inf bdes (1 Palace Guard).
1 para bn.

---

* Excluding expatriate personnel.
† There is no Air Force: the 70-man Army Air Flight
Department operates the aircraft.

1 arty regt.
1 engr regt.
1 sigs regt.
AMX-13 lt tks, 4 3.7-in pack how; 4 4.2-in, 18
 120mm mor; 2 40mm AA guns; 2 *Skyvan,* 3
 DHC-3, 1 HS-748 tpts; 3 *Alouette* III, 2 *Puma* hel.

Para-Military Forces: 12,000 Nepalese Police
 Force.

NEW ZEALAND

Population: 3,200,000.
Military service: voluntary, supplemented by
 Territorial service of 12 weeks for the Army.
Total armed forces: 12,466.
Estimated GNP 1977: $US 12.56 bn.
Defence expenditure 1976–77: $NZ 221 m
 ($US 210.5 m).
 $1 = $NZ 1.05 (1977), $NZ 0.99 (1976).

Army: 5,457.
2 inf bns.
1 arty bty.
Regular troops also form the nucleus of 2 bde gps
 and a log gp; these would be completed by
 mobilization of Territorials.
7 M-41 lt tks; 8 *Ferret* scout cars; 55 M-113 APC;
 17 25-pdr, 10 5.5-in guns; 28 105mm how; 23
 106mm RCL.

DEPLOYMENT: *Singapore:* 1 inf bn with log support.

RESERVES: 1,540 Regular, 5,834 Territorial.

Navy: 2,741.
4 frigates with *Seacat* SAM (2 Type 12, 2 *Leander*-
 class with *Wasp* hel).
4 patrol craft (under 100 tons).
1 survey ship.

DEPLOYMENT: 1–2 frigates in Pacific area.

RESERVES: 3,250 Regular, 302 Territorial.

Air Force: 4,268; 34 combat aircraft.
1 FB sqn with 10 A-4K, 3 TA-4K *Skyhawk.*
1 FB/trg sqn with 16 BAC-167.
1 MR sqn with 5 P-3B *Orion.*
3 med tpt sqns with 5 C-130H, 3 *Devon,* 10 *Andover,*
 3 Bristol *Freighter.*
1 tpt hel sqn with 8 Bell 47G, 2 *Wasp,* 10 UH-1D/H.
Trainers: 6 *Devon,* 13 *Airtrainer,* 4 *Airtourer* ac,
 4 *Sioux* hel.
(6 *Airtrainer* trainers on order.)

DEPLOYMENT: *Singapore:* 1 tpt sqn (3 Bristol
 Freighter tpts, 4 UH-1 hel).

RESERVES: 1,090 Regular, 139 Territorial.

PAKISTAN

Population: 74,190,000.
Military service: voluntary.
Total armed forces: 428,000.
Estimated GNP 1975: $10.1 bn.
Defence expenditure 1977–78: 8.1 bn rupees
    ($819 m).
    $1 = 9.89 rupees (1977), 9.72 rupees (1975).

Army: 400,000 (incl 29,000 *Azad Kashmir* troops).
2 armd divs.
14 inf divs.
3 indep armd bdes.
3 indep inf bdes.
2 AD bdes.
5 army aviation sqns.
M-4, 250 M-47/-48, 50 T-55, 700 T-59 med, PT-76,
    50 M-24 lt tks; 550 M-113 APC; about 1,000 25-
    pdr, 100mm, 105mm, 130mm and 155mm guns/
    how; 270 107mm, 120mm mor; 6-pdr ATK guns;
    75mm, 106mm RCL; *Cobra* ATGW; 37mm,
    40mm, 57mm, 3.7-in AA guns; *Crotale* SAM; 50
    O-1E, 45 Saab *Supporter* lt ac; 12 Mi-8, 20
    Alouette III, 20 Bell 47G hel. (35 *Puma* hel on
    order.)

RESERVES: 500,000.

Navy: 11,000.
3 submarines (*Daphne*-class, 1 on order).
5 SX-404 midget submarines.
1 lt cruiser (trg ship).
4 destroyers (1 ex-British *Battle*-, 1 CH-, 2 CR-
    classes).
1 frigate (ex-British Type 16).
19 patrol boats (ex-Chinese, 6 *Hu Chwan* hydrofoil,
    12 *Shanghai*-class).
7 coastal minesweepers.
2 UH-19, 4 *Alouette* III, 6 *Sea King* SAR hel.

RESERVES: 5,000.

Air Force: 17,000; 247 combat aircraft.
1 lt bbr sqn with 11 B-57B.
4 fighter sqns with 30 *Mirage* IIIEP/DP, 28 VPA.
8 FGA sqns with 60 F-86, 100 MiG-19/F-6.
1 recce sqn with 13 *Mirage* IIIRP.
1 MR sqn with 3 *Atlantic*, 2 HU-16B.
Tpts incl 12 C-130B, 1 L-100, 1 *Falcon* 20, 1 F-27.
10 CH-47, 10 HH-43B, 14 *Alouette* III, 1 *Puma*,
    12 Bell 47 hel.
Trainers incl 15 Saab *Supporter*, 26 T-33, 40 T-37.
(10 *Mirage* VPA fighters, 4 *Super Frelon* hel,
    Sidewinder AAM on order.)

RESERVES: 8,000.

Para-Military Forces: 157,000: 60,000 Civil Armed
    Forces, 22,000 National Guard, 20,000 Federal
    Security Forces, 40,000 Frontier Corps, 15,000
    Pakistan Rangers.

PHILIPPINES

Population: 45,295,000.
Military service: selective.
Total armed forces: 99,000.
Estimated GNP 1976: $16.5 bn.
Defence expenditure 1977–78: 3.08 bn pesos
    ($419 m).
    $1 = 7.35 pesos (1977), 7.43 pesos (1976).

Army: 63,000.
4 lt inf divs.
1 indep inf bde.
21 *Scorpion*, 7 M-41 lt tks; 35 M-113 APC; 100
    105mm, 5 155mm how; 40 4.2in mor; 75mm,
    106mm RCL; *HAWK* SAM. (33 M-113 on order.)

RESERVES: 17,000.

Navy: 20,000 (7,000 Marines and naval engrs).
7 frigates.
3 destroyer escorts.
22 patrol craft.
24 inshore patrol craft (under 100 tons).
4 minesweepers.
2 command ships.
33 landing craft (22 LST, 5 med).
1 SAR sqn with 10 *Islander*.
6 marine bns.

RESERVES: 12,000.

Air Force: 16,000; 104 combat aircraft.
2 FGA sqns with 20 F-5A/B.
2 fighter/trg sqns with 20 F-86F.
2 COIN sqns with 16 SF-260WP, 36 T-28A/D.
1 gunship sqn with 12 AC-47.
1 SAR sqn with 6 HU-16 ac, UH-19, 3 SH-34G, 12
    UH-1H, H-13, Hughes 300 hel.
1 hel sqn with 18 UH-1H.
6 tpt sqns with 9 C-130H, 30 C-47, 9 F-27, 4 L-100-
    20, 4 YS-11, 15 C-123K, 12 *Nomad*.
1 liaison sqn with O-1E, Cessna 180, U-17A/B,
    Cessna 310K, 21 *Beaver*.
Other hel incl 12 UH-1D, 8 FH-1100, 5 UH-19,
    2 H-34, 2 S-62.
Trainers incl 3 F-5B, 12 T-28A, 12 T-33, 17 T-34,
    10 T-41D, 32 SF-260MP.
(11 F-5E FGA, 38 BO-105, 17 UH-1 hel on order.)

RESERVES: 16,000.

Para-Military Forces: 65,000: 40,000 Philippine
    Constabulary, 25,000 Local Self-Defence Force.

SINGAPORE

Population, 2,340,000.
Military service: 24–36 months.
Total armed forces: 36,000.
Estimated GNP 1975: $US 6.5 bn.

Defence expenditure 1976–77: \$S 840 m
  (\$US 340 m).
  \$US 1 = \$S 2.47 (1976), \$S 2.28 (1975).

Army: 30,000.
1 armd bde (1 tk, 2 APC bns).
3 inf bdes (9 inf, 3 arty, 3 engr, 3 sigs bns).
75 AMX-13 tks; 250 V-200 *Commando*, 250 M-113
  APC; some 6 25-pdr, 20 155mm guns/how; 50
  120mm mor; 90 106mm RCL. (155mm how on
  order.)

RESERVES: 45,000, 18 reserve battalions.

Navy: 3,000.
6 FPBG (*Jaguar*-class with *Gabriel* SSM).
6 MGB.
5 patrol craft (4 under 100 tons).
2 coastal minesweepers.
4 ex-US LST and 4 landing craft.
(2 minesweepers, 6 landing craft on order.)

Air Force: 3,000; 92 combat aircraft.
2 FGA/recce sqns with 32 *Hunter* FGA/FR74/T75.
3 FGA sqns with 40 A-4S.
1 COIN/trg sqn with 20 BAC-167.
2 tpt/SAR sqns: 1 with 6 *Airtourer*, 1 with 6 *Skyvan*.
1 SAR hel sqn with 8 *Alouette* III, 3 AB-212.
Hel incl 15 UH-1H.
Trainers incl 4 T-66, 16 SF-260MS, 6 TA-4S.
2 SAM sqns: 1 with 28 *Bloodhound*, 1 with *Rapier*.
(21 F-5E/F FGA, 200 *Sidewinder* AAM on order.)

Para-Military Forces: 7,500 police/marine police;
  Gurkha guard units; Home Guard 30,000.

SRI LANKA (CEYLON)

Population: 14,650,000.
Military service: voluntary.
Total armed forces: 13,300.
Estimated GNP 1976: \$2.8 bn.
Defence expenditure 1977: 352.1 m rupees (\$48.4 m).
  \$1 = 7.28 rupees (1977), 8.56 rupees (1976).

Army: 8,900.
1 bde of 3 bns.
1 recce regt.
1 arty regt.
1 engr regt.
1 sigs regt.
6 *Saladin* armd cars, 30 *Ferret* scout cars; 10 BTR-
  152 APC; 76mm, 85mm, 105mm how.

RESERVES: 12,000; 7 bns and a Pioneer Corps.

Navy: 2,400.
1 frigate (ex-Canadian *River*-class).
5 fast gunboats (ex-Chinese *Shanghai*-class).
23 coastal patrol craft.

Air Force: 2,000; 10 combat aircraft.
1 FGA sqn with 5 MiG-17F, 1 MiG-15UTI, 4 *Jet
  Provost* Mk 51.
1 tpt sqn with 2 Riley, 2 *Heron*, 2 DC-3, 1 CV-440.
1 comms sqn with 4 Cessna 337.
1 hel sqn with 7 AB-206, 2 Ka-26, 6 Bell 47G.
3 Cessna 150, 7 *Chipmunk*, 4 *Dove* trainers.

RESERVES: 750; 4 sqns Air Force Regt, 1 sqn Airfield Construction Regt.

Para-Military Forces: 14,500 Police Force, 4,500
  Volunteer Force.

THAILAND

Population: 45,090,000.
Military service: 2 years.
Total armed forces: 211,000.
Estimated GNP 1975: \$14.7 bn.
Defence expenditure 1976–77: 13.1 bn baht
  (\$639 m).
  \$1 = 20.5 baht (1976), 20.6 baht (1975).

Army: 141,000.
1 cav div.
6 inf divs (incl 4 tk bns).
3 indep regimental combat teams.
4 AB and special forces bns.
1 SAM bn with *HAWK*.
5 aviation coys and some flts.
20 M-24, 150 M-41 lt tks; 20 *Saracen* armd cars;
  250 M-113, LVTP-7 APC; 300 105mm, 50 155mm
  how; 57mm, 106mm RCL; 40mm AA guns; 40
  HAWK SAM; 90 O-1 lt ac; 120 UH-1B/D, 4
  CH-47, 24 OH-13, 16 FH-1100, 3 Bell 206, 2 Bell
  212, 6 OH-23F, 28 KH-4 hel. (24 how, 80 APC
  and armd cars on order.)

RESERVES: 500,000.

Navy: 28,000 (7,000 Marines).
7 frigates (1 with *Seacat* SAM).
14 patrol vessels.
3 FPBG with *Gabriel* SSM.
18 mine warfare ships.
28 river patrol boats.
30 coastal gunboats (29 under 100 tons).
5 LST (1 trg ship), 15 landing craft.
1 MR sqn with 10 S-2F *Tracker*, 2 HU 16B *Albatross*.
1 Marine bde (3 inf, 1 arty bns).
(24 patrol craft, *Exocet* SSM on order.)

Air Force: 42,000; 184 combat aircraft.
1 FGA sqn with 12 F-5A/E, 2 F-5B.
7 COIN sqns with 45 T-28D, 20 T-6G 32 OV-10C, 16
  A-37B, 32 AU-23A *Peacemaker*.
1 recce sqn with 17 T-33, 4 RT-33A, 4 RF-5A.
1 utility sqn with 25 O-1 lt ac.
3 tpt sqns with 20 C-47, 30 C-123B, 2 HS-748, 1
  Islander, 3 *Skyvan*, 10 *Turbo-Porter*.

2 hel sqns with 20 CH-34C, 30 UH-1H.
Trainers incl, 15 *Chipmunk*, 14 T-33A, 14 T-37B, 10 T-41, 12 SF-260, 15 CT-4.
4 bns of airfield defence troops.
(16 F-5E/F FGA, 4 CASA C-212 tpts, 18 *Sidewinder* AAM on order.)

Para-Military Forces: 52,000 Volunteer Defence Corps, 14,000 Border Police, hel and lt ac.

VIETNAM: SOCIALIST REPUBLIC OF*

Population: 46,855,000.
Military service: 2 years minimum.
Total armed forces: 615,000.

Army: 600,000.
25 inf divs,† 2 trg divs.
1 arty comd (of 10 regts).
1 engr comd.
About 15 indep inf regts.
20 SAM regts (each with 18 SA-2 launchers).

---

* Equipment of the former forces of South Vietnam are not included above. It is estimated to have included up to 550 M-48 med and M-41 lt tks; 1,200 M-113 APC; 1,330 105mm and 155mm guns/how (some SP); 2 frigates; 2 patrol vessels; 42 patrol gunboats; 13 landing ships; 17 landing craft; 800 riverine craft; 11 support vessels; 1,000 ac of all types, incl 73 F-5A, 95 A-37B, 10 C-130, 25 A-1H/J, 37 AC-119C/K, 10 AC-47, 114 O-1, 33 *Beaver*, 13 C-47; 36 CH-47, 434 UH-1 hel.
† Inf divs, normally totalling 8–10,000 men, include 1 tk bn, 3 inf, 1 arty regts, and support elements.

50 AA arty regts.
15 indep engr regts.
900 T-34, T-54 and T-59 med, PT-76, Type 60 lt tks; BTR-40/-60 APC; SU-76, ISU-122 SP guns; 85mm, 100mm, 105mm, 122mm, 130mm, 152mm, 155mm guns/how; 82mm, 100mm, 107mm, 120mm, 160mm mor; 107mm, 122mm, 140mm RL; *Sagger* ATGW; 23mm, 37mm, 57mm, 85mm, 100mm towed, ZSU-23-4, ZSU-57-2 SP AA guns; SA-2, SA-3, SA-6, SA-7 SAM.

DEPLOYMENT: 40,000 in Laos (numbers fluctuate).

Navy: 3,000.
3 coastal escorts (ex-Soviet SO-1 type).
3 *Komar*-class FPBG with *Styx* SSM.
22 MGB (*Shanghai*- and *Swatow*-class).
4 MTB (ex-Soviet P-4-, P-6-classes).
About 30 small patrol boats (under 100 tons).
Some 20 landing craft.
10 Mi-4 SAR hel.

Air Force: 12,000; 310 combat aircraft.
1 lt bbr sqn with 10 Il-28.
8 FGA sqns with 120 MiG-15/-17, 30 Su-7.
6 interceptor sqns with 80 MiG-19, 70 MiG-21.
20 An-2, 4 An-24, 12 Il-14, 1 Il-18, 20 Li-2 tpts.
20 Mi-4, 10 Mi-6, 9 Mi-8 hel.
About 30 trainers incl Yak-11/-18, MiG-15/21 UTI.

Para-Military Forces: 70,000 Frontier, Coast Security and People's Armed Security Forces; Armed Militia of about 1,500,000.

Latin America

Continental Treaties and Agreements

In March and April 1945 the Act of Chapultepec was signed by Argentina, Bolivia, Brazil, Chile, Colombia, Costa Rica, Cuba, the Dominican Republic, Ecuador, Guatemala, Haiti, Honduras, Mexico, Nicaragua, Panama, Paraguay, Peru, the United States, Uruguay and Venezuela. This Act declared that any attack upon a member party would be considered an attack upon all and provided for the collective use of armed force to prevent or repel such aggression.

In September 1947 all the parties to the Chapultepec Act – except Ecuador and Nicaragua – signed the Inter-American Treaty of Reciprocal Assistance, otherwise known as the Rio Defence Treaty (Cuba withdrew from the Treaty in March 1960). This Treaty constrained signatories to the peaceful settlement of disputes among themselves and provided for collective self-defence should any member party be subject to external attack.

The Charter of the Organization of American States (OAS), drawn up in 1948, embraced declarations based upon the Rio Defence Treaty. The member parties – the signatories to the Act of Chapultepec plus Barbados, El Salvador, Jamaica and Trinidad and Tobago – are bound to peaceful settlement of internal disputes and to collective action in the event of external attack upon one or more signatory states.*

The United States is also a party to two multilateral defence treaties: the Act of Havana (1940), signed by representatives of all of the then 21 American Republics, which provides for the collective trusteeship by American nations of European colonies and possessions in the Americas should any attempt be made to transfer the sovereignty of these colonies from one non-American power to another; and the Havana Convention, which corresponds with the Act of Havana, signed in 1940 by the same states, with the exception of Bolivia, Chile, Cuba and Uruguay.

A Treaty for the Prohibition of Nuclear Weapons in Latin America (The Tlatelolco Treaty) was signed in February 1967 by 22 Latin American countries; 20 countries have now ratified it (Argentina has signed but not ratified, and Brazil has ratified but reserved her position on peaceful nuclear explosions). Britain and the Netherlands have ratified it for the territories within the Treaty area for which they are internationally responsible. Britain and the Netherlands have signed Protocol I (which commits states outside the region to accept, for their territories within it, the Treaty restrictions regarding the emplacement or storage of nuclear weapons); France has not; the United States has announced her intention of doing so. The United States, Britain, France and China have signed Protocol II to the Treaty (an undertaking not to use or threaten to use nuclear weapons against the parties to the Treaty); the Soviet Union has not. An Agency has been set up by the contracting parties to ensure compliance with the Treaty.

Other Agreements

In July 1965, El Salvador, Guatemala, Honduras and Nicaragua agreed to form a military bloc for the co-ordination of all resistance against possible Communist aggression.

The United States has bilateral military assistance agreements or representation with Argentina, Bolivia, Brazil, Chile, Colombia, the Dominican Republic, El Salvador, Guatemala, Honduras, Mexico, Nicaragua, Panama, Paraguay, Peru, Uruguay and Venezuela. She has a bilateral agreement with Cuba for jurisdiction and control over Guantánamo Bay.† She also has a treaty with the Republic of Panama granting her, in perpetuity, full sovereign rights over the Canal Zone, but negotiations on its revision are at an advanced stage.

The Soviet Union has no defence agreements with any of the states in this area, although she has supplied military equipment to Cuba and Peru.

---

* Legally, Cuba is a member of the OAS but has been excluded – by a decision of OAS Foreign Ministers – since January 1962. Barbados and Trinidad and Tobago signed the Charter in 1967.
† This agreement was confirmed in 1934. In 1960 the United States stated that it could be modified or abrogated only by agreement between the parties, and that she had no intention of agreeing to modification or abrogation.

ARGENTINA

Population: 26,045,000.
Military service: Army and Air Force 1 year,
 Navy 14 months.
Total armed forces: 129,900.
Estimated GNP 1976: $52.1 bn.*
Defence expenditure 1977: 466.24 bn pesos
 ($1.42 bn).*
 $1 = 329 pesos (1977), 149 pesos (1976).

Army: 80,000.
1 armd bde.
1 mech bde.
3 mot inf bdes.
4 inf bdes.
2 mountain bdes.
1 airmobile bde.
5 AD bns.
1 aviation bn.
200 M-4 *Sherman* med, 120 AMX-13 lt tks; 140
 M-113, 150 Mowag, AMX-VCI, M-3, M-16 APC;
 200 105mm and 155mm guns; 105mm pack,
 155mm towed, 24 French Mk F3, some US M-7
 155mm SP how; 120mm mor; 75mm, 90mm,
 105mm RCL; SS-11/-12, *Bantam*, *Cobra* ATGW;
 35mm, 40mm, 90mm AA guns; *Tigercat* SAM; 4
 Turbo Navajo, 2 DHC-6, 2 G-222, 1 *Queen Air*,
 1 *Sabreliner*, 5 Cessna 207, 5 T-41 ac; 7 AB-206,
 7 FH-1100, 20 UH-IH, Bell 47G, 2 Bell 212 hel.
 (5 *Turbo Commander*, 1 G-222, 4 Swearingen
 Metro IIIA on order.)

RESERVES: 250,000: 200,000 National Guard,
 50,000 Territorial Guard.

Navy: 32,900, incl Naval Air Force and Marines.
4 submarines (2 Type 209, 2 ex-US *Guppy*-class).
1 aircraft carrier (15 S-2A/A-4Q/SH-3D).
2 cruisers with *Seacat* SAM, 2 hel.
10 destroyers (2 Type 42 with *Sea Dart* SAM, 5
 Fletcher-class, 3 ex-US).
11 patrol vessels (2 trg, 1 coastguard).
5 large patrol craft (3 in coastguard).
6 coastal minesweepers/minehunters.
2 FPB.
5 landing ships, 28 landing craft (1 LCT).
(6 Type 21 frigates, 2 Type 148 FPBG, *Exocet* SSM,
 Sea Dart SAM on order.)

NAVAL AIR FORCE: 4,000; 60 combat aircraft.
1 FB sqn with 14 A-4Q *Skyhawk*.
2 FB/trg sqns with 8 MB-326GB, 28 T-28.
1 MR sqn with 6 S-2A, 4 P-2H, PBY-5A *Catalina*.
1 SAR sqn with 3 HU-16B *Albatross*.
1 ASW/SAR sqn with 9 *Alouette* III, 4 S-61D hel.
Tpts incl 3 C-45, 8 C-47, 3 C-54, 3 *Electra*, 2 DC-4,
 1 *Guarani* II, 1 HS-125, 3 *Beaver*, 1 DHC-6, 2
 Super King Air 200, 15 Cessna U-17A.

---

* Rapid inflation makes defence expenditure and GNP
figures in local currency and dollar terms unreliable.

Hel incl 5 S-55, 6 Bell 47G (3 *Lynx* on order).
Trainers incl 12 T-6, AT-11.

MARINES: 7,000.
5 bns.
1 cdo bn.
1 fd arty bn.
1 AD regt.
1 engr bn.
1 sigs bn.
7 indep inf coys.
20 LVTP-7, 15 LARC-5 APC; 105mm how; 106mm,
 120mm mor; 75mm, 105mm RCL; *Bantam* ATGW;
 88mm AA guns; 10 *Tigercat* SAM.

Air Force: 17,000; 146 combat aircraft.
1 bbr sqn with 9 *Canberra* B62 and 2 T64.
2 FB sqns with 45 A-4P *Skyhawk*.
1 interceptor sqn with 12 *Mirage* IIIEA, 2 IIIDA.
3 FGA sqns with 16 MS-760A *Paris* I, 25 A-4P.
1 COIN sqn with 15 IA-58 *Pucará*.
1 recce sqn with 20 IA-35 *Huanquero*.
1 hel sqn with 14 Hughes 500M, 6 Bell UH-1H.
1 SAR sqn with 3 HU-16B ac, 6 *Lama* hel.
Tpts incl 1 Boeing 707-320B, 7 C-130E/H, 1
 Sabreliner, 1 HS-748, 8 F-27, 6 F-28, 10 C-47,
 7 DHC-6, 22 IA-50 *Guarani* II, 4 *Commander*, 14
 Shrike Commander.
Hel incl 2 S-61NR, 1 S-61R, 12 UH-1D/F, 6 UH-
 19, 4 Bell 47G.
Trainers incl 35 T-34, 12 MS-760, *Mirage*, *Can-*
 berra.
(15 *Pucará* COIN, 2 *Merlin* IVA, 16 *Turbo Com-*
 mander tpts on order.)

Para-Military Forces: 42,000. Gendarmerie: 11,000;
 M-113 APC, 20 lt ac, 10 hel under Army command, mainly for frontier duties. National Maritime Prefecture: 9,000. *Policia Federal:* 22,000;
 APC, 4 BO-105 hel.

BOLIVIA

Population: 5,910,000.
Military service: 12 months selective.
Total armed forces: 22,500.
Estimated GNP 1976: $2.5 bn.
Defence expenditure 1977: 1.5 bn pesos ($74.2 m).
 $1 = 20.2 pesos (1977), 20 pesos (1976).

Army: 17,000.
4 cav regts.
1 mech regt.
1 mot regt.
13 inf regts (1 Palace Guard).
2 ranger regts.
1 para bn.
3 arty regts.
6 engr bns.

10 *Commando* armd cars; 10 M-706, 18 M-113, 20
Mowag APC; 6 75mm guns; 25 75mm pack, 20
FH-18, 25 M-101 105mm how.

Navy: 1,500.
16 small patrol craft.
1 river transport.

Air Force: 4,000; 45 combat aircraft.
1 fighter/trg sqn with 12 T-33A/N, 4 F-86F.
3 COIN sqns with 10 F-51D *Mustang*, 13 AT-26D
Xavante, 6 T-28A/D.
Tpts incl 1 C-130H, 1 *Electra*, 2 C-54, 1 *Learjet*, 6
Arava, 4 CV-440, 12 C-47, C-45, 2 Cessna 402, 1
Turbo-Porter, 2 *Turbo Centurion*, 15 Cessna 185.
1 hel sqn with 12 Hughes 500M, 3 Hiller OH-23C/D.
Trainers incl Cessna 310, 10 T-6, 6 T-41D, 18
T-23 *Uirapuru*, 8 Fokker S-11.
(1 *Arava*, 1 C-130H tpts on order.)

BRAZIL

Population: 113,240,000.
Military service: 1 year.
Total armed forces: 271,800 (113,000 conscripts).
Estimated GNP 1976: $131 bn.
Defence expenditure 1977: 26.95 bn cruzeiros
($2.07 bn).
$1 = 13.0 cruzeiros (1977), 10.3 cruzeiros (1976).

Army: 180,000 (110,000 conscripts).
8 divs: each up to 4 armd, mech or mot inf bdes.
2 indep inf bdes.
1 indep para bde.
5 lt 'jungle' inf bns.
60 M-4 med, 220 M-3A1, 250 M-41, 25 X-1 lt tks;
120 *Cascavel*, M-8 armd cars; *Urutu*, M-59, 600
M-113 APC; 500 75mm pack, 450 105mm (some
SP), 90 155mm how; 108-R, 114mm RL; 106mm
RCL; *Cobra* ATGW; 40mm, 90mm AA guns; 40
Neiva L-42 *Regente*, O-1E lt ac; 10 AB-206A hel.
(4 *Roland* SAM on order.)

Navy: 49,000 (3,000 conscripts, 13,500 Naval Air
Force, Marines and Auxiliary Corps).
8 submarines (1 *Oberon*-, 7 *Guppy* II/III-class).
1 aircraft carrier.
12 destroyers (1 with *Seacat* SAM).
2 frigates (with *Exocet* SSM, *Seacat* SAM, 1 hel).
10 corvettes (fleet tugs).
5 river patrol ships, 1 river monitor.
6 gunboats.
6 coastal minesweepers.
2 coastal auxiliaries, 2 LST, 39 small landing craft.
(2 *Oberon* submarines, 4 frigates on order.)

NAVAL AIR FORCE:
1 ASW sqn with 5 SH-3D *Sea King*.
1 utility sqn with 5 *Whirlwind*, 4 *Wasp*, 4 FH-1100,
2 Bell 47G, 18 AB-206B.

1 trg sqn with 10 *Hughes* 269/300.
(16 EMB-111 MR ac, 9 *Lynx* hel on order.)

Air Force: 42,800; 131 combat aircraft.
1 interceptor sqn with 11 *Mirage* IIIEBR, 4 DBR.
2 FGA sqns with 33 F-5E.
7 COIN/recce sqns with 60 AT-26 *Xavante* ac, 5
UH-1D, 4 Bell 206, 4 OH-6A hel.
1 ASW sqn with 8 S-2A, 8 S2-E (6 in carrier).
1 MR sqn with 7 P-2E *Neptune*.
3 SAR sqns with 12 SA-16 *Albatross*, 3 RC-130E,
5 SH-1D, 36 UH-1H hel.
10 tpt sqns; some 120 tpts, incl 2 Boeing 737, 13
C-130E/H, 2 KC-130H, 2 BAC-111, 10 HS-125,
12 HS-748, 21 DHC-5, 35 C-47, 6 *Catalina*, 60
C-95 *Bandeirante*, C-119, 5 *Porter*.
60 Bell 47, 11 Bell 206A, 4 OH-4 hel.
Trainers incl 6 F-5B, 100 T-23 *Uirapuru*, 150 T-25
Universal, 25 Cessna T-37C, 8 TC-45T, 50 AT-
26; 34 H-13J hel.
(45 AT-26, 8 T-25, 28 EMB-110 on order.)

Para-Military Forces: Public security forces about
200,000; state militias in addition.

CHILE

Population: 10,940,000.
Military service: 1 year.
Total armed forces: 85,000 (21,600 conscripts).
Estimated GNP 1976: $9.0 bn.*
Defence expenditure 1977: 10.93 bn pesos
($614 m).*
$1 = 17.8 pesos (1977), 12.5 pesos (1976).

Army: 50,000 (20,000 conscripts).
6 divs, incl 7 cav regts (3 armd, 3 horsed, 1 hel-
borne), 20 inf regts (incl 9 mot, 3 mountain), 6
arty regts, some AA arty, support dets.
76 M-4 med, 10 M-3, 60 M-41 lt tks; M-113,
Mowag MR-8 APC; 105mm, M-56 105mm pack
how; 120mm mor; 106mm RCL; 20mm, 40mm
AA guns; 9 T-25 trg ac, 9 *Puma*, 3 UH-1H, 2 AB-
206 hel. (8 T-25 trg ac, AS-11/-12 ASM on order.)

RESERVES: 160,000.

Navy: 24,000 (1,600 conscripts), incl Naval Air and
Marines.
3 submarines (2 *Oberon*, 1 ex-US *Fleet* type).
2 cruisers (1 ex-US *Brooklyn*-, 1 ex-Swedish *Tre
Kroner*-class).
6 destroyers (2 ex-US *Sumner*-, 2 *Fletcher*-, 2
Almirante-class with *Exocet* SSM, *Seacat* SAM).
2 frigates (*Leander*-class) with *Exocet* SSM, *Seacat*
SAM.
3 destroyer escorts (ex-US fast transport).

---

* Rapid inflation makes defence expenditure and GNP
figures in local currency and dollar terms unreliable.

4 corvettes.
2 large patrol craft.
4 MTB.
7 landing ships/craft (4 ex-US LST, 3 medium).

NAVAL AIR FORCE: 500.
Tpts incl 4 C-47, 5 Beech D-18S, 3 EMB-110 *Bandeirante*, 1 *Navajo* (1 F-27 on order).
Hel incl 4 AB-206, 4 UH-19, 2 UH-1D, 14 Bell 47G.
5 T-34 trainers.

MARINES: 3,800.
1 bde; coast-defence units.

Air Force: 11,000; 70 combat aircraft.
3 fighter sqns with 32 *Hunter* F71, 18 F-5E/F.
1 COIN sqn with 20 T-6G.
1 SAR/ASW sqn with 8 HU-16B *Albatross*.
Tpts incl 2 C-130H, 5 C-118, 6 DC-6B, 25 C-47, 10 C-45, 11 DHC-6, 3 EMB-110, 5 *Twin Bonanza*, 1 *King Air*, 10 Cessna 180.
Hel incl 6 S-55T, 6 SL-4, 2 UH-1H, 6 UH-12E, 6 *Lama*.
Trainers incl 30 T-34, 30 T-37B, 8 T-41, 11 *Vampire* T22/55, 4 *Hunter* T77, T-6, 9 Beech 99.
1 AA arty regt.
(16 A-37B COIN, 6 EMB-111 MR ac, 1 F-27 tpt, *Shafrir* AAM on order.)

Para-Military Forces: 30,000 *Carabineros*, with 15 Mowag MR-8 APC, 25 lt ac.

COLOMBIA

Population: 26,320,000.
Military service: 2 years.
Total armed forces: 56,500.
Estimated GNP 1976: $15.2 bn.
Defence expenditure 1977: 5.12 bn pesos ($140.3 m).
  $1 = 36.5 pesos (1977), 34.9 pesos (1976).

Army: 42,000.
10 inf bdes ('Regional Bdes').
1 Presidential Guard.
1 ranger bn.
1 AB bn.
1 AA arty bn.
Some mech cav, 20 inf, 5 arty, 6 engr units.
M-4A3 med, M-3A1 lt tks; M-8, M-20 armd cars; M-101 105mm how; mor; 40mm AA guns.

RESERVES: 250,000.

Navy: 8,000 (1,500 Marines).
6 submarines (4 midget, 2 Type 209).
4 destroyers (2 Swedish *Halland*-class, 2 ex-US *Sumner*-class).
3 frigates.
21 coastal patrol craft (13 under 100 tons).
1 marine bn.

Air Force: 6,500; 28 combat aircraft.
1 bbr/recce sqn with 8 B-26K/RB-26C.
1 fighter/recce sqn with 14 *Mirage* VCOA, 2 VCOR.
4 PBY-5A *Catalina* MR ac.
Tpts incl 2 C-130B, 10 C-54, C-45, 6 C-47, 3 HS-748, 1 F-28, 7 *Beaver*, 4 *Otter*, 6 *Porter*.
Hel incl 16 Bell 47, 6 UH-1B, 12 OH-6A, 6 TH-55, 4 H-23, 6 HH-43B, 27 *Lama*, 1 AB-212, 10 Hughes 500D.
Trainers incl 2 *Mirage* VCOD, 10 T-37, 30 T-41D, 10 AT-33, 30 T-34.

Para-Military Forces: 5,000 National Police Force.

CUBA

Population: 9,580,000.
Military service: 3 years.
Total armed forces: 189,000.
Estimated GNP 1970: $4.5 bn.
Estimated defence expenditure 1971: 290 m pesos ($290 m).
  $1 = 1 peso.

Army: 160,000.
15 inf 'divs' (bdes).
3 armd regts.
Some indep 'regts' (bn gps).
Over 600 tks, incl 60 IS-2 hy, T-34/-54/-55, 50 T-62 med, PT-76 lt; BRDM-1 armd cars; 200 BTR-40/-60/-152 APC; 75mm pack, 105mm, 122mm, 130mm, 152mm guns/how; 100 SU-100 SP guns; 30 *FROG*-4 SSM; 57mm, 76mm, 85mm ATK guns; 57mm RCL; *Snapper* ATGW; ZU-23, 37mm, 57 mm, 85mm, 100mm AA guns.

DEPLOYMENT: *Angola:* 15,000.*

RESERVES: 90,000.

Navy: 9,000.
1 escort patrol vessel (ex-US).
18 submarine chasers (12 ex-Soviet SO-1, 6 *Kronstadt*).
5 *Osa*-I, 2 *Osa*-II, 18 *Komar*-class FPBG with *Styx* SSM.
24 MTB (ex-Soviet P-4 and P-6).
29 armed patrol boats (under 100 tons).
Some 50 *Samlet* coast-defence SSM.

Air Force: 20,000, incl Air Defence Forces; 210 combat aircraft.
4 FB sqns with 75 MiG-17.
5 interceptor sqns with 50 MiG-21, 30 MiG-21MF.
2 interceptor sqns with 40 MiG-19.
1 trg sqn with 15 MiG-15.
Tpts incl 50 Il-14, An-24 and An-2.

---

* Cuban advisers and technicians are reported in Congo, Ethiopia, Guinea, Mozambique, Sierra Leone, Somalia, Tanzania, Uganda, South Yemen.

Hel incl 30 Mi-1, 24 Mi-4.
Trainers incl MiG-15UTI, Zlin 326.
24 SAM bns with 144 SA-2 *Guideline* and SA-3 *Goa*.

Para-Military Forces: 10,000 State Security troops;
    3,000 border guards; 100,000 People's Militia.

DOMINICAN REPUBLIC

Population: 4,970,000.
Military service: voluntary.
Total armed forces: 18,500.
Estimated GNP 1976: $4.0 bn.
Defence expenditure 1977: 43.2 m pesos ($43.2 m).
    $1 = 1 peso.

Army: 11,000.
3 inf bdes.
1 mixed armd bn.
1 mountain inf bn.
1 para 'bn'.
1 Presidential Guard bn.
1 arty regt.
1 AA arty regt.
1 engr bn.
1 armd recce sqn.
20 AMX-13 lt tks; AML, 20 *Lynx* armd cars; APC;
    75mm, 105mm, 122mm how; 40mm AA guns.

Navy: 4,000.
3 frigates (2 ex-US *Tacoma*-, 1 ex-Canadian *River*-
    class).
2 corvettes (ex-Canadian *Flower*-class).
2 fleet minesweepers.
14 patrol craft (12 under 100 tons).
1 landing ship (med), 2 landing craft.
1 cdo bn.

Air Force: 3,500; 45 combat aircraft.
1 FB sqn with 7 B-26, 10 *Vampire*, 20 F-51D
    Mustang.
1 COIN/trg sqn with 6 T-28D.
2 PBY-5 *Catalina* MR aircraft.
1 tpt sqn with 6 C-46, 6 C-47, 3 *Beaver*.
Trainers incl 4 T-6, T-11, 2 T-33, 4 Cessna 172.
2 UH-12, 7 OH-6A, 2 UH-19, 3 *Alouette* II/III hel.

Para-Military Forces: 10,000 Gendarmerie.

ECUADOR

Population: 7,680,000.
Military service: 2 years, selective.
Total armed forces: 23,900.
Estimated GNP 1976: $4.7 bn.
Defence expenditure 1977: 2.85 bn sucres
    ($114 m).
    $1 = 25 sucres (1977), 25 sucres (1976).

Army: 17,500.
11 inf bns (2 mot).
1 para bn.
3 recce, 4 horsed cav sqns.
1 Presidential Guard sqn.
10 indep inf coys.
3 arty gps, 1 AA arty bn.
2 engr bns.
15 M-3, 25 M-41, 41 AMX-13 lt tks; 27 AML-60/
    -90 armd cars; M-113, AMX-VCI APC; 105mm,
    6 155mm SP how; 40mm AA guns; 1 *Skyvan*,
    5 *Arava*, 3 *Porter* tpts, 7 lt ac, 2 hel.

Navy: 3,800 (700 marines).
3 destroyers (1 ex-US fast transport, 2 ex-British
    Hunt-class).
2 coastal escorts (ex-US).
3 FPBG with *Exocet* SSM, 3 FPB.
8 patrol craft (6 under 100 tons).
2 landing ships (med.)
1 *Arava*, 3 DHC-6, 1 *Cardinal* lt tpts, 2 *Alouette* hel.
(2 Type 209 submarines, 3 FPBG on order.)

Air Force: 2,600; 48 combat aircraft.
1 lt bbr sqn with 5 *Canberra* B6.
1 FB sqn with 6 *Jaguar* A/B.
1 COIN sqn with 12 A-37B.
1 recce sqn with 7 *Meteor* FR9.
1 FGA/trg sqn with 16 BAC-167 *Strikemaster*.
2 PBY-5A *Catalina* MR aircraft.
Tpts incl 4 *Electra*, 2 C-130H, 4 DC-6B, 3 *Learjet*,
    5 HS-748, 1 *Skyvan* 3M, 12 C-47, 6 C-45, 2
    DHC-5, 3 *Turbo-Porter*.
Hel incl 2 *Puma*, 6 *Alouette* III, 4 *Lama*, 3 Bell 47G,
    1 FH-1100.
Trainers incl T-28, 12 T-33, 20 T-41, 24 Cessna
    A150.
(6 *Jaguar* A/B, 12 *Super Mystère* B2 FB, 2 DHC-5
    tpts, 14 T-34, 12 SF-260 trainers on order.)

Para-Military Forces: 5,800.

HONDURAS

Population: 3,295,000.
Military service: voluntary.
Total Armed Forces: 14,200.
Estimated GNP 1976: $1.1 bn.
Defence expenditure 1977: 50.5 m lempira
    ($25.3 m).
    $1 = 2 lempira (1977), 2 lempira (1976).

Army: 13,000.
10 inf bns.
1 Presidential Guard bn.
2 arty btys.
1 engr, 1 sigs bn.
12 75mm pack, 8 105mm how; 57mm RCL; 81mm,
    120mm mor.

Air Force: 1,200; 22 combat aircraft.
1 FB sqn with 9 F-4U, 4 F-86K, 1 B-26, 8 *Super Mystère* B2.
Tpts incl 1 C-54, C-45, 3 *Arava*, 1 *Westwind*, 2 Cessna 180.
Trainers incl T-6G, 4 T-28E, 9 T-41, 6 AT-37B, 1 RT-33A.
(4 *Super Mystère* B2 FB on order.)

Para-Military Forces: 3,000.

MEXICO

Population: 64,440,000.
Military service: voluntary, with part-time conscript militia.
Total armed forces: 95,500 regular, 250,000 part-time conscripts.
Estimated GNP 1976: $93.2 bn.
Defence expenditure 1977: 12.26 bn pesos ($543 m).
$1 = 22.6 pesos (1977), 15.4 pesos (1976).

Army: 72,000 regular, 250,000 conscripts.
1 mech bde gp (Presidential Guard).
1 inf bde gp.
1 para bde.
Zonal Garrisons incl:
23 indep cav regts, 64 indep inf bns, 1 arty regt.
AA, engr and support units.
M-3 lt tks; 100 M-3A1, M-8 armd cars; HWK-11 APC; 75mm, 105mm how (some SP).

Navy: 17,500, incl Naval Air Force and Marines.
2 destroyers (ex-US *Fletcher*-class).
1 frigate (ex-US *Edsall*-class).
18 corvettes (ex-US *Auk*-class).
6 transports (5 ex-US, 1 training ship).
16 fleet minesweepers.
23 *Azteca*-class patrol craft (8 on order).
15 river and coastal patrol boats.
2 LST.

NAVAL AIR FORCE: 350.
4 HU-16 *Albatross* MR ac.
Other ac incl 1 *Learjet* 24D, 4 DC-3, 3 Cessna 180.
4 *Alouette* II, 5 Bell 47 hel.

MARINES: 2,000; 19 security companies.

Air Force: 6,000; 105 combat aircraft.
1 COIN sqn with 15 AT-33A.
5 COIN/trg sqns with 45 T-6, 30 T-28.
1 recce sqn with 15 AT-11.
1 SAR sqn with 18 LASA-60 ac, 9 *Alouette* III, 1 Hiller 12E hel.
Tpts incl 1 DC-7, 2 C-118, 5 C-54, 1 *Jetstar*, 7 C-47, 3 *Skyvan*, 12 *Islander*, 10 *Arava*.
Hel incl 14 Bell 47G, 5 AB-206B, 1 AB-212, 10 Bell 205.

Trainers incl 3 T-55, 45 T-6, 30 T-28, T-33, 20 Beech F33-19, 20 *Musketeer*.
1 para bn.

PARAGUAY

Population: 2,765,000.
Military service: 18 months.
Total armed forces: 17,000.
Estimated GNP 1976: $1.7 bn.
Defence expenditure 1977: 4.55 bn guaranies ($36.1 m).
$1 = 126 guaranies (1977), 124 guaranies (1976).

Army: 12,500.
1 cav 'div' (bde) with 1 med, 1 lt tk regt.
6 inf 'divs' (bn gps).
2 indep horsed cav regts.
2 indep inf bns.
1 Presidential Guard bn.
1 arty regt.
5 engr bns.
9 M-4 med, 6 M-3 lt tks; APC; 75mm guns; 75mm, 105mm how.

Navy: 2,000 (500 Marines and Naval Air).
2 large patrol vessels with 1 hel.
3 patrol boats (ex-Argentinian minesweepers).
8 coastal, 2 river patrol craft (under 20 tons).
2 LCT.
1 marine 'regt' (bn).
2 AT-6 *Texan* ac, 4 UH-13 hel.

Air Force: 2,500; 12 combat aircraft.
1 COIN sqn with 12 AT-6 *Texan*.
Tpts incl 5 DC-6B, 2 C-54, 1 CV-240, 10 C-47, 1 DHC-6, 1 *Dove*, 1 DHC-3.
14 Bell UH-13A, 3 H-12E hel.
Trainers incl 8 Fokker S-11, 8 T-23 *Uirapuru*, T-6, 1 MS-760, Cessna 185.
1 para 'regt' (bn).

Para-Military Forces: 4,000 security forces.

PERU

Population: 16,900,000.
Military service: 2 years, selective.
Total armed forces: 70,000 (40,000 conscripts).
Estimated GNP 1976: $10.7 bn.*
Defence expenditure 1977: 30.03 bn soles ($406 m).*
$1 = 74 soles (1977), 57.4 soles (1976).

Army: 46,000 (40,000 conscripts).
1 armd 'div' (bde).
2 armd, 2 horsed regts (cav 'div').

---

* Rapid inflation makes defence expenditure and GNP figures in local currency and dollars unreliable.

8 inf and mech 'divs' (bdes).
1 para-cdo 'AB div' (bde).
1 jungle 'div' (bde).
3 armd recce sqns.
Arty and engr bns.
250 T-54/-55, 60 M-4 med, 110 AMX-13 lt tks;
M-8, *Commando* armd cars; 50 M-3A1 scout
cars; 300 M-113, UR-416, Mowag APC; 75mm,
105mm, 122mm, 130mm, 155mm how; 120mm
mor; 28 40mm, 76mm towed, ZSU-23-4 SP AA
guns; SA-3 SAM; 5 Helio U-10B, 5 Cessna 185
lt ac; 8 Bell 47G hel. (200 T-62 tks, 122mm,
130mm guns, SA-3/-7 SAM, 2 *Nomad* lt tpt ac on
order.)

Navy: 14,000 (incl Naval Air, 1,000 Marines).
8 submarines (2 ex-US *Guppy* I, 4 ex-US *Mackerel*-
class, 2 Type 209).
4 light cruisers (2 ex-Dutch, 2 ex British).
4 destroyers (2 with *Exocet* SSM).
2 destroyer escorts (ex-US *Bostwick*-class).
3 river patrol craft.
6 river gunboats.
2 coastal minesweepers.
4 landing ships/craft (2 LST, 2 med).
9 S-2A *Tracker* ASW, 7 C-47, 2 F-27, 1 *Aztec* tpt ac;
8 Bell 47G, 10 Bell 206, 6 UH-1D, 4 *Alouette* III
hel; 2 T-34 trainers.
(2 Type 209 submarines, 4 *Lupo*-class frigates with
Otomat SSM and *Albatros* SAM, 6 PR72P FPBG,
2 F-27 ac, 6 AB-212 hel on order.)
1 marine bn.

Air Force: 10,000; 136 combat aircraft.
2 lt bbr sqns with 34 *Canberra* B2, B(I)8, B(I)56.
5 fighter sqns: 2 with 36 *Mirage* VP, 1 with 12
F-86F, 1 with 10 *Hunter* F52, 1 with 12 MiG-21.
2 COIN sqns with 24 A-37B.
1 MR sqn with 4 HU-16B *Albatross*, 4 PV-2.
Tpts incl 6 *Hercules*, 4 C-54, 2 *Learjet*, 6 C-47, 2
F-27, 4 F-28, 12 DHC-6, 16 DHC-5, 18 *Queen
Air*, 12 *Turbo-Porter*, 5 Cessna 185.
Hel incl 12 *Alouette* III, 20 Bell 47G, 17 Bell 212,
30 Mi-8.
Trainers incl 2 *Canberra* T4, 1 *Mirage* VDP, 15
T-6, 6 T-34, 8 T-33A, 19 T-41, 24 T-37B, 6 Pitts
Special.
(36 Su-22 FB on order.)

Para-Military Forces: 20,000 *Guardia Civil*.

URUGUAY

Population: 3,140,000.
Military service: voluntary.
Total armed forces: 27,000.
Estimated GNP 1976: $3.5 bn.*

**Rapid inflation makes defence expenditure and GNP
figures in local currency and dollars unreliable.*

Defence expenditure 1977: 316.4 bn pesos
($75 m).*
$1 = 4,220 pesos (1977), 3,300 pesos (1976).

Army: 20,000.
4 regional 'Armies' (divs) comprising:
3 armd regts, 13 inf bns, 6 cav regts, 4 arty 'bns'
(btys), 1 AD bn, 5 engr bns.
17 M-24, 18 M-3A1 lt tks; 10 M-3A1 scout cars;
15 M-113 APC; 25 105mm how.

Navy: 4,000 (incl naval air, naval infantry, coastguard).
3 destroyer escorts.
2 escorts (ex-US minesweepers).
6 patrol craft (all under 100 tons).
1 coastal minesweeper.
3 S-2A MR ac, 3 SNB-5 (C-45) tpts, T-34B, 4 SNJ-4,
4 T-6 trainers, 2 Bell 47G hel.

Air Force: 3,000; 48 combat aircraft.
1 fighter sqn with 8 F-80, 6 AT-33A.
1 COIN sqn with 8 A-37B.
1 recce sqn with 10 T-6, 10 AT-11, 6 U-17.
Tpts incl 12 C-47, 2 F-27, 3 FH-227, 2 *Queen Air*,
5 EMB-110.
Hel incl 6 Bell UH-1H, 2 Hiller UH-12.
Trainers incl 6 T-41.

Para-Military Forces: 2,200.

VENEZUELA

Population: 12,745,000.
Military service: 2 years, selective.
Total armed forces: 44,000.
Estimated GNP 1976: $32.5 bn.
Defence expenditure 1977: 2.2 bn bolivares
($513 m).
$1 = 4.29 bolivares (1977), 4.29 bolivares (1976).

Army: 28,000.
2 med, 1 lt tk bns.
2 mech, 11 inf bns.
13 ranger bns.
1 horsed cav bn.
7 arty gps.
5 AA arty and engr bns.
142 AMX-30 med, 40 AMX-13 lt tks; 12 M-8,
15 *Shorland* armd cars; AMX-VCI, 20 UR-416
APC; 20 AMX 155mm SP guns; 75mm pack, 105
mm how; 120mm mor; 35 M-18 76mm SP ATK
guns; 106mm RCL; 40mm AA guns; some 20 hel
incl 2UH-19D, *Alouette* III, Bell 47G.

Navy: 8,000, incl 4,000 Marines.
4 submarines (1 *Balao*-, 2 *Guppy* II, 1 Type 209).
4 destroyers (1 with *Seacat* SAM).
6 destroyer escorts.

3 FPBG, 3 FPB.
10 patrol craft.
16 coastal patrol craft (21 on order).
6 landing ships (1 LST, 4 med, 1 tpt).
6 S-2E *Tracker*, 4 HU-16 SAR ac, 3 C-47 tpts, 2 Bell 47J hel.
(1 Type 209 submarine, 6 *Lupo*-class frigates with *Albatros* SAM, 6 AB-212 ASW hel on order.)

MARINES: 3 bns.

Air Force: 8,000; 99 combat aircraft.
2 lt bbr sqns with 29 *Canberra*, 16 OV-10E.

3 fighter sqns: 1 with 15 CF-5A, 4 F-5B; 1 with 9 *Mirage* IIIEV, 4 VV, 2 VDV; 1 with 20 F-86K.
2 tpt sqns with 6 C-130H, 1 Boeing 737, 20 C-47, 12 C-123B *Provider*, 1 *Skyvan*.
Hel incl 15 *Alouette* III, 12 UH-1, 10 UH-19.
Trainers incl 12 *Jet Provost* T52, 24 T-2D *Buckeye*, 25 T-34 *Mentor*, 2 Beech 95, 9 *Queen Air*, 12 Cessna 182.
1 para bn.
(2 *Skyvan* tpts, 7 Bell 206, 8 A-109 hel on order.)

Para-Military Forces: 10,000 National Guard.

ARMED FORCES OF OTHER LATIN AMERICAN COUNTRIES*

Country	Estimated population (000)	Estimated GNP 1976 ($m)	Total armed forces	Army — Manpower and formations	Army — Equipment	Navy — Manpower and equipment	Air Force — Manpower and equipment	Para-military forces
El Salvador	4,350	1,800	7,130	6,000 3 inf 'bdes' 1 arty 'bde' 1 mixed cav bn 1 AD bn 1 para 'bn' (coy) 2 cdo/ranger coys	3 M-3 lt tks; 20 UR-416 APC; 30 105mm how	130 4 small patrol boats	1,000 17 Ouragan, 4 Magister FGA; 2 DC-6, 12 C-47, 4 Arava tpts; 1 Alouette III, 3 Lama hel	3,000
Guatemala	6,170	4,200	14,300	13,500 3 bde HQ 10 inf bns 1 para bn 1 engr bn 1 armd coy 1 arty bty	8 M-8, 8 Commando armd cars; 6 M-3A1, 10 M-113, 10 RBY-1 APC; 12 75mm, 12 M-101 105mm how	400 14 small coastal patrol boats; 1 med landing craft	400 11 A-37B con: 1 C-54, 1 DC-6, 11 C-47, 9 Arava tpts; 6 UH-1D, 3 UH-19, 1 OH-23G hel; 7 T-6, 10 T-23, 5 T-33, 3 T-37 trg ac. (3 Arava on order)	3,000
Guyana	820	478	2,000†	2 inf bns	4 Shorland armd cars; 12 81mm mor	3 FPB (1 on order)	8 BN-2A lt tpts; 1 lt ac; 2 Hughes 269, 2 Bell 206B, 1 Bell 212, 1 Alouette hel	2,250
Haiti	4,735	1,100	6,550	6,000 Pres Guard 1 inf bn Garrison dets	M-113 APC; 75mm, 105mm how; 37mm, 57mm ATK guns	300 4 small patrol boats; 1 LCT	250 4 F-51D FGA; 6 Cessna 337/0-2A con; 3 C-47, 2 C-45 tpts; 4 H-34, 3 S-55 hel; 3 T-6, 2 T-28 trg ac	14,900
Nicaragua	2,290	1,800	7,100	5,400 Pres Guard 1 inf bn 1 engr bn 16 inf coys 1 arty bty 1 AA arty bty	Some M-4 med tks; 3 M-3 APC; 4 105mm how; 12 20mm, 8 40mm AA guns	200 8 patrol craft	1,500 4 B-26K bbrs; 6 T-33A, 3 T-28D con; 1 Arava, 5 C-47, 10 Cessna 0-2A tpts; 1 Hughes 269, 5 CH-34, 1 OH-6A hel	4,000

* Costa Rica and Panama maintain para-military forces, numbering 5,000 and 11,000 respectively
† In Guyana the forces are all part of a single service.

2

**TABLES
AND ANALYSIS**

1. NUCLEAR DELIVERY VEHICLES: COMPARATIVE STRENGTHS AND CHARACTERISTICS

(A) UNITED STATES AND SOVIET UNION

(i) Missiles and Artillery

United States

Category[a]	Type	Range (mi)[b]	Warhead yield range[c]	Throw-weight range[d] (000 lb)	First deployment	Number deployed (7/77)
Land-based						
ICBM	*Titan II*	7,000	5–10 MT	7.5	1962	54
	Minuteman II[l]	7,000	1–2 MT	1–1.5	1966	450
	Minuteman III	7,500	3×170 KT	1.5–2	1970	550
M/IRBM						
SRBM	*Pershing*[l]	450	high KT	n.a.	1962	108[m]
	Lance[l]	70	low KT	n.a.	1972	36[m]
	Honest John[l]	25	KT	n.a.	1953	n.a.
Sea-based						
LRCM						
SLBM	*Polaris A3*	2,880	3×200 KT	1,000	1964	160
	Poseidon C3	2,880	10×50 KT[n]	2,000	1971	496
SLCM						

Soviet Union

Category[a]	Type	Range (mi)[b]	Warhead yield range[c]	Throw-weight range[d] (000 lb)	First deployment	Number deployed (7/77)
Land-based						
ICBM	*SS-7 Saddler*	6,900	5 MT	3–4	1961	} 109
	SS-8 Sasin	6,900	5 MT	3–4	1963	
	SS-9 Scarp	7,500	18–25 MT or 3×5 MT[f]	12–15	1965	238
	SS-11 Sego	6,500	1–2 MT or 3×KT[g]	1.5–2	1966	840
	SS-13 Savage[h]	5,000	1 MT	1	1968	60
	SS-17	6,500	4×KT or 1×5 MT[i]	6	1975	40
	SS-18	7,500	15–25 MT or 8×MT[j]	15–18	1975	50
	SS-19	6,500	6×KT or 1×5 MT[i]	7	1975	140
M/IRBM	*SS-4 Sandal*	1,200	1 MT	n.a.	1959	500
	SS-5 Skean	2,300	1 MT	n.a.	1961	100
	SS-20	3,000	3×KT[k]	1.2	1977	(20)
SRBM	*SS-1b Scud A*[l]	50	KT	n.a.	1957	} (750)
	SS-1c Scud B[l]	185	KT	n.a.	1965	
	SS-12 Scaleboard	500	MT	n.a.	1969	
	FROG 7[l]	10–45	KT	n.a.	1957–65	(450)
Sea-based						
LRCM	*SS-N-3 Shaddock* 450	450	KT	n.a.	1962	(100)
SLBM	*SS-N-4 Sark*	350	1–2 MT	n.a.	1961	27
	SS-N-5 Serb	750	1–2 MT	n.a.	1964	54
	SS-N-6 Sawfly[o]	1,750	1–2 MT or 3×KT[p]	1,500	1969	544
	SS-N-8[q]	4,800	1–2 MT	1,500	1972	284
SLCM	*SS-N-3 Shaddock*[r] 450	450	KT	n.a.	1962	324

(i) Missiles (continued)

United States

	Category[t]	Type	Range (mi)[u]	Speed/Yield	Weapons load (000 lb)	First deployment	Number deployed (7/77)
Air-launched	ALCM	Hound Dog	600	KT	n.a.	1961	(400)
	ALBM	SRAM	150	KT	n.a.	1972	1,500
Artillery	SP	M-110 203mm how[t]	10	KT	—	1962	200[m]
		M-109 155mm how[t]	10	2 KT	—	1964	300[m]
	Towed	M-115 203mm how[t]	10	KT	—	1950s	n.a.

Soviet Union

Type	Range (mi)[u]	Speed/Yield	Weapons load (000 lb)	First deployment	Number deployed (7/77)
AS-3 Kangaroo	400	KT	n.a.	1961	n.a.
AS-4 Kitchen	450	KT	n.a.	1962	(800)
M-55 203mm gun/how[t]	18	KT	—	1950s	n.a.

(ii) Aircraft[s]

United States

Category[t]	Type	Range (mi)[u]	Speed (Mach no.)	Weapons load (000 lb)	First deployment	Number deployed (7/77)
Long-range bombers	B-52D	11,500	0.95	60	1956	} 373[w]
	B-52G-H	12,500	0.95	70	1959	
Medium-range bombers	FB-111A	3,800	2.5	37.5	1969	68
Land-based strike (incl short-range bombers)	F-105D	2,100	2.25	16.5	1960	
	F-4C-J	2,300	2.4	16	1962	(350)[m]
	F-111A/E	3,800	2.2/2.5	25	1967	
	A-7D	3,400	0.9	15	1968	
Carrier-based strike	A-4	2,055	0.9	10	1956	
	A-6A	3,225	0.9	18	1963	(200)[m]
	A-7A/B/E	3,400	0.9	15	1966	
	F-4	2,000	2.4	16	1962	

Soviet Union

Type[v]	Range (mi)[u]	Speed (Mach no.)	Weapons load (000 lb)	First deployment	Number deployed (7/77)
Tu-95 Bear	8,000	0.78	40	1956	100
Mya-4 Bison	6,000	0.87	20	1956	35[x]
Tu-16 Badger	4,000	0.8	20	1955	740[v]
Tu-? Backfire B	5,500	2.5	20	1974	65[v]
Il-28 Beagle	2,500	0.8	4.85	1950	
Su-7 Fitter A	900	1.7	4.5	1959	
Tu-22 Blinder	1,400	1.5	12	1962	
MiG-21 Fishbed J/K/L	1,150	2.2	2	1970	} (1,000)[m]
MiG-27 Flogger D	1,800	2.5	2.8	1971	
Su-17-20 Fitter C	1,100	1.6	5	1974	
Su-19 Fencer A	1,800	2.3	8	1974	

[a] ICBM range = 4,000+ statute miles; IRBM range = 1,500–4,000 miles; MRBM range = 500–1,500 miles; SRBM range = under 500 miles; LRCM range = over 350 miles.

[b] Statute miles. Operational range depends upon the payload carried; use of maximum payload may reduce missile range by up to 25 per cent.

[c] Estimated maxima; warhead yields vary greatly. KT range = less than 1 MT.

[d] Figures given are estimated maxima. Throw-weight is the weight of the post-boost vehicle (warheads, guidance systems, penetration aids) that can be delivered over a given range. At maximum range throw-weight will be less than shown here.

(iii) US–Soviet Strategic Balance: Static Measurements[a]

		Deliverable warheads[b]	Equivalent megatonnage[c]	Missile throw-weight (million lb)[a]	Bomber payload (million lb)[a]
USA	ICBM	2,154	1,460	2.2	
	SLBM	5,120	830	1.1	
	Long-range bombers	4,056	4,400		
	Totals	11,330	6,690	3.3	22.8
USSR	ICBM	2,647	2,950	7.8	
	SLBM	909	860	1.3	
	Long-range bombers	270	780		
	Totals	3,826	4,590	9.1	4.7

e Numerical designations of Soviet missiles (e.g. SS-9) are of US origin; names (e.g. *Scarp*) are of NATO origin.

f The SS-9 exists in three operational modes; 18- or 25-MT single-warhead and 3 MRV of 4–5 MT each.

g A 3-MRV version of the SS-11 has replaced some of the single-warhead systems.

h A solid-fuel replacement for the SS-13, the SS-X-16, which has about twice the throw-weight and may also be deployed in a land-mobile mode, is undergoing tests.

i The SS-17 and SS-19 have begun deployment in modified SS-11 silos. Operational missiles are equipped with MIRV, but single-warhead versions have been tested.

j The SS-18, a follow-on to the SS-9, has been tested in two single-warhead and 5–8-MIRV versions.

k The SS-20 has been tested at longer ranges with a single, lower-yield warhead.

l Dual-capable (able to deliver conventional or nuclear warheads). Conventional warheads for US *Lance* and *Pershing* under development. Though shown in the table, it is uncertain whether Soviet 203mm arty is nuclear-capable.

m Figures for systems in Europe only.

n *Poseidon* can carry up to 14 RV over a reduced range.

o A solid propellant replacement for the SS-N-6, the SS-NX-17, has been tested and is thought to be capable of deploying MIRV.

p The SS-N-6 has been tested with new single warhead (MT range) and with 3 MRV.

q A 3-warhead MIRV replacement for the SS-N-8, the SS-NX-18, has been tested.

r A longer-range version of the SS-X-12, is reportedly under development.

s All aircraft are dual-capable, but some in the strike aircraft categories are not presently configured for the nuclear role.

t Long-range bomber = maximum range 6,000+ miles; medium-range bomber = maximum range 3,500–6,000 miles, primarily designed for bombing missions. *Backfire* is classified as a medium-range bomber on the basis of reported range characteristics.

u Theoretical maximum range in statute miles, with internal fuel only, at optimum altitude and speed. Ranges of strike aircraft assume no weapons load. Especially in the case of strike aircraft, therefore, range falls sharply for flights at higher speeds, lower altitude or with full weapons load.

v Names of Soviet aircraft (e.g. *Bear*) are of NATO origin.

w Excluding aircraft in storage or reserve.

x Excluding approximately 45 Mya-4 configured as tankers.

y Including aircraft in the Naval Air Force (some 280 Tu-16 and 30 *Backfire*) but excluding Tu-16 tankers.

a These are estimates of *static* strategic capability derived from Table 1 (i) and (ii) above. These measurements are useful in comparing force size, but provide limited information about force effectiveness. More elaborate *dynamic* presentations of the balance can be used to portray effectiveness, but this requires the enumeration of factors not shown here, such as accuracy and defensive capability. For a more detailed portrayal of the balance and the problems of depicting it, see 'Measuring the Strategic Balance', *Military Balance 1976–1977*, pp. 106–108.

b This measures the number of targets each side can attack. Only separately-targetable delivery vehicles are included in missile totals. Bomber totals assume both stand-off missile and gravity bomb deployment.

c Equivalent megatonnage (EMT) measures damage to unprotected area targets. Assuming that a warhead falls within the boundary of the target area, the EMT of a specific weapon is expressed as the two-thirds power of its explosive yield, or $Y^{2/3}$. Totals assume maximum yield values shown in Table 1 (i) and (ii).

d Neither missile throw-weight nor bomber payload provides a measure of destructive power, but both give some indication of the capacity of a given system to be exploited for different purposes. An ICBM, for example, can be used to deliver a small number of larger-yield warheads (to maximize EMT) or a larger number of smaller warheads (to maximize target coverage). The same is true for bombers, but calculations are complicated by the range versatility of aircraft and the large choice of weapons they can carry. Because bomber payload is a less precise index of potential military capacity than missile throw-weight, the table gives separate estimates for missiles and bombers.

(iv) Historical Changes in Launcher Strength

		1963	1964	1965	1966	1967	1968	1969	1970	1971	1972	1973	1974	1975	1976	1977
USA	ICBM	424	834	854	904	1,054	1,054	1,054	1,054	1,054	1,054	1,054	1,054	1,054	1,054	1,054
	SLBM	224	416	496	592	656	656	656	656	656	656	656	656	656	656	656
	Long-range bombers	630	630	630	630	600	545	560	550	505	455	442	437	432	387	373
USSR	ICBM	90	190	224	292	570	858	1,028	1,299	1,513	1,527	1,527	1,575	1,618	1,527	1,477
	SLBM	107	107	107	107	107	121	196	304	448	500	628	720	784	845	909
	Long-range bombers	190	175	160	155	160	155	145	145	145	140	140	140	135	135	135

(B) OTHER NATO AND WARSAW PACT COUNTRIES

(i) Missiles and Artillery

NATO (excluding USA)

Category[a]	Type[b]	Operated by[c]	Range (mi)[d]	Warhead yield range[e]	First deployment	Number deployed (7/77)
Land-based missiles — IRBM	SSBS S-2	FR	1,875	150 KT	1971	18
SRBM	Sergeant[g]	GE	85	KT	1962	20
	Pershing[g]	GE	450	KT	1962	72
	Lance	BR, GER, IT	70	KT	1976	(44)
	Pluton	FR	75	15–25 KT	1974	24
	Honest John	[i]	25	KT	1953	(112)
SLBM	Polaris A3	BR	2,880	3 × 200 KT	1967	64
	MSBS M-1	FR	1,550	500 KT	1972	32
	MSBS M-2	FR	1,900	500 KT	1974	16
	MSBS M-20	FR	3,000	1 MT	1977	16
Artillery — SP	M-110 203mm how	[j]	10	KT	1962	n.a.
	M-109 155mm how	[k]	10	2 KT	1964	n.a.
Towed	M-115 203mm how	[j]	10	KT	1950s	n.a.

Warsaw Pact (excluding USSR)

Type[f]	Operated by[c]	Range (mi)[d]	Warhead yield range[e]	First deployment	Number deployed (7/77)
SS-1b Scud A[h]	All	50	KT	1957	(130)
SS-1c Scud B[h]	All	185	KT	1965	(130)
FROG 3–7[h]	All	10–45	KT	1957–65	(200)

a IRBM range 1,500–4,000 miles; SRBM range under 500 miles.

b All NATO vehicles are of American origin, with the exception of the SSBS IRBM, MSBS SLBM and *Pluton*, which are of French origin.

c BR = Britain, FR = France, GE = Germany, IT = Italy.

d Statute miles. Use of maximum payload may reduce range by up to 25 per cent.

e Figures given are estimated maxima. KT range = less than 1 MT.

f All Warsaw Pact vehicles are of Soviet origin. Numerical designations (e.g., SS-1b) are of American origin, names (*Scud A, FROG*) of NATO origin.

g These SRBM are operated by Germany but the nuclear warheads for them are in American custody. *Sergeant* and *Honest John* are dual-capable.

h These dual-capable systems are operated by the countries shown, but nuclear warheads for them are in Soviet custody.

i *Honest John* is dual-capable and is operated by Belgium, Germany, Greece, the Netherlands and Turkey, but with the nuclear warheads held in American custody.

j The 203mm (8-in.) how is dual-capable. It is operated by Belgium, Britain, Denmark, Germany, Greece, Italy, the Netherlands and Turkey, but any nuclear warheads for it are in American custody. There are no nuclear warheads on Danish soil.

k The 155mm how is primarily a conventional artillery weapon but is dual-capable. It is operated by Belgium, Britain, Canada, Denmark, Germany, Greece, Italy, the Netherlands, Norway and Turkey, but in very few cases is it likely to have a nuclear role, certainly not in the case of Canada. Any nuclear warheads would be in American custody, none of them being held on either Danish or Norwegian soil.

(ii) *Aircraft*[a]

NATO (excluding USA)

Category[b]	Type[c]	Operated by[d]	Range (mi)[e]	Speed (Mach no.)[f]	Weapons load (000 lb)	First deployment	Deployed (7/77)
Medium-range bombers	*Vulcan* B2	BR	4,000	0.95	21	1960	50
Strike aircraft (incl short-range bombers)[k]	F-104	h	1,300	2.2	4	1958	n.a.[j]
	F-4	{BR GE}	1,600	2.4	16	1962	n.a.[j]
	Buccaneer	BR	2,300	0.95	8	1962	70
	Mirage IVA	FR	2,000	2.2	8	1964	50
	Jaguar	{BR FR}	1,000	1.1	8	{1973 1974}	{72 120}

Warsaw Pact (excluding USSR)

Type[g]	Operated by[d]	Range (mi)[e]	Speed (Mach no.)[f]	Weapons load (000 lb)	First deployment	Deployed (7/77)
Il-28 *Beagle*[i]	PO	2,500	0.81	4.85	1950	n.a.[j]
Su-7 *Fitter* A[i]	{CZ HY PO}	900	1.7	4.5	1959	n.a.[j]
Su-20 *Fitter* C[i]	PO	1,100	1.6	5	1974	n.a.[j]

a All aircraft listed are dual-capable but many would be more likely to carry conventional than nuclear weapons.

b Medium-range bomber = maximum range 3,500–6,000 miles, primarily designed for bombing missions.

c *Vulcan* and *Buccaneer* are of British origin; F-104 and F-4 are of American origin; *Mirage* is of French origin; *Jaguar* is Anglo-French.

d BR = Britain, FR = France, GE = Germany, CZ = Czechoslovakia, HY = Hungary, PO = Poland.

e Theoretical maximum range in statute miles, with internal fuel only, at optimum altitude and speed. Ranges for strike aircraft assume no weapons load. Especially in the case of strike aircraft, therefore, range falls sharply for flights at lower altitude, at higher speed or with full weapons load (e.g., combat *radius* of F-104, at operational height and speed, with typical weapons load, is approximately 420 miles).

f Mach 1 = speed of sound.

g Warsaw Pact aircraft are of Soviet origin; the names listed (e.g., *Beagle*) are of NATO origin.

h The dual-capable F-104 is operated by Belgium, Canada, Denmark, Germany, Greece, Italy, the Netherlands, Norway and Turkey, but the Canadian aircraft no longer have a nuclear role. The nuclear warheads are held in American custody.

i Nuclear warheads for these dual-capable aircraft are held in Soviet custody.

j The absence of figures here reflects the uncertainty as to how many of these dual-capable aircraft actually have a nuclear role.

k Certain other aircraft, such as the *Mirage* III, may also be capable of carrying tactical nuclear weapons.

2. COMPARISONS OF DEFENCE EXPENDITURES 1974–1977

Country	$ million				$ Per head				% Government spending[a]				% of GNP[b]			
	1974	1975	1976	1977	1974	1975	1976	1977	1974	1975	1976	1977	1973	1974	1975	1976
Warsaw Pact[c]																
Bulgaria	403	457	438	538	46	52	50	61	6.0	6.0	6.0	7.3	2.5	2.7	2.7	2.6
Czechoslovakia	1,602	1,706	1,805	1,614	109	116	121	108	7.0	7.3	n.a.	6.2	4.0	3.8	3.8	3.5
Germany, East	2,373	2,550	2,729	2,889	138	148	158	167	8.6	7.9	7.8	7.8	5.4	5.4	5.5	6.0
Hungary	477	506	551	590	46	48	52	56	3.7	3.5	3.6	3.6	2.3	2.4	2.4	2.6
Poland	1,832	2,011	2,252	2,438	54	59	66	70	7.2	7.0	7.0	n.a.	3.2	3.0	3.1	3.6
Romania	626	707	759	824	30	33	35	38	4.1	3.7	4.0	n.a.	1.7	1.7	1.7	1.8
Soviet Union[d]	109,000 / –113,000	124,000	127,000	n.a.	432 / –447	490	492	n.a.	n.a.	n.a.	n.a.	n.a.	— 11–13% —			
NATO[e]																
Belgium	1,506	1,971	2,013	2,476	153	200	204	253	9.8	10.0	10.2	10.4	2.7	2.8	3.0	3.0
Britain	10,041	11,118	10,734	11,214	179	198	190	201	12.9	11.6	11.0	11.4	4.9	5.1	4.9	5.1
Canada	2,944	2,965	3,231	3,348	131	130	140	144	14.3	11.9	10.0	n.a.	2.0	2.1	2.2	1.9
Denmark	741	939	861	1,103	147	185	168	217	7.4	7.3	7.4	6.8	2.1	2.2	2.2	2.8
France	9,970	13,984	12,857	13,740	190	264	241	256	20.3	20.2	20.6	20.4	3.5	3.6	3.9	3.7
Germany*	13,923	16,142	15,220	16,602	224	259	242	263	26.7	24.4	23.5	22.9	3.4	3.6	3.7	3.6
Greece	807	1,435	1,249	1,100	90	159	138	120	25.2	25.5	26.0	n.a.	4.1	4.0	6.9	5.5
Italy	4,415	4,700	3,821	4,416	80	84	68	78	11.0	9.7	8.6	8.3	3.0	2.9	2.6	2.6
Luxembourg	19	22	23	28	56	65	68	80	3.5	3.0	2.9	2.9	0.8	0.9	1.1	1.2[f]
Netherlands	2,406	2,978	2,825	3,357	178	218	205	241	12.2	11.0	9.8	9.7	3.3	3.4	3.6	3.4
Norway	723	929	902	1,194	181	232	223	295	8.5	8.2	7.6	9.9	3.2	3.1	3.1	3.1
Portugal	1,000	1,088	748	508	114	124	85	52	47.3	35.2	n.a.	19.2	6.2	6.6	6.0	3.9
Turkey	1,173	2,200	2,800	2,653	30	55	70	64	19.2	26.6	29.4	21.1	4.1	3.7	9.0	5.6
United States	85,906	88,983	102,691	113,000	405	417	477	523	26.5	23.8	26.0	24.4	6.1	6.1	5.9	6.0
Other Europe																
Austria	323	410	433	534	43	54	57	68	3.7	3.7	3.7	3.7	0.9	0.9	1.0	1.1
Eire	98[g]	128	134	146	32	41	43	45	3.9	4.3	4.3	4.2	1.2	1.4	1.6	1.6
Finland	313	388	364	426	67	83	77	90	5.3	5.0	4.8	n.a.	1.4	1.4	1.4	1.1
Spain	1,372	1,701	1,766	2,154	39	48	49	59	14.1	14.5	15.2	15.3	1.9	1.9	1.8	1.7
Sweden	1,903	2,483	2,418	2,833	233	303	294	343	10.3	10.5	9.6	n.a.	3.7	3.4	3.4	3.7
Switzerland	832	1,047	1,221	1,280	126	160	184	204	19.2	19.3	19.1	20.3	1.8	1.8	1.8	2.3
Yugoslavia[f]	1,295	1,705	1,798	1,640	61	80	84	76	49.5	49.9	40.9	41	5.3	5.1	5.6	n.a.
Middle East																
Algeria[f]	221	285	312	387	14	17	18	23	6.2	4.7	5.5	5.8	1.7	1.8	2.2	n.a.
Egypt	4,071	6,103	4,859	4,365	111	163	128	112	26.8	42.0	n.a.	25	31.0	22.8	n.a.	37
*Incl aid to W. Berlin	16,668	19,540	18,758	21,092	268	313	299	333	28.8	29.2	28.9	29.2	4.1	4.3	4.4	4.2

Iran[f]	5,550	8,800	9,500	7,898	172	268	281	227	27.1	24.9	21.4	16.1	7.0	14.0	17.4	12
Iraq	2,701	1,191[g]	n.a.	1,660	251	107	n.a.	141	59.4	43.7	n.a.	17.6	9.8	18.7	n.a.	n.a.
Israel	3,869	3,552	4,214	4,268	1,173	1,045	1,201	1,178	51.0	50.1	56.7	32.4	40.8	31.8	35.9	35.3
Jordan	142	155	155	201	54	57	55	69	26.6	22.0	19.4	20.2	16.4	12.1	12.2	11.7
Libya	169	203	229	n.a.	72	83	90	n.a.	16.1	13.7	n.a.	n.a.	2.3	1.4	1.7	n.a.
Morocco	190	224	258	346	11	13	15	19	8.6	4.5	6.0	7.8	3.5	3.0	2.8	3.2[f]
Saudi Arabia	1,808	6,771	9,038	7,538	329	1,153	1,506	1,005	25.6	20.0	29.0	24.0	17.9	7.3	18.0	n.a.
Sudan	118	120	n.a.	n.a.	7	7	n.a.	n.a.	14.9	15.1	n.a.	n.a.	4.6	4.3	n.a.	n.a.
Syria[f]	452	706	1,003	1,067	64	96	132	137	24.5	25.3	22.3	23.0	16.0	11.0	15.1	n.a.
Africa																
Ethiopia	89	84	103.4	n.a.	3	3	4	n.a.	19.8	19.4	n.a.	n.a.	2.1	3.3	2.9	n.a.
Nigeria	653	1,786	2,434	n.a.	11	28	38	n.a.	15.2	11.8	16.7	n.a.	4.3	2.9	n.a.	n.a.
Rhodesia	80	102	130	159	13	16	21	23	11.1	12.3	14.1	20.0	2.7	2.6	3.0	3.8
South Africa	1,052	1,332	1,494	1,897	43	53	57	70	16.0	18.5	16.4	n.a.	2.6	3.2	5.3	4.7
Asia																
Australia	2,661	2,492	2,807	n.a.	199	184	204	n.a.	10.0	8.6	9.2	n.a.	3.4	3.6	3.2	2.8
China (Taiwan)	1,000	1,007	n.a.	n.a.	63	61	n.a.	n.a.	40.9	n.a.	n.a.	n.a.	8.0	7.2	n.a.	n.a.
India	2,443	2,660	2,812	3,445	4	4	5	6	22.1	21.1	12.1	19.5	3.4	2.7	3.0	n.a.
Indonesia	601	1,108	1,024	1,349	5	9	8	10	15.8	16.7	6.2	14	2.9	2.6	3.8	n.a.
Japan	4,300	4,620	5,058	6,090	39	42	45	49	6.4	6.6	6.2	5.9	0.9	0.9	0.9	0.9
Korea, South	742	943	1,500	1,800	22	28	42	51	25.3	29.2	34.6	n.a.	3.7	4.3	5.1	n.a.
Malaysia	311	385	353	544	26	31	27	41	17.3	17.3	16.9	n.a.	4.1	3.8	4.0	n.a.
New Zealand	242	243	211	n.a.	80	79	68	n.a.	4.5	4.3	4.3	n.a.	1.6	1.8	1.8	1.7
Pakistan	713	725	807	819	11	10	11	11	12.7	12.3	17.2	22	7.5	8.4	7.2	6.2
Philippines	312	407	410	420	8	10	9	9	24.2	19.3	n.a.	n.a.	1.6	2.1	2.6	2.4
Singapore	263	344	340	n.a.	118	152	149	n.a.	19.1	18.1	17.4	n.a.	4.9	5.1	5.3	n.a.
Thailand	430	542	639	n.a.	10	13	15	n.a.	24.5	25.7	19.0	n.a.	3.4	3.2	3.7	n.a.
Latin America																
Argentina	1,609	1,031	1,287	1,415	65	41	49	54	8.5	9.7	11.7	14.7	1.3	1.9	0.9	2.8
Brazil	1,154	1,283	1,780	2,073	11	12	16	18	11.0	9.3	9.7	9.4	1.2	1.3	1.3	1.3
Colombia	102	106	133	140	4	n.a.	5	5	8.0	n.a.	9.0	8.2	0.9	0.8	0.8	0.9
Mexico[f]	423	586	728	542	8	10	12	8	2.2	2.4	2.3	3.9	0.7	0.7	0.7	0.8
Peru	226	383	n.a.	406	15	24	n.a.	24	9.9	15.3	n.a.	13.5	2.9	2.4	3.1	n.a.
Uruguay	98	82	62	75	n.a.	n.a.	20	24	n.a.	n.a.	15.6	17.2	3.1	2.5	2.3	1.8
Venezuela	406	494	423	513	35	41	34	52	8.9	5.4	5.5	6.1	2.0	1.6	1.7	1.3

[a] This series is designed to show national trends only; differences in the scope of the government sector invalidate international comparisons.

[b] Based on local currency. GNP estimated where official figures unavailable.

[c] This section is not directly comparable with the others. The difficulty of calculating suitable exchange rates makes conversion to dollars imprecise. GNP estimates are at factor-cost (market-price for USSR).

[d] See p. 11.

[e] Defence expenditures based on NATO definition, but some 1976 figures estimated from nationally-defined data, as are 1977 figures for Greece and Turkey. Figures from 1976 are provisional.

[f] Gross domestic product at market prices, not GNP.

[g] Nine-month figure only.

3. COMPARISONS OF MILITARY MANPOWER 1973–77 (in thousands)

Country	Numbers in armed forces					Armed forces 1977				Estimated reservists[a]	Para-military forces
	1973	1974	1975	1976	1977	Army	Navy	Air	% of men 18–45		
Warsaw Pact											
Bulgaria	152.0	152.0	152.0	164.5	148.5	115.0	8.5	25.0	8.3	235.0	40.0
Czechoslovakia	190.0	200.0	200.0	180.0	181.0	135.0	—	46.0	6.0	350.0	10.0
Germany, East	132.0	145.0	143.0	157.0	157.0	105.0	16.0	36.0	4.7	255.0	73.0
Hungary	103.0	103.0	105.0	100.0	103.0	83.0	—	20.0	4.7	143.0	20.0
Poland	280.0	303.0	293.0	290.0	307.0	220.0	25.0	62.0	4.1	605.0	97.0
Romania	170.0	171.0	171.0	181.0	180.0	140.0	10.0	30.0	4.0	345.5	37.0
Soviet Union	3,425.0	3,525.0	3,575.0	3,650.0	3,675.0	1,825.0[b]	450.0[b]	475.0[b]	6.9	4,200.0	450.0
NATO											
Belgium	89.6	89.7	87.0	88.3	85.7	62.1	4.2	19.4	4.5	55.5	16.0
Britain[c]	361.5	354.6	345.1	344.2	339.2	175.3	76.7	87.2	3.2	248.6	—
Canada	83.0	83.0	77.0	77.9	80.0	28.5	13.4	36.6	1.6	19.1	—
Denmark	39.8	37.1	34.4	34.7	34.7	21.8	5.8	7.1	3.4	153.2	—
France	503.6	502.5	502.5	512.9	502.1	330.0	68.5	103.6	4.8	450.0	76.2
Germany	475.0	490.0	495.0	495.0	489.0	341.0	38.0	110.0	3.8	1,179.5	20.0
Greece	160.0	161.2	161.2	199.5	200.0	160.0	17.5	22.5	11.6	310.0	118.0
Italy	427.5	421.0	421.0	352.0	330.0	218.0	42.0	70.0	3.0	694.8	90.0
Luxembourg	0.6	0.6	0.6	0.6	0.6	0.6	—	—	0.2	—	0.4
Netherlands	112.2	113.9	112.5	112.2	109.7	75.0	17.0	17.7	3.9	176.5	7.7
Norway	35.4	34.9	35.0	39.0	39.0	20.0	9.0	10.0	5.2	240.0	—
Portugal	204.0	217.0	217.0	59.8	58.8	36.0	12.8	10.0	3.7	n.a.	23.4
Turkey	455.0	453.0	453.0	460.0	465.0	375.0	43.0	47.0	5.6	725.0	75.0
United States	2,252.9	2,174.0	2,130.0	2,086.7	2,088.0	789.0	728.0	571.0	4.9	870.5	—
Other European											
Austria	52.0	37.3	38.0	37.3	37.3	33.0	—	4.3	2.7	112.7	11.3
Eire	10.6	12.3	12.1	14.0	14.7	13.4	0.6	0.7	2.6	18.7	—
Finland	39.5	35.8	36.3	35.8	39.9	34.4	2.5	3.0	3.9	690.0	4.0
Spain	293.0	284.0	302.3	302.3	309.0	220.0	48.0	41.0	4.5	n.a.	65.0
Sweden	74.8	72.2	69.8	65.4	68.6	46.0	12.0	10.6	4.3	500.0	—
Switzerland	18.5	18.5	18.5	18.5	18.5	18.5	—	—	1.0	621.5	—
Yugoslavia	240.0	230.0	230.0	250.0	260.0	193.0	27.0	40.0	5.5	500.0	616.0

[a] Reservists with recent training. [b] Excludes *PVO-Strany* and Strategic Rocket Forces. [c] Includes men enlisted outside Britain.

Middle East											
Algeria	63.0	63.0	63.0	69.3	75.8	67.0	3.8	5.0	2.5	100.0	10.0
Egypt	323.0	323.0	322.5	342.5	345.0	300.0	20.0	25.0	4.4	515.0	50.0
Iran	211.5	238.0	250.0	300.0	342.0	220.0	22.0	100.0	5.1	300.0	70.0
Iraq	101.8	112.5	135.0	158.0	188.0	160.0	3.0	25.0	9.6	250.0	54.8
Israel	115.0	145.5	156.0	158.5	164.0	138.0	5.0	21.0	24.0	460.0	9.5
Jordan	72.9	74.9	80.2	67.9	67.8	61.0	0.2	6.7	13.1	30.0	10.0
Libya	25.0	32.0	32.0	29.7	29.2	22.0	2.7	4.5	n.a.	n.a.	n.a.
Morocco	56.0	56.0	61.0	73.0	84.7	75.0	4.0	5.7	2.6	n.a.	30.0
Saudi Arabia	42.5	43.0	47.0	51.5	61.5	45.0	1.5	15.0	n.a.	n.a.	41.5
Sudan	38.6	43.6	48.6	52.6	52.1	50.0	0.6	1.5	n.a.	n.a.	3.5
Syria	132.0	137.5	177.5	227.0	227.5	200.0	2.5	25.0	18.1	102.5	9.5
Africa											
Ethiopia	44.6	44.6	44.8	50.8	53.5	50.0	1.5	2.0	0.9	20.0	84.0
Nigeria	157.0	210.0	208.0	230.0	230.5	221.0	3.5	6.0	n.a.	2.0	—
Rhodesia	4.7	4.7	5.7	9.2	9.6	8.3	—	1.3	0.8	55.0	44.0
South Africa	46.0	47.5	50.5	51.5	55.0	41.0	5.5	8.5	1.1	165.5	125.5
Asia											
Australia	73.3	68.9	69.1	69.4	69.7	31.8	16.2	21.7	2.5	32.2	—
China	2,900.0	3,000.0	3,250.0	3,525.0	3,950.0	3,250.0	300.0	400.0	2.2	n.a.	n.a.
China (Taiwan)	503.0	491.0	494.0	470.0	460.0	320.0	70.0	70.0	n.a.	1,170.0	100.0
India	948.0	956.0	956.0	1,055.5	1,096.0	950.0	46.0	100.0	0.8	240.0	300.0
Indonesia	322.0	270.0	266.0	246.0	247.0	180.0	39.0	28.0	1.0	n.a.	112.0
Japan	266.0	233.0	236.0	235.0	238.0	155.0	40.0	43.0	0.9	39.6	—
Korea, South	633.5	625.0	625.0	595.0	635.0	560.0	45.0	30.0	8.6	1,240.0	1,000.0
Malaysia	56.0	66.2	61.1	62.3	64.0	52.5	5.5	6.0	2.7	27.0	213.0
New Zealand	12.8	12.6	12.7	12.5	12.5	5.5	2.7	4.3	2.0	12.2	—
Pakistan	420.0	420.0	392.0	428.0	428.0	400.0	11.0	17.0	4.0	513.0	157.0
Philippines	42.7	55.0	67.0	78.0	99.0	63.0	20.0	16.0	1.2	45.0	65.0
Singapore	20.6	21.7	30.0	31.0	36.0	30.0	3.0	3.0	7.0	45.0	37.5
Thailand	180.0	195.0	204.0	210.0	211.0	141.0	28.0	42.0	2.8	500.0	66.0
Latin America											
Argentina	135.0	135.0	133.5	132.8	129.9	80.0	32.9	17.0	2.5	250.0	51.0
Brazil	208.0	208.0	254.5	257.2	271.8	180.0	49.0	42.8	1.2	n.a.	200.0
Colombia	63.2	63.2	64.3	54.3	56.5	42.0	8.0	6.5	n.a.	250.0	5.0
Mexico	71.0	82.0	82.5	89.5	95.5	72.0	17.5	6.0	0.8	n.a.	n.a.
Peru	54.0	54.0	56.0	63.0	70.0	46.0	14.0	10.0	2.3	n.a.	20.0
Uruguay	21.0	21.0	22.0	23.0	27.0	20.0	4.0	3.0	4.4	n.a.	2.2
Venezuela	37.5	39.5	44.0	42.0	44.0	28.0	8.0	8.0	1.9	n.a.	10.0

4. INDICES OF NATO DEFENCE EXPENDITURE, CURRENT AND CONSTANT PRICES[a] (in local currency, 1970=100)

Country	1960	1966	1967	1968	1969	1970	1971	1972	1973	1974	1975	1976[b]	% Growth[c] 1960–70	1971–76
Belgium	53.9	75.1	81.1	87.1	90.4	100.0	105.8	117.7	130.5	153.0	186.5	212.0	6.4	14.9
	72.5	*85.6*	*89.8*	*93.9*	*94.0*	*100.0*	*101.3*	*107.0*	*110.9*	*115.4*	*124.7*	*129.8*	*3.3*	*5.0*
Britain	67.7	88.1	93.1	95.4	94.2	100.0	115.2	133.3	143.4	172.1	211.3	253.1	4.0	17.0
	100.6	*106.0*	*109.3*	*106.9*	*100.2*	*100.0*	*105.2*	*113.7*	*112.0*	*115.9*	*114.6*	*117.8*	*0*	*1.4*
Canada	80.3	85.7	95.3	93.5	92.1	100.0	103.4	108.6	116.7	138.9	151.7	174.4	2.2	10.9
	105.3	*99.8*	*107.2*	*101.1*	*95.2*	*100.0*	*100.6*	*100.8*	*100.6*	*108.0*	*106.6*	*114.0*	*-0.5*	*2.5*
Denmark	40.4	75.4	81.6	94.0	95.8	100.0	115.9	122.8	127.7	161.0	191.3	206.0	9.5	12.2
	71.4	*97.0*	*97.3*	*103.7*	*102.0*	*100.0*	*109.4*	*108.9*	*103.6*	*113.2*	*122.9*	*121.3*	*3.4*	*2.1*
France	57.7	80.5	87.1	91.0	95.5	100.0	105.4	110.8	121.2	147.4	171.3	196.2	5.6	13.2
	85.7	*97.1*	*102.3*	*102.3*	*101.1*	*100.0*	*99.8*	*99.2*	*101.1*	*108.1*	*112.5*	*116.5*	*1.6*	*3.0*
Germany	53.7	89.7	94.8	85.5	95.6	100.0	112.7	127.2	141.4	157.9	166.5	172.0	6.4	8.9
	70.2	*98.7*	*102.6*	*91.1*	*99.2*	*100.0*	*107.2*	*114.6*	*119.0*	*124.2*	*123.6*	*122.2*	*3.6*	*2.7*
Greece	36.0	50.5	66.1	77.4	89.8	100.0	109.0	121.1	139.8	169.8	309.1	401.8	10.8	24.3
	44.2	*54.3*	*70.0*	*81.7*	*92.6*	*100.0*	*105.8*	*112.6*	*112.9*	*108.1*	*172.6*	*198.4*	*8.5*	*11.0*
Italy	45.5	85.9	87.0	89.8	90.4	100.0	118.6	138.4	153.1	182.6	198.7	227.9	8.2	13.9
	67.0	*97.1*	*95.0*	*96.8*	*94.8*	*100.0*	*113.1*	*125.0*	*124.7*	*124.8*	*116.7*	*113.0*	*4.1*	*0*
Luxembourg	63.2	119.5	99.3	89.9	94.0	100.0	106.3	124.3	144.5	170.7	201.0	236.3	4.7	17.3
	81.5	*134.1*	*109.1*	*96.3*	*98.3*	*100.0*	*101.6*	*112.9*	*124.1*	*133.5*	*141.8*	*151.9*	*2.1*	*8.6*
Netherlands	43.5	70.3	80.6	82.7	92.8	100.0	112.6	125.4	137.7	161.9	182.6	194.4	8.7	11.6
	65.6	*84.0*	*93.1*	*92.0*	*96.1*	*100.0*	*104.7*	*108.2*	*110.0*	*117.9*	*120.7*	*118.1*	*4.3*	*2.5*
Norway	38.1	70.2	75.6	82.9	90.2	100.0	108.9	116.8	126.4	142.0	171.0	188.2	10.1	11.6
	59.2	*86.5*	*89.3*	*94.5*	*99.8*	*100.0*	*102.5*	*102.6*	*103.3*	*106.0*	*115.0*	*115.3*	*5.4*	*2.5*
Portugal	24.1	59.0	76.4	85.3	86.0	100.0	117.2	128.0	133.5	200.3	158.0	147.6	15.3	4.6
	37.3	*76.4*	*93.7*	*98.7*	*91.0*	*100.0*	*104.7*	*103.3*	*95.4*	*114.4*	*78.6*	*60.5*	*10.4*	*-11.6*
Turkey	38.6	64.1	73.7	82.7	86.5	100.0	136.1	159.7	195.5	253.8	532.6	699.2	10.0	31.0
	68.4	*87.0*	*87.7*	*93.0*	*92.6*	*100.0*	*114.3*	*123.6*	*131.1*	*147.0*	*259.8*	*253.2*	*3.9*	*13.3*
United States	58.3	81.7	96.9	103.7	104.6	100.0	96.2	99.7	100.8	110.3	116.8	127.3	5.5	5.7
	76.5	*97.6*	*112.7*	*115.7*	*110.8*	*100.0*	*92.3*	*92.6*	*88.1*	*86.9*	*84.3*	*86.8*	*2.7*	*-1.2*

[a] To produce constant price series (in italics) defence expenditures are deflated by consumer price indices. These reflect general rates of inflation, not rates in the defence sector.

[b] 1976 figures are provisional, those for Greece and Turkey being estimates; hence 1971–76 growth rates are approximate

[c] Average annual compound growth rates over periods shown.

5. COMPARATIVE STRENGTHS OF ARMED FORCES 1956–1977 (in thousands)

Year	USA	Japan	Germany	France	Britain[a]	USSR
1956	2,857	188	66	785	760	4,500
1957	2,800	202	122	836	700	4,200
1958	2,637	214	175	797	615	4,000
1959	2,552	215	249	770	565	3,900
1960	2,514	206	270	781	520	3,623
1961	2,572	209	325	778	455	3,800
1962	2,827	216	389	742	445	3,600
1963	2,737	213	403	632	430	3,300
1964	2,687	216	435	555	425	3,300
1965	2,723	225	441	510	424	3,150
1966	3,123	227	455	500	418	3,165
1967	3,446	231	452	500	417	3,220
1968	3,547	235	440	505	405	3,220
1969	3,454	236	465	503	383	3,300
1970	3,066	259	466	506	373	3,305
1971	2,699	259	467	502	365	3,375
1972	2,391	260	467	501	363	3,375
1973	2,253	266	475	504	352	3,425
1974	2,174	233	490	503	345	3,525
1975	2,130	236	495	503	345	3,573
1976	2,087	235	495	513	335	3,650
1977	2,088	238	489	502	330	3,675

[a] Excluding forces enlisted outside Britain.

6. OFFENSIVE SUPPORT AIRCRAFT CHARACTERISTICS

Model[a]	Country of origin and name	Date in service	Crew	No. of engines	Take-off weight (kg) Clean	Max	Take-off run, typical load (m)	Max level speed (Mach or mph)	Typical combat radius (km)	Ceiling (ft)	Roles[a]
	Britain										
	Hunter FGA Mk 9	1960	1	1	7,000	10,800	685	0.92	980	53,000	FGA/trainer
	Lightning F53	1960	1	2	18,144	22,680	1,203	2.00	740	57,000	AWX, AD
BAC-167	Strikemaster	1968	2	1	2,810	5,125	1,067	410	656	40,000	lt attack
	Buccaneer S2	1969	2	2	20,800	28,123	720	0.95	1,500	40,000	naval strike, FB
	Harrier GR3	1969	1	1	5,896	11,339	VTOL	0.96	540	45,000	VTOL FGA
BAC-145	Jet Provost Mk5	1969	1–2	1	3,170	4,173	410	440	480	36,750	lt attack/trainer
BAC-1182	Hawk	1976	1–2	1	5,035	7,843	549	1.16	920	48,500	lt attack/trainer
	Canada										
CF-5A		1968	1	2	6,600	10,923	808	1.04	346	50,000+	FGA
	China										
F-9	Fantan A	1975	1	2	9,200	10,700	620	2.00	790	51,200	AD
	France										
	Mirage IIIE	1964	1	1	7,050	13,500	700	2.02	1,200	55,775	FGA, AD, strike
	Mirage V	1967	1	1	6,600	13,500	700	2.02	1,300	55,775	FGA
	Mirage F1C	1973	1	1	10,900	14,900	640	1.02	740	65,600	multi-role
	International										
	Jaguar	1973	1	2	10,500	15,500	880	1.4	850	48,000	FGA, strike
	AlphaJet	(1978)	2	2	4,890	7,300	480	0.85	630	46,000	close support/trainer
MRCA	Tornado	(1978)	2	2	n.a.	20,385	700	2.00	925	50,000+	multi-role (VG), strike
	Israel										
	Kfir	1972	1	1	7,200	14,600	700	2.2	370–535	50,000+	AD, FGA
	Kfir C2	1976	1	1	7,285	14,600	700	2.3	1,300	50,000+	FGA, AD
	Italy										
G-91Y		1971	1	2	7,800	8,700	914	0.95	600	41,000	FB
MB-326K		1972	1–2	1	4,645	5,897	411	553	648	39,000	lt attack/trainer
	Soviet Union										
	MiG-15 Fagot	1948	1	1	3,773	6,464	n.a.	0.87	300	48,000	FGA
	MiG-17 Fresco C	1952	1	1	n.a.	5,669	n.a.	0.96	500	57,000	FGA, AD
	MiG-19 Farmer C	1955	1	2	n.a.	9,000	n.a.	1.3	322	58,000	FGA, AD

Yak-25	*Flashlight D*	2	2	1957	n.a.	11,350	n.a.	0.95	1,100	n.a.	AD, FB
Yak-28	*Brewer*	2	2	1961	n.a.	15,875	n.a.	1.1	800	55,000	AD, FB
Su-7B	*Fitter A*	1	1	1961	12,000	13,500	n.a.	1.2	480	49,700	FGA/strike
Tu-28P	*Fiddler*	2	2-3	1962	n.a.	45,000	n.a.	1.75	970	65,000	AWX
Yak-28P	*Firebar*	2	2	1962	n.a.	15,875	n.a.	1.1	925	55,000	AD
Su-11	*Fishpot C*	1	1	1967	8,300	12,457	900	1.8	508	50,000	AD
Su-15	*Flagon A*	2	1	1967	8,720	16,000	n.a.	2.5	650	55,000	AD
MiG-21F	*Fishbed J*	1	1	1970	7,840	9,400	800	2.1	550	46,000	FGA
MiG-23	*Flogger B*	1	1	1971	14,800	20,400	650	2.3	1,017	50,000	FB, AD (VG)
MiG-25	*Foxbat A*	2	1	1971	15,425	33,995	1,380	3.2	462	75,000	AWX
MiG-27	*Flogger D*	1	1	1971	14,400	20,400	775	1.6	1,017	45,000	FB/strike
Su-17	*Fitter C*	1	1	1972	14,000	19,000	620	1.3	600	50,000	FGA (VG)
Su-19	*Fencer A*	2	2	1974	16,000	30,804	600	2.0	740	44,000	strike (VG)
Yak-36	*Forger A*	1+2	1	1976	5,215	9,977	VTOL	0.9	370	n.a.	VTOL naval/FGA
Sweden											
J35A	*Draken*	1	1	1960	11,400	15,000	650	2.0	635	55,000+	AD
AJ-37	*Viggen*	1	1	1971	16,500	22,500	400	2.0	1,000	50,000	FGA, AD
Saab 105G		2	1-2	1973	4,860	6,500	700	0.86	695	42,650	lt attack/trainer
United States											
F-106	*Delta Dart*	1	1	1956	12,471	15,875	n.a.	2.31	920	57,000	AWX
F-8	*Crusader*	1	1	1957	8,150	13,300	n.a.	2.0	965	55,000	naval FB
F-4B	*Phantom*	2	2	1958	20,865	24,765	1,525	2.0+	1,450	58,050	multi-role, strike, naval
F-105	*Thunderchief*	1	1	1958	n.a.	24,495	610	2.25	1,110	52,000	FB, strike
A-6A	*Intruder*	2	2	1963	11,900	27,500	497	620	600	41,660	naval strike, tanker
F-104G	*Starfighter*[b]	1	1	1963	6,387	13,054	902	2.2	1,200	58,500	AD, strike
F-111A		2	2	1964	35,400	41,500	915	2.2	1,700	51,000	FGA, strike (VG)
A-7D	*Corsair II*	1	1-2	1968	8,972	19,050	1,525	698	825	n.a.	FB, strike, naval
A-37B	*Dragonfly*	2	2	1968	4,200	6,350	531	524	245	41,765	lt attack
A-4M	*Skyhawk*	1	1	1970	4,747	11,113	823	645	1,100	45,000	naval strike, FGA
F-14A	*Tomcat*	2	2	1972	25,007	33,724	366	2.3	n.a.	50,000	naval AD (VG)
F-5E	*Tiger II*	2	1	1973	4,275	11,561	610	1.57	1,080	52,000	FGA
F-15	*Eagle*	2	1	1974	18,900	25,400	274	2.5	1,100	65,000	multi-role, strike (VG)
A-10A		1	1	1977	16,800	21,148	1,152	518	485	45,000	close support
F-16A		1	1	(1978)	9,850	14,968	533	2.0	925	50,000+	FGA

vg = variable geometry.

[a] The characteristics quoted are for the particular mark or model shown (e.g., F-104G). The alternative roles shown may be performed by other marks/models.

Recce and ecm roles not listed, since many ac can be adapted to them.

[b] Built as F-104S (interceptor) in Italy. F-104G were also built in Belgium, Netherlands and West Germany, in Canada as CF-104, and in Japan as F-104J (fighter-bomber).

7. MAJOR NAVAL SHIP CONSTRUCTION, WARSAW PACT & NATO, 1957–1976ᵃ

		1957–66	1967	1968	1969	1970	1971	1972	1973	1974	1975	1976	Totalᵇ	Ten years 1967–76	Five years 1972–76
Submarines															
Ballistic missile, nuclear	WP	9	2	4	6	8	6	6	6	6	6	6	65	54	30
	NATO	40	2	2	1	—	1	—	1	1	—	1	49ᶜ	9	3
Ballistic missile, diesel	WP	29ᵈ	—	—	—	—	—	—	—	—	—	—	29	—	—
	NATO	—	—	—	—	—	—	—	—	—	—	—	—	—	—
Cruise missile, nuclear	WP	31ᵉ	4	2	2	3	2	2	1	—	1	—	48	17	4
	NATO	1ᶠ	—	—	—	—	—	—	—	—	—	—	1	—	—
Cruise missile, diesel	WP	23ᵍ	2	2	—	—	—	—	—	—	—	—	27	4	—
	NATO	1ᶠ	—	—	—	—	—	—	—	—	—	—	1	—	—
Torpedo attack, nuclear	WP	14	2	2	2	2	3	3	2	2	2	2	36	22	11
	NATO	25	8	5	9	4	9	4	3	4	2	3	76	51	16
Torpedo attack, diesel	WP	91	5	5	3	2	1	—	1	1	1	1	111ʰ	20	4
	NATO	61	8	6	4	3	1	5	7	5	8	2	110	49	27
Aircraft Carriers															
Attack, over 60,000 tons	WP	—	—	—	—	—	—	—	—	—	—	—	—	—	—
	NATO	6	—	1	—	—	—	—	—	—	1	—	8	2	1
Attack, 30–60,000 tons	WP	—	—	—	—	—	—	—	—	—	—	—	—	—	—
	NATO	2	—	—	—	—	—	—	—	—	—	—	2	—	—
Attack, under 30,000 tons	WP	1	—	—	—	—	—	—	—	—	—	—	1	—	—
	NATO	—	—	—	1	—	—	—	—	—	—	—	1	—	—
ASW, 30–60,000 tons	WP	—	—	—	—	—	—	—	—	—	1ⁱ	—	1	1	1
	NATO	—	—	—	—	1ʲ	—	—	—	—	—	—	1	1	—
ASW Cruisers															
15–30,000 tons	WP	—	1	1	—	—	—	—	—	—	—	—	2ᵏ	2	—
	NATO	—	—	—	—	—	—	—	—	—	—	—	—	—	—
8–15,000 tons	WP	—	—	—	—	—	—	—	—	—	—	—	—	—	—
	NATO	—	—	—	1	—	—	—	—	—	—	—	1ˡ	1	—
Surface Ships															
Over 11,000 tons	WP	—	—	—	—	—	—	—	—	—	—	—	—	—	—
	NATO	9	—	—	—	—	—	—	—	—	—	—	9	—	—

8–11,000 tons	WP	—	1	1	1	1	1	1	5^m	5	5
	NATO	1	1	—	—	1	1	—	4	3	2
5,500–8,000 tons	WP	5	1	1	1	2	1	1	17^n	12	6
	NATO	32	1	—	1	1	2	8	51°	19	12
3,500–5,500 tons: new construction	WP	30	2	2	3	3	3	3	56^p	26	15
major modification	WP	1	1	3	3	2	2	2	23^p	22	11
	Total	31	3	4	6	5	5	5	79	48	26
	NATO	53	3	3	12	8	4	1	117^q	64	27
1,000–3,500 tons	WP	51	6	5	—	2	2	—	75^r	24	—
	NATO	114	11	6	4	8	8	5	177^s	63	19
Amphibious Ships											
Assault ships, over 30,000 tons	WP	—	—	—	—	—	—	—	—	—	—
	NATO	—	—	—	1	—	1	1	1^t	1	1
Under 30,000 tons	WP	5	—	1	—	—	—	—	7^u	—	—
	NATO	—	1	—	—	—	—	—	—	2	—
LPD and LSD, 10–17,000 tons	WP	—	—	—	—	—	—	—	23^v	15	2
	NATO	8	3	1	2	2	3	2	—	—	—
LSD, 8–10,000 tons	WP	—	—	—	—	—	—	—	2^w	—	—
	NATO	1	—	—	—	1	—	—	—	1	—
LST, over 8,000 tons	WP	—	—	—	—	1	1	1	23^x	20	4
	NATO	3	2	7	7	4	1	3	—	—	—
LST, 4–8,000 tons	WP	2	2	2	1	1	1	3	21^y	19	11
	NATO	9	3	1	—	—	—	3	13^z	4	—

LCM = landing craft, mechanized
LCPL = landing craft, personnel, large
LCU = landing craft, utility
LCVP = landing craft, vehicle/personnel
LPD = landing platform, dock
LSD = landing ship, dock
LST = landing ship, tank
LVT = landing vehicle, tracked

a This table is effectively confined to contrasting NATO naval shipbuilding with that of the Soviet Union (since other Warsaw Pact navies are very small). The Soviet Union does, however, also have to take into account the navies of other Western allies of the United States, and, of course, China.

b These totals will be greater than the aggregates of the vessels shown in the country entries, since they include ships that have been retired or lost. They also include ships transferred to other countries outside the two alliances unless specifically mentioned above.

c 31 *Poseidon* conversions completed 1970–1976.
d Incl 6 Z-V class retrofitted with SS-N-3.
e Incl 5 E-I class later converted to ssn.
f Experimental only.
g Incl 12 W-class retrofitted with SS-N-3.
h 8 F-class transferred to India not included.
i Incl 8 F-class (40,000 tons). Fitted with asw msls and 2 SA-N-3 SAM systems; can carry 15–20 vtol ac and 20 hel.
j *Ark Royal* modernization 1967–1970.
k *Moskva*-class (17,500 tons). Fitted with asw msls and two SA-N-3 SAM systems; can carry 15 hel.
l *Vittorio Veneto* (8,850 tons). Fitted with *Terrier/ASROC* msl system, carries 9 AB-204B hel.

m *Kara*-class (9,500 tons). Carry asw msls.

n Incl 13 *Kresta* I- and II-class (8,000 tons), both designated 'large asw ship'), 4 *Kynda*-class (6,000 tons); all fitted with ssm and sam system.

o Incl 7 British *County*-, 1 Type 82, 9 US *Belknap*- and 8 *Spruance*-class, all comparable to 'large asw ships'.

p 19 *Kashin*, 14 *Krivak* average 4,000 tons; major modifications incl 8 sam *Kotlin* 8 *Kanin*, 4 *Kildin*. All except sam *Kotlin* are 'large asw ships'. *Kashin*, *Kanin* and sam *Kotlin* carry SA-N-1 sam. *Krivak* carries SA-N-3 sam. None carry hel.

q 57 ships are armed with sam and 62 carry hel.

r *Mirka/Petya*-classes (average 1,050 tons), designated 'escort ship', are only comparable to NATO ships under 2,000 tons (28 included in this category).

s 82 carry hel. The asw capabilities of 58 NATO ships over 2,000 tons in this category are comparable to the *Kashin*.

t *Tarawa* (39,300 tons). Carries 1,825 troops, 30 troop-carrying hel.

u *Iwo Jima*-class (18,300 tons). Carry 2,090 troops, 20–24 med, 8 hy and 4 lt hel.

v 12 *Austin*-class LPD (16,900 tons) carry 930 troops, 6 hel; 3 *Raleigh*-class LPD (13,900 tons) carry 930 troops, 6 hel; 5 *Anchorage*-class LSD, (13,700 tons) carry 376 troops, 3 LCU, 1 LCM and 1 LCPL; 9 *Thomaston*-class LSD (11,270 tons) carry 340 troops, 21 LCM (or 3 LCU and 6 LCM, or 50 LVT) in docking well, plus 30 LVT on upper decks; 2 British LPD (12,120 tons) can carry 580 troops, 4 LCM in dock, 4 LCVP at davits.

w 2 *Ouranga*-class LSD (8,500 tons) can carry 350 troops, 18 LCM.

x 20 *Newport*-class (8,342 tons) can carry 386 troops; 3 *Suffolk County* class (8,000 tons) carry 575 troops, 23 tanks.

y 14 *Alligator*-class (5,800 tons) capacity 1,700 tons, one naval inf bn, 20–25 med, 30–40 lt tks. 7 *Ropucha*-class (4,000 tons).

z 5 French LST (4,225 tons) carry 4 LCVP, 1,800 tons freight, 335 troops; 2 Italian *De Soto County* class (8,000 tons) carry 575 troops; 6 British log landing ships (5,674 tons) carry 340 troops.

8. COMPARISON OF DIVISIONAL ESTABLISHMENTS, PRESENT AND PROPOSED[a]

	Armoured Divisions							Mechanized Divisions				
	USSR[b]	USA		West Germany		Britain		USSR[b]	USA		West Germany	
		Present	New[c]	Present	New[d]	Present[e]	New[f]		Present	New[c]	Present	New[d]
Personnel in div	11,000	16,500	17,800	17,000	15,000	11,700	8,500	12,700	16,000	18,000	17,500	15,000
Armd bdes/regts[g]	3	3[h]	3	2	2	2	—	1	—	1	1	1
each of: tk bns	3	2	3	2	3	2	—	4[i]	—	3	2	3
inf bns	—	1	2	1	1	2	—	—	—	2	1	1
Mech bdes/regts[g]	1	—	—	1	1	—	—	3	3[h]	2	2	2
each of: tk bns	1	—	—	1	2	—	—	1	1	2	1	2
inf bns	3	—	—	2	3	—	—	3	2	3	2	3
Major units in div:												
tk bns	10	9	9	5	8	4	2	7	4[h]	7	4	7
inf bns	3	6[h]	6	4	5	4	3	9	6[h]	8	5	7
recce bns	1	1[j]	1[j]	1	1	—[k]	1	1	1[j]	1[j]	1	1
ATK bns	—	—	—	—	—	—	—	1	—	—	—	—
arty bns	4	4	4	5	5	2	2	4	4	4	5	5

Major equipments in div:

Tanks												
med	325[l]	324	360	300	264	212	148	266[l]	216	288	250	231
lt	22	54[m]	—	—	—	—	72	22	54[m]	—	—	n.a.
Anti-tank weapons												
Tank destroyers	—	—	—	16	—	—	—	18	—	—	32	—
ATGW[n]	153[o]	380[p]	480	34	186	72[q]	78[r]	165[s]	426[t]	534	29	222
Artillery												
hy guns[u]	—	12	16	18	18	—[v]	3	—	12	16	18	18
med guns[u]	60	54	96	54	54	36	36	96	54	96	54	54
hy mor	18	53	—	30	30	—	—	54	49	—	36	36
multiple RL	18	—	—[w]	16	16	—	—	18	—	—[w]	16	16
SSM	4	—[x]	—[x]	4	4	—[x]	—[x]	4	—[x]	—[x]	4	4

[a] Countries tend to have more than one manpower establishment for a div (e.g. peacetime and wartime) or variations to fit different theatre requirements. The figures shown here apply to Central Europe, and to operations rather than peacetime. They include only regular units that are a permanent part of the formation.

[b] Figures refer to tk divs with 1 BMP mech regt and to mech divs with 1 BMP and 2 BTR-60 mech regts.

[c] Figures for new US divs refer to div structures being tested, based on more but smaller bns and an increase in arty and ATGW; details may well change.

[d] Figures for new West German divs refer to divs based on a new bde structure; several bdes have already been converted. Figures for numbers of weapons are provisional only and may change.

[e] The div strength would be increased in war to 12,700 by inclusion of reservists.

[f] Britain is converting her divs into smaller ones, eliminating the bde. One has already been converted. Div strength will be increased in war to 11,500 by inclusion of reserve units.

[g] The number of bdes in a div and, in particular, the number of bns in a bde, will vary with operational needs; regrouping of units would be normal. The composition given here is only a guide in each case to standard peacetime dispositions. Soviet regts are the equivalent formation to bdes in the West.

[h] US bdes in the armd div have a total of 11 tk and inf bns; those in the mech div have a total of 10 tk and inf bns, flexibly assigned according to need.

[i] Incl one indep tk bn.

[j] An armd cav sqn, strength 860.

[k] Recce bns are Corps units, alloted one to a div. They include 8 ATGW AFV.

[l] Divs in Eastern Europe only; others have fewer tks, particularly in mech divs.

[m] In Europe; elsewhere normally 27.

[n] AFV with multiple launchers counted as one ATGW. Figures exclude weapons carried in tks shown in this table or on hel.

[o] 12 manpack, 132 BMP-, 9 BRDM-mounted *Sagger*.

[p] 134 *TOW*, 246 *Dragon*.

[q] 40 *Swingfire* AFV with armd regts and recce bn plus 32 *Milan* (16 per inf bn).

[r] 30 *Swingfire* AFV, 48 *Milan*.

[s] 36 manpack, 102 BMP-, 27 BRDM-mounted *Sagger*.

[t] 148 *TOW*, 278 *Dragon*.

[u] Med guns incl 105mm and 155mm; larger calibres are classified as hy.

[v] Hy guns are held at Corps level, the div share would be 8 175mm, 4 203mm.

[w] A multiple RL system is being developed.

[x] Held at Corps level.

9. INDEX OF NATO CODE NAMES FOR SOVIET AIRCRAFT

Name	Aircraft	Role	Name	Aircraft	Role
Backfire	Tu-?	med bbr	*Flagon*	Su-15	interceptor
Badger	Tu-16	med bbr, MR, ECM, tanker	*Flashlight* A–D	Yak-25	interceptor, FB, recce
			Flogger A, B, C, E	MiG-23	interceptor
Beagle	Il-28	lt bbr, recce, ECM	*Flogger* D, F	MiG-27	FGA
Bear	Tu-95	LR* bbr, MR	*Fresco*	MiG-17	FGA, interceptor
Bison	Mya-4	LR bbr, tanker	*Forger*	Yak-36	VTOL FGA
Blinder	Tu-22	med bbr, recce, ECM	*Foxbat*	MiG-25	interceptor, recce
Brewer	Yak-28	FGA, recce, ECM			
			Hare	Mi-1	lt hel
Cab	Li-2	2-engine tpt	*Harke*	Mi-10	flying crane hel
Camel	Tu-104	2-engine tpt	*Haze*	Mi-14	ASW hel
Candid	**Il-76**	4-engine tpt	*Hind*	Mi-24	assault hel
Careless	Tu-154	3-engine tpt	*Hip*	Mi-8	tpt hel
Clank	An-30	2-engine aerial survey	*Homer*	Mi-12	hy GP hel
Classic	Il-62	4-engine tpt	*Hoodlum*	Ka-26	lt hel
Cleat	Tu-114	4-engine tpt	*Hook*	Mi-6	hy tpt hel
Clod	An-14	2-engine lt GP	*Hoplite*	Mi-2	GP lt hel
Cock	An-22	4-engine tpt	*Hormone*	Ka-25	ASW, GP hel
Codling	Yak-40	3-engine tpt	*Hound*	Mi-4	tpt, ASW, GP hel
Coke	An-24	2-engine tpt			
Coot	Il-18	4-engine tpt	*Maestro*	Yak-28U	trainer
Crate	Il-14	2-engine tpt	*Maiden*	Su-9U	fighter/trainer
Crusty	Tu-134	2-engine tpt	*Mail*	Be-12	2-engine MR amphibian
Cub A, C	An-12	4-engine tpt, ECM	*Mandrake*	Yak-?	LR recce
Curl	An-26	2-engine tpt	*Mangrove*	Yak-26	fighter, recce
			Mantis	Yak-30	basic trainer
Fagot	MiG-15	FGA	*Mascot*	Il-28UTI	bbr/trainer
Farmer	MiG-19	FGA	*May*	Il-38	4-engine ASW, MR
Fencer	Su-19	FGA	*Maya*	L-29	trainer
Fiddler	Tu-28P	interceptor	*Max*	Yak-18	trainer
Firebar	Yak-28P	interceptor	*Midget*	MiG-15UTI	fighter/trainer
Fishbed	MiG-21	multi-role fighter	*Mongol*	MiG-21UTI	fighter/trainer
Fishpot B	Su-9	interceptor	*Moss*	Tu-126	airborne control
Fishpot C	Su-11	interceptor	*Moose*	Yak-11	trainer
Fitter A	Su-7	FGA	*Moujik*	Su-7BUTI	fighter/trainer
Fitter C	Su-17/-20/ -22	FGA	*Mouse*	Yak-18A/P	fighter/trainer

* Long-range.

10. PEACE-KEEPING FORCES

United Nations Truce Supervisory Organization (UNTSO)

Set up in 1948 to supervise the cease-fire arranged by the Security Council between Egypt, Jordan, Lebanon, Syria and Israel.

Members: Argentina, Australia, Austria, Belgium, Canada, Chile, Denmark, Finland, France, Ireland, Italy, Netherlands, New Zealand, Sweden, USSR, USA.

Activities: Military observation duties since 1948 and assistance with application of the 1949 Armistice Agreements.

After the October 1973 war observers marked the lines of the zone of disengagement in the Suez sector and continue to report incidents and inspect the agreed area of limited armaments and forces. Observation posts are maintained and inspection carried out on the Golan Heights.

HQ: Jerusalem. Field stations and liaison offices in Amman, Beirut, Cairo, Damascus, Gaza, Qneitra and Tiberias.

Composition: Staff consists of 190 international civilians, 298 military observers (90 are assigned to UNDOF) and 160 local personnel.

United Nations Emergency Force (UNEF)

Set up in October 1973 to supervise the cease-fire on the Suez Canal front between Egyptian and Israeli forces.

Activities: Patrols the zone of disengagement and conducts bi-weekly inspections of the areas of limited armaments and forces.

HQ: Ismailia.

Composition: Australia 44, Canada 871, Finland 640, Ghana 597, Indonesia 510, Poland 865, Sweden 687.

United Nations Disengagement Observer Force (UNDOF)

Established in May 1974, following the Geneva disengagement agreement between Syria and Israel.

Activities: Initial task was to take over the territory evacuated by Israel in accordance with the disengagement agreement, and to occupy a buffer zone. Subsequent tasks have included regular inspection of the thinning out of forces of both sides.

HQ: Damascus.

Composition: Austria 520, Canada 164, Iran 388, Poland 88.

United Nations Peace-Keeping Forces in Cyprus (UNFICYP)

Set up in March 1964 to keep the peace between the Greeks and Turkish Cypriot communities.

HQ: Nicosia.

Composition: Austria 312, Britain 823, Canada 505, Denmark 360, Eire 5, Finland 290, Sweden 425.

Arab Peace-Keeping Force in Lebanon

Set up in June 1976 by a number of Arab countries to try to maintain peace in the Lebanon.

HQ: Beirut.

Composition: Saudi Arabia 700, Sudan 1,000, Syria 30,000+, United Arab Emirates 700, Yemen Arab Republic (North) 500, Yemen, People's Democratic Republic (South) 500. Libya originally provided a contingent but it has now been withdrawn.

11. MAJOR IDENTIFIED ARMS AGREEMENTS, JULY 1976–JUNE 1977

(A) WESTERN EUROPE AND NATO

Recipient	Primary supplier	Approximate date of agreement	System	Quantity	Cost ($m)	Expected date of delivery
Belgium	Eire	1976	BDX APC	40	17	n.a.
Britain	France/Germany	Oct 1976	*Milan* ATGW msls	5,000*	n.a.	1977 on
	USA	Mid-1977	*Pave Spike* laser weapon guidance	12	8.5	n.a.
		Mid-1977	*Sidewinder* AAM	1,709	119	n.a.
Canada	Britain	n.a.	*Scorpion* tk turrets	152	14.5	1977–81
Eire	Sweden	n.a.	PV1110 90mm RCL	n.a.	n.a.	1976–77
Germany	Britain	Late 1976	105mm tk guns	375	n.a.	n.a.
	France	Aug 1976	*Exocet* SSM	150	n.a.	1977–78
Greece	France	1976	*Exocet* SSM	20	n.a.	n.a.
		Late 1976	*Combattante* FPBG	6	40	n.a.
	USA	n.a.	Destroyers	7	n.a.	n.a.
		n.a.	Landing ships	2	n.a.	n.a.
		Early 1977	*Sidewinder* AAM	300 ⎫	35	n.a.
			Hel	35 ⎬		
		Early 1977	F-4 fighters	18	161	n.a.
Netherlands	USA	n.a.	*Sidewinder* AAM	840	n.a.	n.a.
Norway	USA	n.a.	*Roland* SAM	40 ⎫	170	1980s
			Roland SAM msls	900 ⎬		
Portugal	USA	Sept 1976	C-130H tpt ac	2	n.a.	1977
Spain	Switzerland	n.a.	*Skyguard* AD systems	12	n.a.	n.a.
	USA	Early 1977	AV-8A v/STOL fighters	5	n.a.	n.a.
		n.a.	C-130H tpt ac	5	n.a.	n.a.
Sweden	Britain	Late 1976	*Skyflash* AAM	n.a.	6	1979
	USA	n.a.	*Maverick* ASM	n.a.	20	n.a.
		n.a.	*Improved Hawk* SAM	100	n.a.	n.a.
Turkey	France/Germany	n.a.	*Milan* ATGW	483 ⎫	n.a.	n.a.
			Milan ATGW msls	6,250 ⎬		
	Germany	Mid-1976	*AlphaJet* trg ac	56	n.a.	1979 on
		Feb 1977	*Leopard* med tks	193	494	n.a.
	Italy	Late 1976	AB-205 hel	56	n.a.	n.a.
		Mid-1977	AB-212 ASW hel	6	n.a.	n.a.
	USA	1977	*Harpoon* SSM	33	n.a.	Feb 1977
USA	Belgium	Early 1977	MAG 58 machine guns	10,000	n.a.	n.a.
	Britain	Late 1976	F-16 avionics	n.a.	59.5	n.a.
	Israel	Mid-1977	M-48 tk cupolas	600	35	1976 on

* Part purchase, part to be manufactured in Britain.

(B) MIDDLE EAST AND NORTH AFRICA

Recipient	Primary supplier	Approximate date of agreement	System	Quantity	Cost ($m)	Expected date of delivery
Egypt	France	Mid-1976	*Crotale* SAM	n.a.	n.a.	1977
		Early 1977	*Agosta-class* submarines	2	n.a.	n.a.
Iran	Britain	Nov 1976	*Rapier* SAM on tracked vehicles	n.a.	680	1979 on
		1976	*Scorpion* lt tks	110	108.7	1977
	Italy	1976	AS-61 hel	2	n.a.	n.a.
	USA	1976	*Sidewinder* AAM	350	261	1978
		1976	*Sparrow* AAM	350	n.a.	n.a.
		Late 1976	*Phoenix* AAM	424	304	1976
		1976	RH-53D hel	6	25	n.a.
		*Late 1976	F-16 fighters	160	3,400	1979–83
		Mid-1976	*Improved Hawk* SAM	6 btys	n.a.	n.a.
		Mid-1976	P-3C *Orion* MR ac	3	n.a.	1977
		March 1977	Bell 214A hel	6	4	1978
		Early 1977	CH-47 tpt hel	50	425	n.a.
	USSR	Nov 1976	SA-7/-9 SAM, ASU-85 SP ATK guns, ZSU-23-4 SP AA guns, BMP MICV	n.a.	414	n.a.
Iraq	France	1976	*Super Frelon* hel	10	n.a.	1976–77
	USSR	Oct 1976	T-62 tks, *Scud* SSM	n.a.	300	1979
Israel	USA	Oct 1976	M-60 med tks	125	100	n.a.
		1976	155mm how	94	n.a.	n.a.
		1976	175mm SP guns	n.a.	n.a.	n.a.
		Oct 1976	*Sidewinder* AAM	n.a.	n.a.	n.a.
		June 1977	M-113 APC	700	115	n.a.
			TOW ATGW	200		
Jordan	USA	Mid-1976	*Vulcan* 20mm AA guns	100	n.a.	n.a.
		Late 1976	*Improved Hawk* SAM	14 btys	540	n.a.
Kuwait	USSR	Dec 1976	SA-7 SAM and arty	n.a.	400	n.a.
Libya	Brazil	Early 1977	EE-9 *Cascavel* and EE-11 *Urutu* AFV	400	400	n.a.
	France	1976	LST	1	n.a.	1977
		1976	PR 72 FPBG	10	186	n.a.
		1976	*Otomat* SSM	80	201.3	n.a.
	Italy	Mid-1977	CH-47C hel	16	n.a.	n.a.
Morocco	France	Early 1977	*Mirage* F-1 fighters	25	n.a.	n.a.
	Italy	1976	SF-260 trg ac	28	n.a.	1976–77
	Spain	June 1976	Frigates	5	170	n.a.
			Corvette	1		
	USA	Sept 1976	T-2 *Buckeye* trg ac	20	89	n.a.
		1976	M-113 APC	334	n.a.	1977 on
Oman	Britain	Mar 1977	Log spt ship	1	n.a.	n.a.
	Netherlands	n.a.	Minesweepers	2	0.65	n.a.

Recipient	Primary supplier	Approximate date of agreement	System	Quantity	Cost ($m)	Expected date of delivery
Saudi Arabia	Britain	1976	*Strikemaster* COIN/trg ac	11	n.a.	n.a.
	USA	Mid-1976	*Maverick* ASM	400	n.a.	n.a.
		1976	*Improved Hawk* SAM	6 btys	1,034	1976–81
		Late 1976	*Sidewinder* AAM	2,000	n.a.	n.a.
Sudan	Canada	Mid-1977	DHC-5D tpt ac	4	n.a.	n.a.
	France	May 1977	*Mirage* V fighters	15	n.a.	n.a.
		May 1977	*Puma* hel	10	n.a.	n.a.
		May 1977	AMX-10 APC	n.a.	n.a.	n.a.
	USA	1976	C-130 tpt ac	6	n.a.	n.a.
Syria	Austria	Feb 1977	Pinzgauer trucks	2,000	n.a.	n.a.
	France	1976	*Milan* ATGW msls	2,000	n.a.	n.a.
	France	Oct 1975	*Gazelle* hel	n.a.	n.a.	n.a.
	Italy	1976	CH-47C hel	6	n.a.	n.a.
Tunisia	Austria	Late 1976	*Kuerassier* SP ATK guns	40	344	n.a.
	Italy	Oct 1976	MB-326 COIN/trg ac	12	n.a.	1977
	USA	Late 1976	*Chaparral* SAM	n.a.	58	n.a.
United Arab Emirates	Canada	Mid-1977	DHC-5D tpt ac	4	n.a.	n.a.
	France	n.a.	*Mirage* V fighters	10	n.a.	1977
Yemen Arab Republic	USA	1976	How, AA guns	n.a.	139	1977 on

*Subject to US Congressional approval.

(C) SUB-SAHARAN AFRICA

Recipient	Primary supplier	Approximate date of agreement	System	Quantity	Cost ($m)	Expected date of delivery
Angola	Switzerland	1976	*Turbo-Porter* lt ac	2	n.a.	1976
Cameroon	USA	Late 1976	C-130 tpt ac	2	n.a.	Dec 1977
Gabon	France	1976	*Mirage* V fighters	6	n.a.	n.a.
Ghana	Germany	Early 1977	FPB	4	n.a.	n.a.
	Italy	Late 1976	MB-326F COIN ac	6	n.a.	n.a.
Ivory Coast	France	1976	Landing ship	1	n.a.	n.a.
Kenya	Britain	1976	Vickers med tks	40	n.a.	n.a.
Mauritania	Britain	Late 1976	*Defender* MR/COIN ac	2	n.a.	n.a.
	France	1976	AML armd cars	n.a.	n.a.	n.a.
	Spain	July 1976	Patrol boats	2	n.a.	n.a.

Recipient	Primary supplier	Approximate date of agreement	System	Quantity	Cost ($m)	Expected date of delivery
Mozambique	USSR	1976–77	T-34/-54 tks, SA-7 SAM, 122mm how	n.a.	n.a.	1976–77
South Africa	France	1976	*Exocet* SSM	n.a.	n.a.	1977–78
	Israel	1976	*Reshef* FPBG	2	n.a.	1977
Togo	Brazil	Nov 1976	*Xavante* COIN ac	3	n.a.	Dec 1976
	France	Mid-1977	*AlphaJet* trg ac	5	n.a.	n.a.
Uganda	Switzerland	1976	*Bravo* trg ac	6	n.a.	n.a.
	USSR	1976	MiG-21 fighters	12	n.a.	1977
Zaire	Canada	Sept 1976	DHC-5 tpt ac	3	n.a.	n.a.
Zambia	Italy	1976	AB-47G hel	10	n.a.	n.a.

(D) ASIA AND AUSTRALASIA

Recipient	Primary supplier	Approximate date of agreement	System	Quantity	Cost ($m)	Expected date of delivery
Australia	Britain	Early 1977	*Blindfire* radars	10	42	n.a.
	Germany	1977	*Leopard* med tks	14	17.4	n.a.
	USA	1976	GW frigates	2	375	1981–82
		Late 1976	P-3B *Orion* MR ac	2	21	1978
		Mid-1976	C-130 tpt ac	12	115	1978
		1976	M-113 APC	69	n.a.	n.a.
		1976	S-2G ASW ac	6	2.1	1977
		Early 1977	S-2G ASW ac	10	5.3	1977
Brunei	Britain	1976	*Scorpion* lt tks	16	n.a.	n.a.
India	Britain	June 1977	*Sea King* ASW hel	5	n.a.	n.a.
	USSR	1976	*Nanuchka* escorts	8	n.a.	n.a.
Indonesia	Australia	Sept 1976	*Attack* patrol boats	6	n.a.	n.a.
		Mid-1977	*Nomad* MR ac	6	n.a.	n.a.
		Mid-1977	T-34C trg ac	16	n.a.	n.a.
	France	Nov 1976	*Exocet* SSM	n.a.	n.a.	1978–80
	Germany	1976	*Palau* MCM ships	5	n.a.	n.a.
		Feb 1977	Type 206 subs	2	221	n.a.
	Italy	1976	AB-205 hel	16	n.a.	n.a.
	South Korea	Early 1977	FPBG	4	n.a.	n.a.
	Spain	1976	CASA C-212 tpt ac	22	n.a.	n.a.
Malaysia	France	1977	*Gazelle* hel	20	n.a.	n.a.
	France	1976	*Exocet* SSM	n.a.	n.a.	n.a.
	Sweden	Aug 1976	*Spica* MTB	4	68	1977–79
	USA	1976	LST	2	n.a.	n.a.
			105mm how	12		
			V-150 armd cars	32		
			M-16 rifles	60,000		

Recipient	Primary supplier	Approximate date of agreement	System	Quantity	Cost ($m)	Expected date of delivery
Pakistan	France	Jan 1977	*Puma* tpt hel	35	n.a.	n.a.
		Jan 1977	*Mirage* V fighters	10	n.a.	n.a.
	USA	1976	*Sidewinder* AAM	n.a.	14.2	n.a.
Philippines	USA	1976	F-5E fighters	11	61.4	n.a.
		1976	UH-1 hel	17	40	n.a.
		1976	M-113 APC	33	n.a.	n.a.
Singapore	Israel	1976	155mm how	n.a.	n.a.	1977
	USA	1976	Minesweepers	2 }	n.a.	n.a.
			Landing craft	6 }		
		1976	*Sidewinder* AAM	200	n.a.	n.a.
		1976	F-5E/F fighters	21	118	n.a.
South Korea	USA	1976	*Sidewinder* AAM	733	20.8	1977
		1976	OV-10 COIN ac	24	58.2	1977 on
		Oct 1976	Hughes 500D hel	100	50	Dec 77–80
Taiwan	Israel	1976	*Gabriel* SSM }	n.a.	n.a.	n.a.
			Shafrir AAM }			
	USA	1976	UH-1H hel	118	n.a.	n.a.
		Mid-1976	F-5E fighters	60	95	n.a.
		June 1976	*Improved Hawk* SAM	24	185	n.a.
Thailand	France	July 1976	*Exocet* SSM	n.a.	n.a.	1979
	Spain	1976	CASA C-212 tpt ac	4	n.a.	n.a.
	Italy	July 1976	FPBG	3	n.a.	1979
	USA	1976	Hel	10 }		
			Patrol craft	24 }		
			How	24 }	n.a.	n.a.
			Armd cars and APC	80 }		
			Sidewinder AAM	18 }		

(E) LATIN AMERICA

Recipient	Primary supplier	Approximate date of agreement	System	Quantity	Cost ($m)	Expected date of delivery
Argentina	Britain	1976	*Lynx* hel	3	n.a.	n.a.
	USA	Early 1977	*Merlin* III tpt ac	4	n.a.	n.a.
		Early 1977	*Merlin* IVA med evac ac	2	n.a.	1977
Brazil	USA	1976	KC-130 tanker ac	2	n.a.	n.a.
Chile	Brazil	1976	EMB-110 COIN/trg ac	3	n.a.	1977
		Early 1977	EMB-111 lt MR ac	6	n.a.	n.a.
	Israel	1976	*Shafrir* AAM	n.a.	n.a.	n.a.
	Netherlands	1976	F-27 tpt ac	1	n.a.	n.a.

Recipient	Primary Supplier	Approximate date of agreement	System	Quantity	Cost ($m)	Expected date of delivery
Ecuador	Israel	1977	*Super Mystère* B2 fighters	12	n.a.	n.a.
	Italy	Early 1977	SF-260 trg ac	12	n.a.	n.a.
	USA	1976	T-34 trg ac	14	5	n.a.
Guatemala	Israel	Mid-1976	*Arava* tpt ac	3	n.a.	n.a.
Honduras	Israel	1976	*Super Mystère* B2 fighters	12	n.a.	1976
Mexico	Israel	1976	*Arava* tpt ac	5	n.a.	n.a.
Peru	France	Sept 1976	*Mirage* VP fighters	16	250	Dec 1976
		Early 1977	PR72 FPBG	6	n.a.	n.a.
	Germany	1976	Type 209 subs	2	n.a.	n.a.
	Italy	1976	AB-212 ASW hel	6	n.a.	n.a.
	Netherlands	1976	F-27 MR ac	2	n.a.	n.a.
		Early 1977	Cruiser	1	n.a.	1977
	USSR	Dec 1976	Su-22 fighters	36	250	n.a.
		Early 1977	SA-3, SA-7 SAM	n.a.	n.a.	n.a.
		Early 1977	Mi-8 hel	23	n.a.	n.a.
		1977	T-62 med tk	200	n.a.	n.a.
		1977	122mm, 130mm guns, AA guns	n.a.	n.a.	n.a.
Venezuela	Britain	1976	*Skyvan* tpt ac	3	n.a.	1977
	Italy	1976	A-109 hel	8	n.a.	n.a.
		1976	AB-212 hel	6	n.a.	n.a.
	USA	1976	Bell 206 hel	7	n.a.	1976–77

The Theatre Balance between NATO and the Warsaw Pact

Any assessment of the military balance between NATO and the Warsaw Pact involves comparison of the strengths of both men and equipment, consideration of qualitative characteristics, factors such as geographical advantages, deployment, training and logistic support, and of differences in doctrine and philosophy. It must be set within the context of the strategic nuclear balance, of military forces world wide and, in particular, of the relative strengths of the navies of the two sides.

Certain elements in the equation are of special importance. Warsaw Pact equipment is standardized, whereas that of NATO is not and is therefore subject to limitations on interoperability and thus flexibility. NATO has certain strengths, such as the striking power of its tactical air forces, but there is little depth in the NATO central sector, which presents problems in its defence. On the other hand, the Warsaw Pact has its own vulnerabilities, and there may be doubts about the reliability of some of its members and the value of their forces.

The appraisal which follows should therefore be regarded as primarily a quantitative guide, since there are difficulties in giving, in so short a space, values to qualitative factors and deciding on their relevance. It is military only, and thus one-dimensional. Furthermore, any single, static comparison of opposing forces can only give a limited insight into what might happen under the dynamic conditions of conflict. The two sides do not have the same military requirements: Soviet forces are designed for an offensive; NATO forces for defence, for creating at least a reasonable Soviet doubt about the possibility of the speedy success of a conventional attack and the nuclear consequences that might follow. This presentation necessarily over-simplifies what is by its nature a complex problem, not easily responsive to analysis.

The characteristics of the military balance are central to any consideration of Mutual and Balanced Force Reductions (MBFR), but the geographical area covered by the MBFR negotiations is only part of NATO territory to be defended. A section at the end of this essay shows the figures relating to this area with which MBFR negotiators will be concerned.

Land and Air Forces

The three major NATO subordinate commands, Northern, Central and Southern Europe, at first seem to offer a convenient basis for making a direct comparison with the opposing forces of the Warsaw Pact, but there are problems. The Northern European Command covers not only Norway but also the Baltic area, including Denmark, Schleswig-Holstein and the Baltic Approaches, which is intimately linked with the Central sector. It is not possible to make precise judgments as to which Warsaw Pact formations would be committed towards NATO's Northern rather than towards its Central European Command, since in both land and air forces there is a considerable degree of flexibility to do either. For the Warsaw Pact this geographical area is a coherent front, though a number of Soviet divisions stationed well to the north, discussed later, are undoubtedly directed towards Norway. Northern and Central Europe have therefore been grouped together in the tables which follow. Southern Europe is shown separately.

GROUND FORMATIONS

A traditional basis of comparing strengths is the number of combat divisions that the two sides have, shown in the table below. This is far from an adequate guide by itself, since not only do divisions vary greatly in their organization, size and equipment (see the comparisons on pp. 92–3), but there are many combat units outside divisional structures. As one very broad indication of the front-line combat resources on the ground in peacetime a divisional count has some utility provided it is taken in conjunction with the various tables which follow, in particular that for combat manpower.

Ground Forces Available in Peacetime (div equivalents)[c]	Northern and Central Europe[a]			Southern Europe[b]		
	NATO	Warsaw Pact	(of which USSR)	NATO	Warsaw Pact	(of which USSR)
Armd	10	32	22	4	6	2
Mech	13	33	20	7	24	7
Inf and AB	4	5	3	26	3	2

[a] Includes, on the NATO side, the commands for which AFCENT and AFNORTH commanders have responsibility (see p. 17). France is not included, nor are any allied ground forces in Portugal or Britain. On the Warsaw Pact side it

Greek forces are included in the table, since their withdrawal from the integrated military organization is still under discussion. French formations are not; if included they would add two mechanized divisions to the NATO totals.[d] Though these divisions are stationed in Germany and there has been some joint planning with NATO military commanders, they are not committed to NATO; they have no operational sectors, and there has been far from full agreement on the military strategy under which they might be employed. All the appropriate forces of the East European Warsaw Pact countries are included, though the military value of some of them might be suspect for political reasons, dependent on circumstances. In addition to the Soviet divisions in Eastern Europe, a number that are stationed in the Western military districts of the Soviet Union are included in the table. They consist of those Category 1 and 2 formations that are judged to be intended for immediate or very early operations in the NATO area; they total about one third of the divisions listed under Northern and Central Europe and one half of those in Southern Europe. A proportion of the Warsaw Pact strength shown is, therefore, some distance away in the Soviet Union, while the NATO divisions in the central sector are mainly in Germany, where they are wanted. The figures for Northern and Central Europe therefore show what is, from a NATO viewpoint, the worst case; those for Southern Europe, for different reasons, show the best, as noted below.

There are a number of disparities which the table does not bring out. The first is a marked imbalance in North Norway. In Norway there are only Norwegian forces, a brigade group being located in the north. There are strong Soviet forces in the Kola peninsula, some two divisions and a marine brigade, and some nine divisions in the Leningrad Military District, with more formations to the south in the Baltic states. While many of these formations may have other missions, it is clear that large forces could be brought against Norway (and indeed Denmark) and could be rapidly reinforced. The Soviet naval strength in the region is massive, and sea power, including amphibious capacity, is an important element in the military and, particularly, regional balance. The wide disparity highlights the problem of the defence of North Norway against surprise attack. To meet this difficulty a system of self-defence, based on a strong Home Guard and rapid mobilization has been designed to take maximum advantage of the ruggedness of the country and the poor road and rail communications, but it is clear that defence against attack of any size depends on timely external assistance, including air and naval support.

Two further imbalances are worth noting. In Southern Europe the whole of the Italian land forces, included in the table under Southern Europe, are stationed in Italy and are thus at some distance from the areas of potential confrontation in the South-east and the Centre. Indeed the NATO forces in the South are effectively in three separate land sectors, with scant possibility of being able to move reinforcing units from one national contingent to assist another. It will also be noted that the Warsaw Pact is much stronger in mechanized formations.

The third imbalance, a legacy from the post-war occupation zones, is a certain maldeployment in the Central European Command, where the strong US formations are stationed in the southern sector, where the terrain often lends itself to defence, while in the north German plain, across which the routes to allied capitals run and where there are fewer obstacles, certain of the forces are less powerful. (This pattern of deployment also leaves US forces reliant on logistic communications running north–south, since they can no longer use French territory.) In wartime, lateral movement of forces might have to be made and, in particular, reinforcements would have to be directed to the sector where they were most needed rather than to existing national sectors. A partial adjustment of this maldeployment is now taking place with the stationing of one of the two additional US brigades in the north, making emergency reinforcement of this area by US troops easier.

MANPOWER

A comparison of front-line combat manpower deployed on the ground in normal peacetime circumstances (as distinct from total manpower, which is referred to later) fills out the picture further. The figures shown reflect the variations in divisional establishments mentioned above but also include combat troops in formations higher than divisions. They take some account of under-manning as well – many NATO and Warsaw Pact divisions are kept well below strength in peacetime. Figures calculated on this basis, which

---

includes the command for which the Pact High Commander has responsibility, but excludes the armed forces of Bulgaria, Hungary and Romania; certain Soviet units stationed in the western USSR, including those that might be committed to the Baltic and Norwegian areas of operations, have, however, been included.
[b] Includes, on the NATO side, the Italian, Greek and Turkish land forces (including those in Asian Turkey) and such American and British units as would be committed to the Mediterranean theatre of operations, and, on the Warsaw Pact side, the land forces of Bulgaria, Hungary and Romania and such Soviet units normally stationed in Hungary and south-western USSR as might be committed to the Mediterranean theatre.
[c] Divisions, brigades and similar formations, aggregated on the basis of three brigades to a division.
[d] These are the two divisions stationed in Germany. There are eight more in France, outside the area of the NATO command. French divisions are in process of reorganization, however.

can only be very approximate, are shown in the table which follows. The figures do not include French forces; if those stationed in Germany are counted, the NATO figure for Northern and Central Europe might be increased by perhaps 40,000. Again, they include Greece.

	Northern and Central Europe[a]			Southern Europe[b]		
	NATO	Warsaw Pact	(of which USSR)	NATO	Warsaw Pact	(of which USSR)
Combat manpower in all types of formations	630	945	640	560	390	145

The table still reveals a marked advantage to the Warsaw Pact in Northern and Central Europe (subject to the caveat about the value to be placed on the forces of the East European countries). It does not, of course, include the men in the US dual-based brigades, because they are not physically present in Europe, but does include on the Warsaw Pact side combat troops in Category 1 and 2 divisions and higher formations in the western military districts of the Soviet Union, since they are clearly designed for operations in the NATO area.

In Southern Europe the figures appear to favour NATO but do not, of course, show that the forces are widely separated while those of the Warsaw Pact can be more flexibly deployed.

It must be remembered that the figures only cover land forces. Of course, any operations would be heavily influenced by air forces, the figures for which are given later, and indeed by naval action as well.

REINFORCEMENTS

The movement of external reinforcements to the theatre and the mobilization of indigenous first-line reserves would materially alter the above figures. Indeed there is only limited utility in comparing just

	Divs			Bdes/regts			Marines
	Armd	Mech	Other	Armd	Mech	Other	Divs
Active Formations							
United States[e]	2	3	5	1	1	1	2
Britain	—	—	1	—	—	2	—
Canada	—	—	—	—	—	1	—
Germany	—	—	—	—	—	—	—
France	—	3	2	—	—	—	—
Totals	2	6	8	1	1	4	2
Reserve Formations[f]							
United States[e]	2	1	5	3	6	13	1
Belgium	—	—	—	—	1	1	—
Britain	—	—	—	—	—	—	—
Canada	—	—	—	—	—	—	—
Germany	—	—	—	—	—	6	—
Netherlands	—	1	—	—	—	1	—
Norway	—	—	—	—	—	11	—
Totals	2	2	5	3	7	32	1
Grand Totals	4	8	13	4	8	36	3

[e] Including light divisions (infantry and airborne) and armoured cavalry regiments.
[f] Some countries, particularly Britain, Canada, the Netherlands and France, have plans to mobilize battalion-sized units in some numbers in addition to the formations shown here. France also has formations earmarked for territorial defence.

peacetime strengths, since in crisis or conflict the total combat manpower that can be brought to bear in time becomes the key indicator. There are, however, acute difficulties in making a numerical comparison of anything other than the numbers of reinforcements potentially available, since there are so many variables and a good many unknowns affecting the speed with which reinforcements and reserves could or would be deployed operationally.

Implicit in NATO defence plans is the concept of political warning time: that there will be enough warning of a possible attack for forces to be brought to a higher state of readiness and for reinforcement and mobilization to take place. This does, of course, assume the willingness – which applies to both sides – to reinforce in a crisis situation, at the risk of heightening tension by doing so. Advantage here will generally lie with an attacker, who can start mobilization first, hope to conceal his intentions and finally achieve some degree of tactical surprise. The point of attack can be chosen and a significant local superiority built up. The defender is likely to start more slowly and will have to remain on guard at all points.

There is obvious military advantage in surprise, and there has been speculation that the all-round improvement in the fire-power and mobility that has taken place in the Warsaw Pact forces is designed to enable them to launch an attack without being reinforced beforehand, so as to give no warning to NATO through the movement or mobilization of Soviet reserves. This would involve attacking with only those forces now in place, forfeiting the possibility of building up greater superiority and of making preparations beforehand that could not be made later (for example, the moving to sea of missile submarines and other naval forces that are kept in port rather than at operational stations, thus giving warning). It would assume that these forces were considered certain to be adequate to the task, and perhaps also that the alternative setting, of both sides carrying out a degree of reinforcement first, yielded less advantage. In fact Warsaw Pact reinforcement in the early stages could be significantly faster than that of NATO (a point to which NATO is paying much attention).

NATO forces would be built up from two sources: the mobilization of reserves to increase the strength or the number of existing formations, and external reinforcement by the movement of active army formations stationed outside the theatre in peacetime.

Potentially the most rapid build-up of any size would be that from the mobilization of reserves in Europe, which could occur within days. This applies particularly to Germany, where reserves would bring units up to wartime strength (but not increase their number) and mobilize the Territorial Army of some 500,000 men, designed to assist with rear area defence. Other European nations could also use mobilized reserves to strengthen units and, in certain cases, increase their number. Formations from outside the immediate area would come from Canada, Britain and possibly France, but principally from the United States. There are two divisions and an armoured cavalry regiment in the United States with equipment stockpiled in Germany; their personnel could be moved very quickly, using the very considerable airlift available.[g] There are in the United States another 10, largely infantry, active divisions (some with heavy equipment) and 2 brigades also available for use in Europe, but, though they might be available very early, much of their equipment would have to be moved by sea. The same would apply to the 8 divisions and some 19 independent brigades in the National Guard (excluding 4 incorporated in active divisions); these could nominally be ready perhaps five weeks after mobilization but might need further training (as might some Soviet reserves). The table above summarizes the formations that NATO countries have available to provide reinforcements for the critical Central and Northern sectors.

Warsaw Pact reinforcement plans follow a rather different pattern. There are a large number of active Soviet divisions, but they are kept at three different manning levels, as are Warsaw Pact formations (see pp. 9 and 13). Reinforcement depends on filling out these divisions by mobilization and on moving some forward from the Soviet Union. All Soviet divisions stationed in East Germany, Poland or Czechoslovakia are in Category 1 and would need little if any reinforcement, but some of the East European countries' divisions in the central sector are at a much lower level. The divisions in the Soviet Union which would move forward first would be those in the western part of the country, of which about a half of those designed for use in the central sector are normally in Category 1 or 2. While Category 2 divisions might take 72 hours or so to be ready, it is possible that they might be committed to battle early, even if only at three-quarter strength, leaving reinforcements to come behind. With more time and risk, reinforcing divisions could also be deployed from elsewhere in the Soviet Union, even from as far away as the Sino–Soviet Border area. The total number and state of readiness of Soviet and East European divisions (which, it will be remembered, are smaller than those of NATO) is shown in the table overleaf.

As far as can be judged, mobilization by the Soviet Union in particular could be very speedy (though it would be impossible to conceal it on any scale); it has been estimated that the 27 Soviet divisions in Eastern Europe could be increased in a few weeks to between 50–60, and the total number of Warsaw Pact divisions to perhaps 80 – if mobilization were unimpeded. Of course it might not be. If hostilities had already started,

---

[g] Equipment is nominally stockpiled for $2\frac{2}{3}$ divisions, but two newly-formed brigades have been equipped from this stockpile.

	Armd divs			Mech divs			Other divs		
	Category			Category			Category		
	1	2	3	1	2	3	1	2	3
Czechoslovakia	3	—	2	3	—	2	—	—	—
East Germany	2	—	—	4	—	—	—	—	—
Poland	5	—	—	3	2	3	—	2	—
Soviet divs									
In above area	14	—	—	13	—	—	—	—	—
Elsewhere[h]	5	13	13	18	20	64	8	—	—
Soviet totals	19	13	13	31	20	64	8	—	—

movement by rail and road could be interdicted and the build-up slowed considerably. Nonetheless, the Soviet Union, a European power operating on interior lines, has geographical advantages and in the early weeks should be able to move reinforcements with heavy equipment faster overland than the United States could by sea, and she could also use heavy airlift. American ability to bring back the men of the dual-based brigades in days by air has been demonstrated on exercises, and for the two divisions with equipment in Germany the airlift of personnel would be a matter of another week or so. As with Soviet Forces, this would depend on movement not being hindered, on a secure air environment and safe airfields to fly into; and quick dispersal from airfields could be difficult once fighting had started. The increase of manpower strengths of combatant units (as distinct from an increase in their number) could take place rapidly, both from the United States and from the European NATO countries, but the real problem for NATO in achieving a fast build-up of the number of combat divisions lies in the inevitable time-lag before the American follow-up formations, dependent on sealift for their heavy weapons, could be ready for operations.

A fair summary of the initial reinforcement position might be that the Warsaw Pact is intrinsically capable of a much faster build-up of formations in the first two or three weeks, particularly if local surprise is achieved, having a large pool of reserves on which to draw and the formations to absorb them; that NATO can only attempt to match such a build-up if it has, and takes advantage of, sufficient warning time; that the subsequent rate of build-up of formations also favours the Warsaw Pact substantially, suggesting that comparative advantage is to be found in this. Only if the crisis develops slowly enough to permit full reinforcement could the West eventually reach a better position. Apart from having greater economic resources, Alliance countries, including France, maintain rather more men under arms than the Warsaw Pact. For Army/Marines the figures (in thousands) are: NATO 2,842; Warsaw Pact 2,647. And the Soviet Union has a large number of her divisions and men on her border with China. Clearly, Soviet plans will put a premium on exploiting a fast build-up of forces, and NATO's on having adequate standing forces to meet any attack and on augmenting them in good time.

EQUIPMENT

In a comparison of equipment one point stands out: the Warsaw Pact is armed almost completely with Soviet or Soviet-designed material and enjoys the flexibility, simplicity of training and economy that standardization brings. NATO forces have a wide variety of everything from weapons systems to vehicles, with consequent duplication of supply systems and some difficulties of interoperability; they do, however, have some weapons qualitatively superior. As to numbers of weapons, there are some notable disparities, of which that in tanks is perhaps the most significant. The relative strengths are:

	Northern and Central Europe			Southern Europe		
	NATO	Warsaw Pact	(of which USSR)	NATO	Warsaw Pact	(of which USSR)
Main battle tanks in operational service[i]	7,000	20,500	13,500	4,000	6,700	2,500

[h] Included here are four Category 1 divisions in Hungary and a number of divisions that might reinforce Southern Europe rather than the central sector. Soviet naval infantry are not included.

Tanks in French formations are not included in the above figures. If the two divisions stationed in Germany are taken into account, 325 tanks should be added to the NATO total; if the three divisions in eastern France are also counted, a further 485 should be added.

It will be seen that in Northern and Central Europe NATO has only a third as many operational tanks as the Warsaw Pact, though NATO tanks are generally superior (not, perhaps, to the T-72 now being issued to the Soviet forces).[j] This numerical weakness in tanks (and in other armoured fighting vehicles, where the Soviet forces are notably well-equipped both in numbers and quality) reflects NATO's essentially defensive role and has in the past been offset to some extent by a superiority in heavy anti-tank weapons, a field in which new air- and ground-launched missiles rapidly coming into service could increasingly give more strength to the defence. NATO is indeed introducing large numbers of such weapons, but so is the Warsaw Pact (see the comparison of divisional weapons on pp. 92–3). At the moment the Pact probably has more ground-launched weapons (and anti-tank guns), but NATO has more effective airborne anti-tank (and other precision air-to-ground) weapons carried by fighter aircraft and helicopters.

The Warsaw Pact has also built up a marked advantage in conventional artillery in Northern and Central Europe: counting field, medium and heavy guns, mortars and rocket launchers with formations, NATO has only some 2,700 against a Warsaw Pact total of over 10,000. In Southern Europe the position is more nearly equal, NATO having 3,500 against some 4,000 in the Warsaw Pact, though about one-third of the NATO total is in Italy. To some extent the imbalance is redressed by the greater lethality of NATO ammunition, and hitherto by a greater logistic capacity to sustain higher rates of fire, stemming from a relatively higher transport lift. Soviet forces have, however, been augmenting their logistics substantially, particularly with formations, and new self-propelled guns are replacing older towed models. NATO is also modernizing its artillery, in which it has achieved a fair degree of standardization, and in particular is developing a precision-guided shell and other munitions which would give artillery, *inter alia*, a much improved anti-tank capability.

LOGISTICS

NATO has an inflexible logistic system, based almost entirely on national supply lines with little central co-ordination. It cannot now use French territory and has many lines of communication running north to south near the area of forward deployment. Certain NATO countries are, furthermore, short of supplies for sustained combat, but Warsaw Pact countries may well be no better off. The Soviet logistic system has been greatly augmented in recent years. The organization has been improved and formations have been given more support. The former NATO superiority in forward-area logistics has probably now gone, though there is some inherent advantage in operating on home territory.

AIR POWER

If NATO ground formations are to be able to exploit the mobility they possess by day as well as by night, they must have a greater degree of air cover over the battlefield than they now have. Such cover is provided by a combination of rapid warning and communications systems, fighter aircraft and air defence weapons both

Tactical Aircraft in Operational Service	Northern and Central Europe[k]			Southern Europe[k]		
	NATO	Warsaw Pact	(of which USSR)	NATO	Warsaw Pact	(of which USSR)
Light bombers	150	125	125	—	50	50
Fighter/ground-attack	1,500	1,350	925	625	325	125
Interceptors	400	2,050	900	200	1,000	425
Reconnaissance	300	550	350	125	200	150

[i] These are tanks with formations or earmarked for the use of dual-based or immediate reinforcing formations (some 600). They do not include those in reserve or small stocks held to replace tanks damaged or destroyed. In this latter category NATO has perhaps 2,500 tanks in Central Europe. There are tanks in reserve in the Warsaw Pact area, but the figures are difficult to establish. The total Pact tank holdings are, however, materially higher than the formation totals shown in the table.

[j] Soviet tank production is high; more than 2,000 T-72 have been built in the last two years.

[k] The area covered here is slightly wider than for ground troops as described in note *a*. Many aircraft have a long-range capability and in any case can be redeployed very quickly. Accordingly, the figures here include the appropriate British and American aircraft in Britain, American aircraft in Spain and Soviet aircraft in the western USSR. They do not, however, include the American dual-based squadrons, which would add about 100 fighter-type aircraft to the NATO totals, nor French squadrons with perhaps another 400 fighters. Carrier-borne aircraft of the US Navy are excluded, but so are the medium bombers in the Soviet Air Force, which could operate in a tactical role.

for defence of key areas or in the hands of forward troops. In numbers of aircraft NATO is inferior but has, however, a higher proportion of multi-purpose aircraft of good performance over their full mission profiles, especially in range, payload and all-weather capability; considerable power can be deployed in the ground-attack role in particular. Both sides are modernizing their inventories. The Soviet Union is producing multi-role fighters to replace the large numbers of aircraft at present used only in an air defence role, thus giving increased ground-attack capacity. In addition, fighters have for the first time been specifically designed for deep strike and interdiction (bringing European capitals within range of tactical aircraft).[l] NATO is also bringing into service new fighter aircraft of many types, and the United States has recently substantially augmented her F-15 and F-111 squadrons in Europe. US aircraft in particular can now be assumed to have available very advanced air-delivered weapons, such as laser-guided and other precision-guided munitions.

The air forces of the two sides have tended to have rather different roles; long range and payload have in the past had lower priority for the Warsaw Pact, while NATO has maintained a long-range deep-strike tactical aircraft capability. (The Soviet Union has chosen to build an MRBM force which could, under certain circumstances, perform analogous missions – though not in a conventional phase of any battle). The introduction of more advanced, longer-range, Soviet aircraft now presents a much greater air defence problem for NATO, whose strike aircraft have to meet the increased air defence capability that Soviet forces have built up. The Soviet Union has always placed heavy emphasis on air defence, evident not only from the large number of interceptor aircraft in the table but from the strength of her deployment of high-quality surface-to-air missiles and air defence artillery both in the Soviet Union and with units in the field. These defences would pose severe problems for NATO strike aircraft, drawing off much effort into defence suppression. NATO territory and forces are much less well provided with air defence, but heavy expenditure is now going into new systems of many sorts, both low- and high-level, missiles and artillery (and into electronic warfare equipment for aircraft).

The Warsaw Pact enjoys the advantage of interior lines of communication, which makes for ease of command and control and logistics. It has in the past had a relatively high capability to operate from dispersed natural airfields serviced by mobile systems, but the introduction of new high-performance fighters will reduce this. It does, however, have more airfields with protective shelters and the great advantage of standard ground support equipment which stems from having only Soviet-designed aircraft. These factors make for greater flexibility than NATO has, with its wide variety of aircraft and support equipment. NATO suffers from having too few airfields, which are thus liable to be crowded, and has been slow to build shelters. It undoubtedly still has superiority in sophistication of equipment but this technological edge is being eroded as the newer Soviet aircraft, which are very advanced, are brought in. The capability of NATO air crews (which in general have higher training standards and fly more hours) and the versatility of its aircraft, gives all-weather operational strength, and the quality of Western electronic technology is such that ground and airborne control equipment is almost certainly superior to that of the Warsaw Pact. The introduction of AWACS, so much discussed but not yet decided, would give NATO an airborne control system that would offer significant advantage. Since squadrons can be moved quickly, the NATO numerical inferiority shown above could rapidly be redressed if enough airfields were available. While the total tactical aircraft inventories of the two sides are not dissimilar in size, the Soviet Union keeps about a third of her force on the Chinese front.

THEATRE NUCLEAR WEAPONS

NATO has been said to have some 7,000 nuclear warheads, but the composition of this armoury has undoubtedly changed as weapon systems have been modernized and redeployed. They are deliverable by a variety of vehicles (over 3,000 in all): aircraft, short-range missiles and artillery of the types listed in Table 1 on pp. 77–81.[m] There are also nuclear mines. Yields are variable but are mainly in the low kiloton range. The ground-based missile launchers and guns are in formations down to divisions and are operated both by American and allied troops, but in the latter case warheads are under double key (except in the case of

---

[l] The latest versions of the MiG-23/-27 *Flogger*, Su-17/-20 *Fitter* and Su-19 *Fencer* are reported to have substantially improved range, payload, avionics and ECM capabilities. This may well be at the expense of overall numbers in future, since there has been an increase of some 1,300 tactical aircraft in the Warsaw Pact during the last seven years or so.

[m] These nuclear weapons are in general designed for use against targets within the battlefield area or directly connected with the manoeuvre of combatant forces – which could be described as a 'tactical' use. However, the warheads include a substantial number carried by aircraft such as the F-4 or F-104, which could be delivered on targets outside the battlefield area or unconnected with the manoeuvre of combatant forces, and thus to put to 'strategic' use. There is inevitably some overlap when describing delivery vehicles, aircraft and missiles capable of delivering conventional or nuclear warheads as 'tactical' or 'strategic'. The warhead total also includes nuclear warheads for certain air defence missiles and nuclear mines.

France). The figure for Soviet warheads is probably about 3,500, similarly delivered by aircraft and missile systems (see Table 1). Soviet warheads are thought to be somewhat larger, on average, than those of NATO, and the delivery systems, both ground and air, notably less accurate. Soviet doctrine has concerned itself more with area targets than precision (it also appears to contemplate the use of launchers for the delivery of chemical weapons, with which Warsaw Pact forces are extensively equipped). Some of the delivery vehicles, but not the nuclear warheads, are in the hands of non-Soviet Warsaw Pact forces.

It is not appropriate to attempt to strike any balance of these theatre-based nuclear systems, since each side also has the ability to deliver warheads into the theatre from outside it, increasingly with accuracies and yields suitable for military targets. The Soviet Union has a large medium-bomber force being equipped with *Backfire*; Long-Range and Naval Air Force aircraft; IRBM and MRBM, including the new mobile SS-20, with its accurate multiple warhead; and cruise missiles on submarines and surface ships. NATO has strike aircraft on carriers and on airfields in Britain (now augmented by extra F-111 squadrons) and could use SLBM for certain theatre roles.

This comparison of nuclear weapons must not, though, be looked at in quite the same light as the conventional comparisons preceding it, since on the NATO side the strategic doctrine is not based on the use of such weapons on this sort of scale. The warhead numbers were accumulated to implement an earlier, predominantly nuclear, strategy, and an inventory of this size now has the chief merit of affording a wide range of choice of weapons, yield and delivery system if controlled escalation has to be contemplated. A point that does emerge from the comparison, however, is that the Soviet Union has the ability to launch a battlefield nuclear offensive on a massive scale if she chooses, or to match any NATO escalation with broadly similar options, though at present with less ability to limit collateral damage.

CHANGES OVER TIME

The comparisons above begin to look rather different from those of a few years ago. The effect of small and slow changes can be marked, and the balance can alter. In 1962 the American land, sea and air forces in Europe totalled 434,000; now the figure is around 300,000. There were 26 Soviet divisions in Eastern Europe in 1967; now there are 31, and they are larger in size (despite the increase of some 25 divisions on the Chinese front over the same period). The numerical pattern over the years so far has been a gradual shift in favour of the East, with NATO relying on offsetting this by a qualitative superiority in its weapons that is now being eroded as new Soviet equipment is introduced. While NATO has been modernizing its forces, the Warsaw Pact has been modernizing faster and expanding as well. In some areas (for example, SAM, certain armoured vehicles and artillery) Soviet weapons are now superior, while in other fields (such as tactical aircraft) the gap in quality is being closed. The advent of new weapons systems, particularly precision-guided munitions and new anti-tank and air defence missiles, may again cut into the Warsaw's Pact's advantage in tank and aircraft numbers, but in general the pattern is one of a military balance moving steadily against the West.

SUMMARY

It will be clear from the foregoing analysis that a balance between NATO and the Warsaw Pact based on comparison of manpower, combat units or equipment is an extraordinarily complex one, acutely difficult to analyse. In the first place, the Pact has superiority by some measures and NATO by others, and there is no fully satisfactory way to compare these asymmetrical advantages. Secondly, qualitative factors that cannot be reduced to numbers (such as training, morale, leadership, tactical initiative and geographical positions) could prove dominant in warfare. However, three observations can be made by way of a summary:

First, the overall balance is such as to make military aggression appear unattractive. NATO defences are of such a size and quality that any attempt to breach them would require major attack. The consequences for an attacker would be incalculable, and the risks, including that of nuclear escalation, must impose caution. Nor can the theatre be seen in isolation: the central strategic balance and the maritime forces (not least because they are concerned to keep open sea lanes for reinforcements and supplies, and because of their obvious role in the North and in the Mediterranean) play a vital part in the equation as well.

Second, NATO has emphasized quality, particularly in equipment and training, to offset numbers, but this is now being matched. New technology has strengthened the defence, but it is increasingly expensive. If defence budgets in the West are maintained no higher than their present level and manpower costs continue to rise, the Warsaw Pact may be able to buy more of the new systems than NATO. Soviet spending has been increasing steadily, in real terms, for many years. Furthermore, technology cannot be counted on to offset numerical advantages entirely.

Third, while an overall balance can be said to exist today, the Warsaw Pact appears more content with the relationship of forces than is NATO. It is NATO that seeks to achieve equal manpower strengths through equal force reductions while the Pact seeks to maintain the existing correlation.

Force reductions

Negotiations on the mutual reduction of forces and armaments and associated measures in Central Europe[n] have been under way since 30 October 1973. 'Central Europe' was not defined in the communiqué agreed in the preparatory consultations, but the talks have been concerned with forces and armaments in Poland, Czechoslovakia, East Germany, West Germany, the Netherlands, Belgium and Luxembourg (the so-called NATO Guidelines Area, or NGA). France is taking no part in the discussions, so her forces are presumably excluded (except that French forces in Germany might be taken into account), as are any Soviet or NATO troops not stationed in the area described. Forces stationed in Berlin under quadripartite jurisdiction are unlikely to be covered *per se*, but would almost certainly be embraced by overall ceilings.

Since the area is a narrower one than that with which this appraisal has largely been concerned, and total manpower rather than combat strength is a main yardstick, the table below has been constructed to show the broad figures with which NATO negotiators are concerned, so that they can be compared with the figures for the theatre as a whole. The manpower strengths are in thousands; those for ground forces exclude marines. The tanks represent those on formation establishments and exclude reserve stocks. Aircraft figures do not include naval aircraft.

NATO	Manpower		Equipment		Warsaw Pact	Manpower		Equipment	
	Ground	Air	Tanks	Aircraft		Ground	Air	Tanks	Aircraft
United States	193	35	2,000	335	Soviet Union	475	60	9,250	1,300
Britain	58	9	575	145	Czechoslovakia	135	46	2,500	550
Canada	3	2	30	50	East Germany	105	36	1,550	375
Belgium	62	19	300	145	Poland	220	62	2,900	850
Germany	341	110	3,000	509					
Netherlands	75	18	500	160					
	732	193	6,405	1,344					
France	50	–	325	–					
Total	782	193	6,730	1,344	Total	935[o]	204[o]	16,200	3,075

[n] The full acronym for the talks is MUREFAAMCE.

[o] The Warsaw Pact negotiators have offered significantly lower manpower figures for their forces (reported as 805,000 ground forces, 182,000 air forces), but the basis on which they have been calculated is unclear, and they may not be comparable with the figures given here.

Index for last seven years*

* Of the continents and regions, only Latin America is in this index, since all the others have been included in *The Military Balance* for each of the seven years.

OTHER IISS PUBLICATIONS

Available from: Publications Department, IISS, 18 Adam Street,
London WC2N 6AL
(see cards between pages 56 and 57 for subscription terms.)

Survival

Essential reading for those wanting to keep up with strategic thought and international security matters. *Survival* carries original contributions on issues of current interest, reprints significant documents and articles, and provides a guide to the international literature in its book review section. Bi-monthly; single copy 75p ($1.75).

Adelphi Papers

Analyses of issues of topical importance in the field of international affairs and strategic policy, prepared by experts from many nations. Eight to ten a year; 50p ($1.50) each.

Strategic Survey

A retrospective review of the events and trends of world security and arms limitation during the previous year, which is of constant value for interpreting subsequent developments. Published each April; latest edition (*Strategic Survey 1976*) £1.85 ($4.00).

IISS BOOKS

Published in the United Kingdom by Chatto & Windus.

Recent titles include:

The International Trade in Arms. John Stanley & Maurice Pearton. £2.25
(cased), 80p (paper).
South Asian Crisis: India, Pakistan, Bangladesh.* Robert Jackson. £4.00.
Nations in Arms: Theory and Practice of Territorial Defence.* Adam Roberts.
£7.50.
Arms Control and European Security: A Guide to East–West Relations.* J. I.
Coffey. £10.00.

Orders for books (UK): Chatto, Bodley Head & Cape Services Ltd,
9 Bow Street, London WC2E 7AL

*Enquiries (USA): Praeger Publishers, 200 Park Avenue, New York,
NY 10017